NATIONALISM AND HISTORICAL LOSS IN RENAISSANCE ENGLAND

NATIONALISM AND HISTORICAL LOSS IN RENAISSANCE ENGLAND

Foxe, Dee, Spenser, Milton

ANDREW ESCOBEDO

CORNELL UNIVERSITY PRESS

Ithaca and London

First published 2004 by Cornell University Press

Printed in the United States of America

Library of Congress Cataloging-in-Publication Data

Escobedo, Andrew, 1967–
   Nationalism and historical loss in Renaissance England : Foxe, Dee, Spenser, Milton / Andrew Escobedo.
      p. cm.
   Includes bibliographical references and index.
      ISBN 0-8014-4174-9 (acid-free paper)
   1. English literature—Early modern, 1500–1700—History and criticism. 2. Nationalism and literature—England—History—16th century. 3. Nationalism and literature—England—History—17th century. 4. Spenser, Edmund, 1552?–1599—Knowledge—History. 5. Milton, John, 1608–1674—Knowledge—History. 6 Foxe, John, 1516–1587. Actes and monuments. 7. Dee, John, 1527–1608—Knowledge—History. 8. Literature and history—England—History. 9. Medievalism—England—History. 10. Loss (Psychology) in literature. 11. Renaissance—England. 12. Arthur, King. I. Title.
PR428.N37 E83 2004
820.9'358—dc22

                         2003020142

Cornell University Press strives to use environmentally responsible suppliers and materials to the fullest extent possible in the publishing of its books. Such materials include vegetable-based, low-VOC inks and acid-free papers that are recycled, totally chlorine-free, or partly composed of nonwood fibers. For further information, visit our website at www.cornellpress.cornell.edu.

Cloth printing 10 9 8 7 6 5 4 3 2 1

For Beth,
those thousand decencies

CONTENTS

PREFACE

I have modernized the poetry and prose of all Renaissance texts that I quote, with the following three exceptions: Spenser's *The Faerie Queene*, Drayton's *Poly-Olbion*, and Milton's prose—in the first two cases for the sake of maintaining the deliberately archaic orthography, in the last case for the sake of conforming to a nearly universal convention in Milton studies. For Milton's English tracts I quote from *The Complete Prose Works of John Milton*, 8 volumes, edited by Don M. Wolfe (New Haven: Yale University Press, 1953–82); for Milton's Latin tracts I quote from *The Works of John Milton*, 18 volumes, edited by Frank Allen Patterson (New York: Columbia University Press, 1931–38). I refer parenthetically to the various sixteenth-century editions of Foxe's *Acts and Monuments* by date and, because of the unreliable pagination, by signature (signature notations include asterisks and pointing hands for frontmatter, and letters A through YYYY for main text).

Nations are imagined communities, but within them dwell communities of friends and colleagues that at least approach the real. Such a community helped me write this book. My early interest in *The Faerie Queene* emerged from studying it with two great Spenserians. Harry Berger, Jr., showed me a poem of deep mysteries, while Paul Alpers offered a poem of brilliant rhetorical effects. I remain deeply grateful for their generous willingness to teach me, especially for Alpers's patient guidance as I wrote a dissertation about Spenser and nationalism. Jeffrey Knapp offered tireless support and detailed advice as I developed my ideas for this book, and out of sheer generosity Timothy Hampton read and commented on anything I gave him. John N. King has repeatedly answered my calls for help with John Foxe, and William Sherman has done the same for my work on John Dee. I still feel astonishment at the amount of time and effort these people have exerted on my behalf.

I have accumulated many other debts while writing this book. Todd Berliner, Thomas Betteridge, Andrew Gow, Linda Gregerson, Paul Stevens, and Gordon Teskey have all read parts of this project in various forms, offering me kind encouragement and advice. Anna Dzirkalis provided me with able research assistance. Colleagues at Berkeley, who endured early drafts of what are now the chapters of this book, can certainly claim their due from me: thank you, Mary Ann Koory, Lisa Lampert, Michael Cudahy, and Wendy Roth. My parents, in addition to unstinting emotional support, showed great forbearance in listening to me describe my book in nonacademic language. My colleagues at Ohio University, especially Samuel Crowl, Thomas Scanlan, and Roy Flannagan, lent me sympathetic ears and shrewd suggestions. My thanks also to the Ohio University Research Committee, which made it possible to spend part of the summer of 1999 in London reading John Dee's sprawling autograph.

A portion of chapter 3 appeared as "_The Book of Martyrs_: Apocalyptic Time in the Narrative of the Nation," in _Prose Studies_ 20.2 (1997); I thank Frank Cass Publishers for their permission to reprint that portion here. Chapter 2 appeared as "The Tudor Search for Arthur and the Poetics of Historical Loss," in _Exemplaria_ 14.1 (2002); my thanks to Pegasus Press for allowing me to reprint that essay here.

This book argues that the Renaissance English nation labored under a sense of bad timing, and appropriately enough, unexpected schedule changes occurred throughout its composition. Andrew Gow kindly asked me to submit an article on Milton and millennialism for a collection he was editing with Brill Press, forcing me—when I had no time to spare—to write the piece that I eventually reworked into chapter 5 of this book. I ended up revising the entire book much earlier than anticipated because Bernhard Kendler at Cornell University Press was absurdly efficient about sending my manuscript out to readers (Theresa Krier and another kind reviewer), who responded with detailed, thoughtful comments in a ridiculously short time. Worse still, during the final month of revision my son Garey was born, a full four inconvenient weeks early, altering my sense of priorities in shocking, profound, and irreversible ways. The most egregious example of bad timing that I encountered was the generosity of my wife, Beth Quitslund, who read, reread, commented on, and copyedited my entire project, from its origins to articles to book, who kept my spirits up with good humor and love, doing all this when she had precious little time for her own work and often scant energy to spare for reading yet another chapter, sacrificing her own schedule quite imprudently in order to make my book better. To her most of all I am happy to acknowledge the debt of time.

NATIONALISM AND HISTORICAL LOSS IN RENAISSANCE ENGLAND

INTRODUCTION
The Nation in Time

National Novelty and Historical Loss

It is probably no coincidence that two of the most influential studies of national consciousness in recent years conclude by invoking Walter Benjamin's angel of history. Both Tom Nairn and Benedict Anderson quote from the following passage of *Theses on the Philosophy of History:*

> A Klee painting named "Angelus Novus" shows an angel looking as though he is about to move away from something he is fixedly contemplating. His eyes are staring, his mouth is open, his wings are spread. This is how one pictures the angel of history. His face is turned toward the past. Where we perceive a chain of events, he sees one single catastrophe which keeps piling wreckage upon wreckage and hurls it in front of his feet. The angel would like to stay, awaken the dead, and make whole what has been smashed. But a storm is blowing from Paradise; it has got caught in his wings with such violence that the angel can no longer close them. This storm irresistibly propels him into the future to which his back is turned, while the pile of debris before him grows skyward. This storm is what we call progress.[1]

[1] Walter Benjamin, *Illuminations*, ed. Hannah Arendt (New York: Schocken, 1969), 257–58.

Each author finds this striking image of modern *time* an appropriate symbol for the nation: Nairn seems to feel that it expresses the catastrophic effects of the "uneven development of history since the eighteenth century," whereas for Anderson the image appears to represent the "small grounds for hope" that the nationalist precedents of violent conflict will change in the near future.[2] Both of them imply, by means of the quasi-apocalyptic quality of Benjamin's figure, that the nation has reached a *late* phase of development in the twentieth century, producing an effect of modern weariness that has no clear sense of where to go next. Not even the angel can make history whole again. Friedrich Nietzsche, to whom Benjamin himself refers in his essay, had in fact said the same thing about his fellow Germans in 1874, calling his own generation "latecomers . . . faded last shoots of mighty and cheerful generations, to whom Hesiod's prophecy applies that men would one day be born with grey hair and that Zeus would destroy this generation as soon as that sign had become visible in it."[3] Modern nationhood in these texts appears marked by a latecomer's perspective on history.

Early English national consciousness emerged out of a similar sense of belatedness. In this book I take Nairn's and Anderson's concluding focus as my central concern: to what degree did the English nation articulate itself in terms of an interpretation of historical origins? Conversely: how did a latecomer's view of history, marked by an isolation from origins, limit the ways in which England could represent itself as a nation? I offer such questions as an alternative to the more usual topographical and spatial approaches to English Renaissance nationhood: How is a nation like an island? Did England, Scotland, and Wales compose a nation called Britain? To what degree did regional identity conflict with national identity? To what degree did national selfhood depend on colonial otherness? I certainly do not propose abandoning these questions—this work addresses most of them—but rather I try to rethink them in terms of the nation's place in time. As often as possible, I supplement the question "*Where* is the nation?" with the question "*When* is the nation?" Linda

---

[2] Tom Nairn, *The Break-up of Britain: Crisis and Neo-Nationalism* (London: New Left Books, 1977), 335, 359–60; Benedict Anderson, *Imagined Communities: Reflections of the Origin and Spread of Nationalism* (London: Verso, 1983), 146–47.

[3] Friedrich Nietzsche, *On the Advantage and Disadvantage of History for Life*, trans. Peter Preuss (Indianapolis: Hackett, 1980), 43–44.

Gregerson, in a searching look at imperialism and early English nationhood, has recently suggested that the nation always emerges from
what it is not: "What constitutes the nation? It must have some substance and some boundedness, some 'us not them,' some 'here not
there.' "[4] This book focuses on a third differential configuration: now,
not then.

English nationhood in the Renaissance, I argue, was linked to a perception of historical loss, the sense that the past was incommensurate with and possibly lost to the present. Partly for this reason I use
the term "Renaissance" (their fiction) rather than "early modern"
(our fiction) to describe the sixteenth- and seventeenth-century rhetoric of rebirth as a compensation for a missing history. Despite the
explosion of historical writing in the sixteenth century (in chronicles, chorographies, poetry, and drama), much of this writing regis-
tered a profound sense that the English past was missing and unre-
coverable, even as it celebrated English history. The more the Tudors
investigated the past, the more they felt that their nation's history
was alien to the present. Worse still, this temporal isolation seemed
to be a distinctively English fate, as John Higgins, one of the editors of
the *Mirrour for Magistrates*, unhappily suggested: "amongst diverse
and sundry Chronicles of many Nations, I think there are none
(gentle reader) so uncertain and brief in the beginning as ours."[5] This
book examines how four English writers—John Foxe, John Dee, Edmund Spenser, and John Milton—use narrative representations of nationhood to mediate what they perceive as a troubling breach in history and in the process attempt to bring together the English past,
present, and near future in a complete and continuous story. Yet
these narratives end up contributing to the problem they ostensibly
solve, exposing in detail the imperfect grasp the English have on their
past. Because the sense of the latter-day nation's isolation from tradition in fact motivates their narrative projects, these writers are forced
to acknowledge that the historical otherness confronting them may
be irreducible, and thus potentially disruptive to their narrative accounts of the English nation. Their narratives resemble long tapes-

---

[4] Linda Gregerson, "Colonials Write the Nation: Spenser, Milton, and England on
the Margins," in *Edmund Spenser: Essays on Culture and Allegory,* ed. Matthew
Greenfield (Burlington, Vt.: Ashgate, 2000), 98.

[5] John Higgins, ed., *Mirrour for Magistrates* (London, 1574); reprinted in *Parts
Added to "The Mirror for Magistrates,"* ed. Lily B. Campbell (Cambridge: Cambridge
University Press, 1946), 35.

tries that, even as they grow longer, produce their own rips and tears, forcing the weaver to go back and repair them.

John Higgins's lament about the "uncertain and brief" quality of English origins stems in part from his culture's sense of the unsettling novelty of early national consciousness. There is no denying the continuities between the Tudor conception of Englishness and earlier conceptions. Yet many of the developments linked to England's emerging national identity highlighted the difference between past and present—what Samuel Daniel referred to as "strange alterations."[6] Several elements of Renaissance culture have long been credited for encouraging a sense of English nationalism, elements that play an important part in the arguments of this book. The Reformation united many of the English under "true" religion, in opposition to most of Europe. Protestant historiography replaced earlier Catholic "distortions" with an ostensibly accurate accounting. The Tudor and Stuart political machine imposed, albeit unevenly, a national uniformity over regional affiliations. A revival of Arthurian narratives convinced some writers of the nation's past imperial grandeur. Yet every one of these nationalizing developments brought along with it a sense of historical discontinuity. The Reformation broke with centuries of devotional and ecclesiastical tradition, and when Tudor and Stuart Protestants looked for their medieval past they saw Catholics staring back at them. The spoliation of the monastic libraries in the 1530s and after, performed in part to dispose of previous Catholic "propaganda," represented for some English antiquaries the destruction of the nation's past. The centralization of power by the Tudor and Stuart crowns, while always carried out under the aegis of traditional royal prerogative, struck some writers as an encroachment on the earlier, regional organization of social life. The increased interest in the ancient British past, relying on historical records of dubious accuracy, led some historians to suspect that the only origins the nation possessed were fictional ones. Furthermore, the disagreements about where England should look for its past (to the Britons? the Saxons? the Normans?) exacerbated the perception that the nation's present identity was incommensurate with any identity it could find in its history. As the urgency for national unity

---

[6] Samuel Daniel, *The Collection of the History of England* in *The Complete Works in Verse and Prose*, 5 vols., ed. Alexander B. Grosart (London: Spenser Society, 1885–96), 4:77.

deepened during the sixteenth century, the anxiety about heterogeneity in England's past increased. Foxe, Dee, Spenser, and Milton are all torn, to a certain degree, between the etiological impulse to remember the past and the suspicion that the national present may require certain aspects of this past to be forgotten.

Although England's particular circumstances made it especially vulnerable to the experience of historical loss, in more general terms the phenomenon of early national consciousness in Europe necessitated a new vision of time, as an increasing number of scholars have begun to argue. Anderson has suggested that national consciousness begins to emerge as the concept of time undergoes an important shift, a transition from a medieval, figural "simultaneity of past and future in an instantaneous present" to a conception of "homogeneous, empty time, in which simultaneity is, as it were, transverse, cross-time, marked not by prefiguration and fulfillment, but by temporal coincidence, and measured by clock and calendar."[7] No doubt Anderson exaggerates the difference between medieval and modern time, especially to the degree that the Christian understanding of God's unfolding plan required a linear as well as typological model of history. Yet his thesis calls attention to the role of historical perception in national consciousness. Indeed, it is in the historical threshold *between* these two conceptions of time that we ought locate early English nationhood, especially if we rely on Homi K. Bhabha's qualification of Anderson's "homogeneous, empty time" in terms of the uncanniness of modern temporality: the "repetitive time of the alienating anterior . . . the alienating and iterative time of the sign." In contrast to Anderson's homogeneity is Bhabha's observation that the modern conception of time, so crucial to the development of the nation, potentially isolates the present from the past. That is, the present does indeed see the past as a version of itself ("repetitive"), but in a relation that emphasizes the difference between the two, so that the past emerges, as Bhabha suggests, "as an anteriority that continually introduces an otherness or alterity within the present."[8] Indeed, Renaissance writers often find the national present eerily empty, temporally isolated from both past and future, either lost in decaying manuscripts or falling victim to God's apocalyptic wrath. Such a de-

---

[7] Anderson, *Imagined Communities*, 30.

[8] Homi K. Bhabha, "DissemiNation," in *Nation and Narration*, ed. Homi K. Bhabha (New York: Routledge, 1990), 309, 308.

scription echoes and seeks to expand on recent accounts of the provisional nature of national temporality, what Michel Foucault once called "a limited history" and what Claire McEachern has suggestively described as "an ideal of community that is, by definition, either proleptic or passing, ever just beyond reach."[9]

The sense of temporal provisionality fostered by early national consciousness forces many historical writers into a double gesture of recognition and denial, a process in which reuniting the novel present with its estranged history calls uncomfortable attention to the chasm between now and then that the writers were attempting to close. Michel de Certeau has argued that this paradoxical combination of recovery and loss itself functions as the defining characteristic of Renaissance (and, indeed, contemporary) historiography. Certeau observes that "the 'return to origins' always states the contrary of what it believes, at least in the sense that it presupposes a *distancing* in respect to a past . . . and a will to *recover* what in one fashion or another seems lost in a received language. In this way, the 'return to origins' is always a modernism as well."[10] This perspective on the nature of historical consciousness suggests that the Tudors were able to pursue their origins only in as far as they perceived these origins to be missing. Even William Camden's optimistic statement of purpose in his *Britannia* hints at the loss that underlies his project: "I would restore antiquity to Britain, and Britain to . . . antiquity . . . that I would renew ancientry, enlighten obscurity, clear doubts, and recall home Verity by way of recovery."[11] The sense of belatedness in Camden's sentence—"*restore . . . renew . . . recall . . . recovery*"—suggests that the act of pursuing a link between past and present emphasizes the fact that this past is missing. Thus, although Camden suggests that "the studies of antiquity . . . hath a certain resemblance with eternity," linking earthly time to a full, divine temporality, he also acknowledges the unsettling difference between past and present:

---

[9] See Michel Foucault, "The Political Technology of Individuals," in *Technologies of the Self*, ed. Luther H. Martin, Huck Gutman, and Patrick H. Hutton (Amherst: University of Massachusetts Press, 1988), 152; and see Claire McEachern, *The Poetics of English Nationhood, 1590–1612* (Cambridge: Cambridge University Press, 1996), 6.

[10] Michel de Certeau, *The Writing of History*, trans. Tom Conley (New York: Columbia University Press, 1988), 136.

[11] William Camden, *Britain*, trans. Philemon Holland (London, 1610), *4r.

"who is so skilful that, struggling with time in the foggy dark sea of antiquity, may not run upon the rocks?" (*4v and *5v). Even as the feeling of historical solitude prompted the Tudors to search out their past, their search itself reinforced the feeling of solitude. These writers, in both relying on and denying the loss of their past, are compelled to carry out what Certeau describes as "an odd procedure that posits death, a breakage everywhere reiterated in discourse, and that yet denies loss by appropriating to the present the privilege of recapitulating the past as a form of knowledge. A labor of death and a labor against death."[12]

For many English Renaissance writers, then, the nation refuses to fit neatly in time but rather remains a community that emphasizes the impression of historical difference. Literary studies of the Renaissance have approached the issue of historical difference from a variety of perspectives. Three interpretations in particular have aided my own work immensely: Thomas M. Greene's discussion of imitation and anachronism, wherein the search for literary models from the past produces a distance from these models; Debora Shuger's account of Protestant historiography and biblical exegesis, in which the attempt to articulate the Bible's historical content ends up producing an alienated Bible in the present; and Timothy Hampton's interpretation of Renaissance exemplarity, in which the invocation of virtuous figures from the classical past calls attention to the gap between classical and Christian.[13] All three of these influential studies link the experience of anachronism to the rise of humanism in this period, and the authors I examine owe much of their historicist sensibilities to the humanist interest in the past. Yet I extend the arguments of these works, in the case of Renaissance England at least, by demonstrating that the past comes to seem most alien to these writers when they try to represent the nation and its attendant phenomena. The search for a *native* literary tradition, the desire for a specifically *English* reformed church, the invocation of distinctly *national* heroes from the past—these are the historical activities that cause the

[12] Certeau, *Writing of History*, 5.

[13] Thomas Greene, *The Light in Troy: Imitation and Discovery in Renaissance Poetry* (New Haven: Yale University Press, 1982); Debora Shuger, *The Renaissance Bible: Scholarship, Sacrifice, and Subjectivity* (Berkeley: University of California Press, 1994); Timothy Hampton, *Writing from History: The Rhetoric of Exemplarity in Renaissance Literature* (Ithaca: Cornell University Press, 1990).

strings of poetry, religion, and humanist exemplarity to resonate anachronistically.[14]

We should not, of course, exaggerate the feeling that historical loss was inevitable. Renaissance historical writers repeatedly express confidence that their new sense of perspective, brought about by the restoration of "true" religion and improved historiographic methodologies, will allow them to recover the national past with a fullness and accuracy unattainable for previous historians. Although the astrologer and antiquarian John Dee made historical claims we now find farfetched, Dee himself believed that his generation of historians was in a position to surpass previous generations, to "shape sundry other things as to St. Jerome and our predecessors did seem rather impossible or untrue, [which] we now (by farther experience) do well know to be likely or, as possible, true & commendable."[15] Remarks such as this one should remind us to what degree historiographical discouragement was mixed, or at least alternated, with optimism. Nor should we assume that the Renaissance sense of historical loss emerged out of nowhere. William of Malmesbury was perfectly able in the twelfth century to describe historical writing as an "uncovering to the light what lay hidden in ancient heaps."[16] The recent work of D. R. Woolf has suggested some of the ways in which the "historical revolution" thesis of F. Smith Fussner, F. J. Levy, and others oversimplifies and perhaps exaggerates the difference between medieval

[14] More recently, in his excellent study of Renaissance French nationalism, Hampton has explored the effects of historical dislocation produced by specifically national consciousness: "the nation-state [pries] 'pre-national' events loose from local or municipal struggles to give them histories they never knew they had . . . new national identity is forged out of earlier identities, which nonetheless leave their traces—as a kind of resistance—on the text. . . . The new community of the modern nation-state thus comes at the expense of some earlier community or shared sense of identity. Literature measures the costs of this transition." Timothy Hampton, *Literature and Nation in the Sixteenth Century: Inventing Renaissance France* (Ithaca: Cornell University Press, 2001), 13. Hampton stresses the tendency of the pre-national past to "resist" the allegorizing efforts of early-modern national representation, whereas I emphasize the impression of national historical writers that the past has escaped them altogether. Nonetheless, there is a substantial compatibility between our views.

[15] John Dee, *Of Famous and Rich Discoveries* (British Library MS Cotton Vitellius C.VII), fol. 201r.

[16] Quoted in Andrew Galloway, "Writing History in England," in *The Cambridge History of Medieval English Literature*, ed. David Wallace (Cambridge: Cambridge University Press, 1999), 264.

and Renaissance historiography.[17] Nonetheless, in England especially, a *generally* heightened sense of historical difference was
strengthened by a new religion, a newly centralized locus of political
authority, and widespread destruction of manuscripts in the 1530s.
English historical writers were deeply enthusiastic about their investigation of their nation's past, but they frequently hint at how this investigation is motivated by a gap that they cannot reduce. Historical
loss is neither something that these writers "solve" nor something
that makes them abandon history but rather a recurring absence that
structures many of their narratives. This historical absence leads national writers to a variety of conclusions: (1) they must link the past
to the present; (2) they must lament the gap between past and present; and (3) they must forget the (alien) past to make sure that it does
not infect the present.

One of the best examples I know of this interplay between remem-
bering, lamenting, and forgetting, an example I return to in nearly
every chapter of this book, is Edmund Spenser's representation of
Prince Arthur, just after the prince has suffered a severe *historia in-
terrupta*. While visiting the chamber of Eumnestes in book II of *The
Faerie Queene*, Arthur finds an old book titled *Briton moniments*
that contains the history of the British people from the founding of
the nation by the Trojan Brutus to the reign of Uther Pendragon in
the fifth century C.E. After reading through the often brutal exploits
of the ancient Britons, Arthur is famously annoyed by the sudden interruption of the narrative, an interruption made all the more conspicuous by Spenser's ironic insertion of the final word, "succeed-
ing":[18] the narrative does not "succeed" at all but rather breaks off
just before it reaches Arthur himself. The prince overcomes his an-
noyance, however, and, "ravished with delight" (II.x.69.1), cries out:

> Dear countrey, O how dearely deare
> Ought thy remembraunce, and perpetuall band
> Be to thy foster Childe, that from thy hand
> Did commun breath and nouriture receave?

[17] D. R. Woolf, *The Idea of History in Early Stuart England: Erudition, Ideology,
and "The Light of Truth" from the Accession of James I to the Civil War* (Toronto:
University of Toronto Press, 1990).
[18] Edmund Spenser, *The Faerie Queene*, ed. A. C. Hamilton (New York: Longman,
2001), II.x.68.2. All subsequent references to the poem are from this edition. In-text
references in parentheses, if not obvious, are identified as *FQ*.

> How brutish is it not to understand,
> How much to her we owe, that all us gave,
> That gave unto us all what ever good we have.
>
> (II.x.69.3–9)

The phrase "commun breath and nouriture," as well as Arthur's and Sir Guyon's earlier experience of "burning both with fervent fire, / Their countries auncestry to understand" (ix.60.6–7), emphasizes the sense of a *national* affiliation over that of class or religion. For Spenser, this sense of national identity naturally leads one to desire a knowledge of national history, because history will fulfill national identity, a point he underlines by offering a narrative in which the fictional reader (Arthur) will someday play a prominent part. The English must remember their past to achieve the identity they desire in the present. At the same time, this image of Arthur at his history lesson implies that national consciousness to some degree depends on the caesura between past and present. Arthur can appreciate ("ravished with delight") his national identity not only in spite of the interruption but also because of it. If Arthur could reach the point in the narrative after Uther Pendragon, he could become part of it, escaping his alienation from history. Yet reaching that point would also mean Arthur's extinction, because the narrative includes his own death. The history that celebrates Arthur also annihilates him. Spenser thus presents us with the peculiar scenario of a reader who must be alienated from the history he studies in order to achieve the identity he seeks. He is the Tudor emblem of national consciousness, a sense of self and community hankering after a knowledge of its origins ("how brutish is it not to understand") yet nonetheless predicated on its isolation from these origins.

What Nation? Which Nation?

One of the primary difficulties for any examination of Renaissance nationalism resides in convincing scholars of modernity, on the one hand, that national consciousness existed at all in the sixteenth century, and persuading scholars of medieval culture, on the other hand, that nationalism was something other than old news in the sixteenth century. One thus starts off with few friends. Many historical studies of national development locate its origins post-Renaissance, citing the period's lack of democratic organization, the absence of wide-spread literacy, the lack of communication between isolated locali-ties, and the universalizing thrust of early Protestantism.[19] In part, I oppose these claims with recent research on Tudor culture that has uncovered the role of republican thinking in Elizabethan political theory, the surprisingly high number of readers of the English Bible, the emergence of a "standard" English over regional dialect as en-couraged by the dissemination of books such as *Acts and Monu-ments*, and the national effects of the English Church. National sen-timent was "real" in this period, in the sense that it amounted to more than only convenient rhetoric, as is sometimes argued. No doubt, when Shakespeare's Henry V demotically assures his humble soldiers that "he today that sheds his blood with me / Shall be my brother; be he ne're so vile, / This day shall gentle his condition" (IV.3.61–63),[20] the king (and the play) may have propagandistic goals. Yet even if so, the king, and playwright, must assume that the audi-ence will recognize and potentially identify with this vision of specif-ically English comradeship. Indeed, is postmonarchical, modern na-tionalism in no way propagandistic? How do we distinguish between politically coerced and real national identity? As McEachern has ar-gued, "[t]o assume that, because early modern England was a monar-chy, its ideologies of order were inimical to expressions of social unity is as naïve as to assume that the reigning democratic myth of twentieth century America . . . guarantees either social equality or unanimity."[21]

On the other hand, my focus on the nation's temporal dimension leads me to insist that Renaissance nationalism differed importantly from later manifestations. Americans, however fervent their love of country, are obliged to acknowledge that their community formally began only in 1776, one event out of many in history. Tudor and Stu-art writers, accustomed to a religious cosmology in which a commu-nity's past extended back to the early events of history, found it more difficult to say when their "nation" began. If I try to mark this differ-

---

[19] For two important examples out of many, see Eric Hobsbawm, *Nations and Na-tionalism since 1789* (Cambridge: Cambridge University Press, 1991), 74–76; and John Breuilly, *Nationalism and the State*, 2d ed. (Chicago: University of Chicago Press, 1994), 2–5.

[20] *Henry V*, in *The Complete Works of Shakespeare*, ed. David Bevington (Glen-view, Ill.: Scott, Foresman, 1980).

[21] McEachern, *Poetics of English Nationhood*, 19.

ence with the term "*early* national consciousness," I do so not to invoke an organic-developmental model of nationalism but rather to assert that some of the customary ways we think of nations as historically limited begin to emerge in the Renaissance.

When I come to the medievalist objection to my repeated claim that national consciousness "emerged" in the sixteenth century, I stand on even shakier ground. How can one deny that many "national" phenomena were alive and well in the Norman period, and perhaps earlier? And if one grants the phenomena, why not the nation? If, as I argue, Spenser uses the myth of Saint George to imbue apocalyptic theology with a sense of provincial English community, he can do so only because of the centuries-old populist significance this figure held for England.[22] If John Dee uses the figure of Arthur as a sign of his nation's imperial destiny, he draws on a long tradition of English and Welsh redactions.[23] Recent studies in premodern culture have argued for medieval nationalism in a variety of ways.[24] Patricia Clare Ingham has even described Anderson's postmedieval emphasis as "an account of nation that medievalists love to hate."[25] To a great extent, I sympathize with the criticism of a narrow-minded link between nation and modernity; there are ways to define nationhood so that the continuities rather than distinctions between medieval and

---

[22] See Jonathan Bengtson, "Saint George and the Formation of English Nationalism," *Journal of Medieval and Early Modern Culture* 27, 2 (1997): 317–40.

[23] See Patricia Clare Ingham, *Sovereign Fantasies: Arthurian Romance and the Making of Britain* (Philadelphia: University of Pennsylvania Press, 2001).

[24] Kathleen Davis and Alfred Smyth have both argued for well-developed conceptions of Englishness in the Saxon period. Davis, "National Writing in the Ninth Century: A Reminder for Postcolonial Thinking about the Nation," *Journal of Medieval and Early Modern Studies* 28, 3 (1998): 611–37; and Smyth, "The Emergence of English Identity, 700–1000," in *Medieval Europeans: Studies in Ethnic Identity and National Perspectives in Medieval Europe*, ed. Alfred P. Smyth (New York: St. Martin's Press, 1998), 24–52, esp. 26. Anthony D. Smith argues for a variety of definitions of the national state that would place it in the middle ages, although he concludes that "It is only from the late fifteenth century that we can confidently speak of a growing sense of English national identity, in a wider national state." Smith, "National Identities: Modern or Medieval?" in *Concepts of National Identity in the Middle Ages*, ed. Simon Ford, Leslie Johnson, and Alan V. Murray (Leeds: School of English, University of Leeds, 1995), 35. Derek Pearsall is one of the few medievalists who argues that before the Reformation "there was no steadily growing sense of national feeling." Pearsall, "The Idea of Englishness in the Fifteenth Century," in *Nation, Court and Culture: New Essays on Fifteenth-Century English Poetry*, ed. Helen Cooney (Dublin: Four Courts Press, 2001), 15.

[25] Ingham, *Sovereign Fantasies*, 8.

modern become primary. Nonetheless, I argue for a distinctly Renaissance national consciousness, one caught between two dispensations of time, a period in which the question "What is English?" becomes deeply tied to the question "When did England begin?" Again, the joining of these questions emerges from the sense that the nation's link to its past has become precarious in often overwhelming ways. Whatever the precedents in English history, the Tudors appear to experience phenomena such as the Reformation and the royal centralization of power as violent caesurae, breaks with the past that they furiously try to repair or repress.

One of my central arguments is that English national consciousness emerges at a point in history *before* the English had constructed a narrative of progress to accommodate the nation's seeming novelty. Their sense of national development in history thus tended to be eschatological rather than progressive, drawn forward by a totalizing future moment rather than pushed from behind by contingent yet determining past events. Yet English writers perceived the eschaton that loomed before them as an imminent end of time, not as a doorway to a new, earthly future. As I have suggested, the surge of historiographic discourse in the period resulted in part from a new sense of perspective, looking back at history from a standpoint of an elderly present. Tudor writers commonly voiced the impression that the world had physically grown old and decrepit. Arthur Golding, translating Augustine Marlorat's biblical commentary, spoke of "the perishing world now hasting to his end."[26] Thomas Rogers took recent climatic and geological disturbances as a sign of the earth's decay: "There are besides these other signs of the oldness of the world, and of his overthrow."[27] An old man can see his life whole in a way youth cannot, but he suffers from a foreshortened future. This sense of the elderly state of the world, a world whose future was now limited, contributed deeply to the apocalyptic expectation regarding the nation that flourished to an almost unprecedented degree in Renaissance England. As we will see in Foxe, Dee, and Spenser, apocalyptic imminence, like the world's old age, permits a special view of the past but also denies the present a worldly future. (Interestingly, although

---

[26] Arthur Golding, *A Catholic Exposition upon the Revelation of Saint John* (London, 1574), A2v.

[27] Thomas Rogers, *Of the End of this World, and the Second Coming of Christ* (London, 1577), D2v.

Nietzsche diagnoses his nation's latecomer weariness as a symptom of modernity, he also identifies the phenomenon as a holdover from Christian apocalypticism.)[28] We ought not underestimate the continuity between apocalyptic imminence and historical loss in this period, especially to the extent that they both respond to the nation's *novelty*. Although historiographers of the sixteenth and seventeenth centuries begin to supplement their typological understanding of history with a linear, causal one, they do not yet experience history in a fully "modern" sense, equipped with the notion of historical progress. National consciousness emerges in England before the Enlightenment idea of historical progress catches up to and compensates for the perception of historical difference, thus awkwardly linking the optimistic hope for a national future to a pessimistic sense of historical loss. It is only in the mid-seventeenth century that historical writers such as Milton begin in a sustained manner to explore the possibility of embracing national innovation as a positive phenomenon, and even then, as I discuss in chapter 5, they try to link this idea to a millenarian providentialism.

This interplay between tradition, novelty, and modernity reveals that, despite my reliance on the retrospective emphasis of "Renaissance," the story I have to tell also invokes the forward-looking gaze of "early modern." My interpretation of early English national consciousness as one of belatedness depends on the assumption that post-Renaissance nationhood embraced the innovation of modernity. As Habermas has influentially described the phenomenon, "the secular concept of modernity expresses the conviction that the future has already begun: It is the epoch that lives for the future, that opens itself up to *the novelty of the future*."[29] More recently, the association between modernity and nationhood has been promoted strenuously by Liah Greenfeld, both in the title of her book—*Nationalism: Five Roads to Modernity*—and in her bold but perhaps reductive claim that "[t]he original modern idea of the nation emerged in sixteenth-century England, which was the first nation in the world."[30] Some

---

[28] "Does not this paralyzing belief in an already withering mankind rather harbour the misunderstanding, inherited from the Middle Ages, of a Christian theological conception, the thought that the end of the world is near, of the fearfully expected judgment?" (Nietzsche, *Advantage and Disadvantage of History*, 44).

[29] Jürgen Habermas, *The Philosophical Discourse of Modernity*, trans. Frederick G. Lawrence (Cambridge: MIT Press, 1987), 5 (my emphasis).

[30] Liah Greenfeld, *Nationalism: Five Roads to Modernity* (Cambridge: Harvard University Press, 1992), 14.

scholars have responded to this progressivism by noting the mystifying effects of national identity wherein the historically contingent *nation* becomes superseded by the transcendental fiction of *nationalism*.[31] Yet this examination does not so much insist on a dichotomy of pre-Renaissance traditionalism and post-Renaissance modernity as it describes the Renaissance attempt to interpret national novelty as historical continuity. Looking back centuries after the fact, we may indeed find it difficult not to see English Renaissance nationalism as an "early" sign of modernity. Yet, if so, it is also a reluctant sign of modernity, one that keeps trying unsuccessfully to realign itself with tradition. This is not to say that the post-Renaissance nation simply abandons tradition in order to embrace novelty but rather to try to understand why nations have often emerged as figures of mediation between a community's need for historical origins and its anticipation of historical change. Even late-nineteenth-century skeptics of the idea of "natural" progress in history often continue to describe the nation in terms of its dual temporal imperatives of recollection and repression. Ernest Renan insists both that "[f]orgetting . . . is a crucial factor in the creation of a nation" and that the nation depends on "the possession in common of a rich legacy of memories." If Renan has a "modern" view of the nation, it may lie in his calm recognition of this community's historical contingency: "nations are not something eternal. They had their beginnings and they will end."[32] Renaissance national consciousness, by contrast, begins to conceive of a form of English community circumscribed by this sort of extreme time-boundedness and yet at the same time tries to reinscribe it in the earlier Virgilian terms of *imperium sine fine*, in which the nation's temporality becomes coextensive with the earliest and final events of civilized history.

As is probably becoming clear from the foregoing discussion, my emphasis on time leads me to treat the nation less as the ideological field of conformity and resistance that it has been in recent critical debates, and more as a community that both motivates and comes

[31] In their introduction to a special issue of *Representations*, Carla Hesse and Thomas Laqueur complain that Greenfeld uses "nationalism" inconsistently, "both as a historically specific and as a transhistorical category of analysis" (2), and they conclude that modern nationalism "continues to seek transparency and transcendence" (12); *Representations* 47 (1994): 1–12.

[32] Ernest Renan, "Qu'est-ce qu'une nation?" originally delivered as a lecture at the Sorbonne in 1882, translated by Martin Thom, and reprinted as "What Is a Nation?" in Bhabha, *Nation and Narration*, 11, 19, 20.

into being by means of the narratives of history that I examine. In
this emphasis I am indebted to the work of Richard Helgerson, who,
although certainly not ignoring the political dimension of national
consciousness, stressed the manner in which textual and visual
forms helped to call this consciousness into existence.[33] Yet my account of the nation's temporality does have implications for the recent polemics of revisionist and postrevisionist scholarship regarding
Renaissance England's political modernity. Revisionist studies, seeking to reverse "anachronistic" assumptions of the Whig view of history about citizenship and republican theory in the sixteenth and seventeenth centuries, have argued for a conservative English culture
little influenced by the isolated radical ideas of Machiavelli or Mon-
taigne. As Kevin Sharpe has recently insisted, "[t]here is little sign . . .
that in the early seventeenth century new theories or ideas affected
the course of politics," and from this he concludes that the Civil War
of the 1640s was the cause rather than effect of a new radical vocabu-
lary about "rights."[34] Before the Civil War, in this view, national
identity functions largely as a traditional form of political uniformity. On the other hand, postrevisionist scholars such as Annabel
Patterson and David Norbrook contend that the language of republicanism extends through national consciousness as far back as the Reformation.[35] Patterson especially has argued for a progressive interpretation of Renaissance nationalism, describing Holinshed's
Chronicles (1577) in terms of "protoliberalism" and an interest "in
what we now call rights theory, specifically in constitutional and
legal rights."[36]

---

[33] Richard Helgerson, *Forms of Nationhood: The Elizabethan Writing of England*
(Chicago: University of Chicago Press, 1992).

[34] Kevin Sharpe, *Remapping Early Modern England: The Culture of Seventeenth-
Century Politics* (Cambridge: Cambridge University Press, 2000), 115, 118. Sharpe
opens this informative study by positioning himself as a slightly reformed revisionist
who pays attention to more than court factions (see 3–37). He does indeed address an
impressive variety of cultural phenomena in the Stuart period, but his basic conclusions about the essentially traditional and conservative nature of this period do not
differ markedly from other revisionist scholars.

[35] Annabel Patterson, *Reading Holinshed's "Chronicles"* (Chicago: University of
Chicago Press, 1994); and David Norbrook, *Writing the English Republic: Poetry,
Rhetoric and Politics, 1627–1660* (Cambridge: Cambridge University Press, 1999).

[36] Patterson, *Reading Holinshed's "Chronicles,"* 7. See also Patterson's thoughtful
discussion about the criteria for "revolution" in modern scholarship: "The Very
Name of the Game: Theories of Order and Disorder," in *Literature and the English
Civil War,* ed. Thomas Healy and Jonathan Sawday (Cambridge: Cambridge Univer-

My examination does not seek to solve this productive debate. Yet to the degree that these positions rely on the Renaissance sense of history, I am able to offer some qualifications. A difficulty with linking early nationalism to an explicit program of progressive politics is that Renaissance writers almost never talk about history as progressive, at least not in the modern sense of embracing innovation. Although uprisings in the Tudor and Stuart era do occur in the name of "England," their authors do not seem to conceive of them with the post-Enlightenment revolutionary mission—however qualified by tradition—to rebuild society from scratch. As I have suggested and continue to demonstrate throughout this volume, until the 1640s they usually attempt to mitigate the sense of novelty with a recourse to precedent. Yet Sharpe's claim that, before the Civil War, radical ideas were stymied because "past and present were not conceived as different" misstates the matter to a considerable degree.[37] His claim matches the conclusions of D. R. Woolf that before 1642 "there was fundamental agreement on the main points of English and classical history," and that "[i]t would take civil war and the suspension of censorship in the 1640s to bring about a framework of historical discussion that was truly dialectical."[38] The validity of these conservative interpretations of Renaissance historicism depends, I suppose, on what counts as "truly dialectical." It is true that English writers became willing to abandon precedent in a sustained manner only in the 1640s and after, but it is inaccurate to conclude that before then they never saw the past as alien to the present. Indeed, it did sometimes appear unfamiliar to them, and there seems to have been no fundamental agreement about how to close the gap between past and present aside from the basic idea that this gap ought to be closed. The historical dilemma of the Renaissance nation derives from its bad timing, cultivating a sense of historical loss before it develops a model of historical progress. Its "pre-progress" status may keep the early nation from affiliating itself with an explicitly radical program, yet its historical dislocation did turn it into a lens through which some traditional forms of identity began to lose their naturalness and inevitability.

---

sity Press, 1990), 21–37. She concludes that "there *was* a continuous radical tradition available in the culture of earlier periods" (36, emphasis in the original).

[37] Sharpe, *Remapping Early Modern England*, 87.

[38] Woolf, *Idea of History in Early Stuart England*, 30, 33.

Even if one grants the emergence of a certain pattern of national consciousness in the sixteenth century, one may still be unclear as to *which* nation we mean. Tudor and Stuart writers in "England" commonly refer to themselves as "British." Depending on context, "British" in this period could comprise England, Scotland, and Wales; or it could designate the pre-Saxon identity persisting in England, especially through the modern Welsh; or, more rarely, it appears simply to be synonymous with "English." This ambiguity in contemporary usage pointed to a persistent historical problem: was the national past an English or a British one? Historical writers disagreed about where England's true ancestry lay. Richard Harvey excluded the Saxons from historical consideration in his *Philadelphus* (1593), explaining that they were barbarous and ought to be subordinated to the Britons, whom he calls "Brutans":

> If I omit some histories of Saxons I do but my duty; what have I to do with them, unless it were to make them tributary to *Brutans*. . . . Let them lie in dead forgetfulness like stones . . . let their names be clean put out. . . . Arise, ye sons of Ebranke, and ye kinsmen of the true ancient Brutans and make those stone-hearted creatures know that they are made to be your servants and drudges: let not any double-forked tongue persuade you that *Brutanie* is under any part of the earth.[39]

On the other hand, the antiquary Sir Henry Spelman, arguing against the proposed transformation of the name "England" to "Great Britain" in 1604, insists that emphasizing England's ancient "Briton" past degrades the present-day nation:

> if the honorable name of England be buried in the resurrection of Albion or Britannia, we shall change the golden beames of the sun for a cloudy day, and drown the glory of a nation triumphant through all the world to restore the memory of an obscure and barbarous people [the Britons], of whom no mention almost is made in any notable history author but is either to their own disgrace or at least to grace the trophies and victories of their conquerors the Romans, Picts and Saxons.[40]

---

[39] Richard Harvey, *Philadelphus* (London, 1593), 97.
[40] Henry Spelman, "Of the Union," 1604; reprinted in *The Jacobean Union: Six Tracts of 1604*, ed. Bruce R. Galloway and Brian P. Levack (Edinburgh: Scottish History Society, 1985), 170.

A "British" position such as Harvey's celebrates national antiquity in the face of a growing impression that these antiquities were mere fables (as I discuss in chap. 4); an "English" position such as Spelman's celebrates national purity in the present at the risk of historical belatedness. Neither account of identity is completely safe, yet both attempt to mediate the difficult question of England/Britain in terms of national history.

Many sixteenth-century writers hint at their unease about this etiological uncertainty by Anglicizing obviously pre-Saxon subject matter, seemingly striving to impose uniformity on a heterogeneous history. Foxe calls Helen, the mother of fourth-century Constantine, "an English woman,"[41] and Richard Robinson refers to Arthur when he was "returned into England."[42] David Baker has recently suggested that English nationalism was born out of a need to compensate for this etiological indeterminacy:

> it is because no one of the British peoples [Scottish, Irish, or English] . . . can call upon a seamless, unadulterated history reaching back to pristine origins that one of those peoples—the English—must emerge as a nation-state capable of subordinating all of the British people to it. . . . British history is a history of chronic instability, and it puts "national" identity on the islands profoundly in question—so profoundly that it must be answered with a fervent and compensatory Englishness.[43]

The Tudor insistence on a pure, homogeneous English identity in the present attempted to mitigate the fragmentation of this identity in the past. No serious investigation of English/British nationalism can afford to neglect Baker's insight. Although I focus on so-called English national identity rather than Welsh or Scottish or Irish national

---

[41] John Foxe, "To the Queen's Most Excellent Majesty," in *Acts and Monuments* (London, 1563), B1r.

[42] Richard Robinson, *A Learned and True Assertion of the Original, Life, Acts, and Death of the Most Noble, Valiant, and Renowned Prince Arthur, King of Great Britain* (London, 1582), fol. 6r. Robinson is translating John Leland's tract, *Assertio Inclytissimi Arturii Regis Britanniae* (London, 1544.)

[43] David Baker, "Spenser and the Uses of British History," in *Worldmaking Spenser: Explorations in the Early Modern Age*, ed. Patrick Cheney and Lauren Silberman (Lexington: University Press of Kentucky, 2000), 201. This insight also governs much of Baker's earlier book-length study of Spenser, Shakespeare, and Marvell; see Baker, *Between Nations: Shakespeare, Spenser, Marvell, and the Question of Britain* (Stanford: Stanford University Press, 1997).

identity, I do not pretend that Englishness was comprehensible apart from these other identities. Yet I want to think the dynamic of history and heterogeneity from the *reverse* direction: to what degree did the novelty of national consciousness *produce* a vision of the past that lacked "pristine origins" and was characterized by "chronic instability"? The answer to this question, as I try to demonstrate in this book, lies in the manner in which English nationalism did not only compensate for historical loss but also helped to create it, depending on this gap between past and present as the condition of its success.

Modes of Historical Recovery

I have deliberately chosen to write about four authors who produced a disparate body of work: Protestant martyrology, allegorical drama, treatise on navigation, antiquarian study, epic romance, colonialist anthropology, historiography, and antiprelatical polemic. These writers also differ importantly in their career trajectories and professional identifications. All four are Protestants, but with different levels of commitment and varying conceptions of their faith (John Dee appears to have been quite content working under Mary I). Two are considered literary writers, two generally regarded as nonliterary. Two wrote some of their work while exiled from England. Only one of them produced a text typically thought of as a history in the strict sense. Yet these differences help me show all the more clearly the crucial commonalty in the work of Foxe, Dee, Spenser, and Milton: they all share a persistent interest in their nation's place in time, and they all explicitly conceive of this temporality as stretched between an obscure past and a foreshortening apocalyptic future. Repeatedly in their work, the national present emerges as a rather precarious threshold. The generic differences in their writing lead them to manifest this conception of national time in importantly distinct ways, yet they all construct narratives, or, in Dee's case, a prospectus of a narrative, that attempt to consolidate England's fractured temporality. In this sense, I conceive of this study primarily as a literary one. Although it certainly tries to read texts within their historical moment, it ultimately focuses on the manner in which these writers use storytelling, even discourse about storytelling, to fashion national identities within history.

Foxe, Dee, Spenser, and Milton are the stars of this book, but so are the *kinds* of narrative solutions these writers try to apply to the problem of historical loss. For this reason, the chapters that follow (except for chap. 1) are organized not by author but by three historical modes: the antiquarian, the apocalyptic, and the fictional. Each mode represents an umbrella concept for a variety of texts, institutions, practices, genres, and vocations that the Renaissance recognized as primary forms of historical thought. These modes are thus broadly conceived but self-consistent, bringing with them assumptions about history and conventions for historical writing. *The Faerie Queene* is not an antiquarian treatise, but it invokes beliefs about historical evidence, physical artifacts, and Arthurianism. *Acts and Monuments* is not an apocalyptic commentary, but it juxtaposes the prophecies of Revelation with English history. The *History of Britain* is not historical poetry, but it elaborates the bare facts of history with fictional speculations. For each mode I consider two authors, which allows me to emphasize the diachronic dimension of that chapter's historical problem. We understand Foxe's apocalypticism in the 1560s better if we compare it with Spenser's in the 1580s and 1590s, and we understand Spenser's fictionalization of history in 1590 better if we compare it to Milton's in the 1640s. All three modes derive their power from qualities that also limit their capacities: the antiquarian artifact consumes itself in time, apocalyptic history forecloses the future, and fiction empties history even as it provides continuity.

In chapter 2, I am concerned with antiquarian history, one of the most important methodological developments of sixteenth-century historical study, and focus on the manner in which the Tudor effort to discover the remains of King Arthur's ancient realm takes the form of a dialectic between the "monument" and "prophecy," between material and transcendental forms of historical knowledge. The figure of the monument, as antiquaries often referred to the physical remains of the past, produces a double effect: it reminds the English nation of its history, closing the gap between past and present, but its materiality assures that it will itself disappear some day, signaling the loss or death of history. The manuscript spoliation of the 1530s exposed the fragility of the monument all too painfully. Both John Dee and Edmund Spenser shift from a precarious investment in the material monument to historical narratives inspired by prophecy, conceiving it as a spiritual form of knowledge free from the burden of material transience. By linking Dee and Spenser, I attempt to demonstrate that *The Faerie Queene* participates seriously in historiographical debate rather than simply taking historiography as a poetic metaphor. The emphasis on the dialectic between the monument and prophecy reveals how commonly antiquarian writing in the period turns on both a fascination with the material past and on a sense of the material as a limitation it would like to escape. At the same time, this escape from the material risks its own historical loss, in the form of a prophetic eschatology that absorbs England's history into a vision of the coming Apocalypse.

This problematic slip from the prophetic to apocalyptic moment leads me, in chapter 3, to consider the impact of apocalyptic theology on nationalism. Early Elizabethan Protestant writers increasingly used a historical interpretation of the Book of Revelation to impose a continuity on the English past, wherein specific national events turn out to have been divinely predicted. In this manner they worked to reverse the impression of historical loss by imbuing English history with a divine inevitability. Yet in a dynamic I call "postmillennial foreclosure," England's recent success against Antichrist—as the Reformers referred to the Roman Church—fuels the desire for a glorious English future, but the expectation of an imminent, earth-destroying Apocalypse closes off the national future. Foxe responds to this problem by narratively deferring the conclusion of his *Acts and Monuments*, adding more and more national details to his story as the eschatological conclusion of his book approaches. Spenser changes the terms of the problem in the first book of *The Faerie Queene*, hinting that the nation, before the end of history, may be able to contribute positively to Christ's final victory. The diachronic dimension makes all the difference here in that Foxe, at the beginning of Elizabeth's reign, conceives of the Apocalypse only as the judgment of national history, whereas Spenser, writing after the English victory over the Armada, begins to imagine the Apocalypse as the culmination of national history.

Fictional history, what Renaissance writers often referred to as "poesy historical," represents in some ways a last-ditch attempt to imagine the nation firmly grounded in ancient tradition. Fiction and history intermixed in a variety of ways during the period, but I contextualize my discussion in chapter 4 with the proposed union between England and Scotland in the early seventeenth century, in which the pro-Union celebration of ancient British origins (à la Geoffrey of Monmouth) coincided with the increasing conviction that these origins were mere fables. If "England" as opposed to "Britain" emerges in these debates as a latter-day community, a product of modernity, its history is at least verifiable. Spenser, writing a decade before these debates, and Milton, writing over two decades after they ceased, both meditate on ancient British origins in relation to national heterogeneity in the present. They both try to imagine a relationship between fact and fable wherein fiction ornaments the bare thread of history, making it possible to represent a homogenous origin that the nation's multinational past (Britons, Saxons, Danes, Normans) otherwise makes impossible. As poets, Spenser and Milton are both alert to the value of fiction to promote continuity; as historical writers, they realize the manner in which fictional ornament may empty their narratives of historical content. Again, their disparate historical moments influence their responses to the problem of fiction, to a considerable degree. What Spenser can claim about the historical existence of Arthur in 1590 differs substantially from what Milton can say in 1649.

Chapter 5 does not so much introduce a new mode of historical engagement as it considers how emerging ideas about historical innovation begin to change the terms of the national problem in the seventeenth century. The development and spread of millenarianism (in which the Apocalypse ushers in a national paradise) led some English thinkers to anticipate a glorious and radically different future on earth, one in which England might have an elect place. They qualified this vision in numerous ways, deferring the end time until that point at which the nation would achieve sufficient godliness and reform the church fully. Yet it is in the seventeenth-century discourse of millenarian nationalism that the narrative of historical progress begins to take shape in English thought, making it possible to interpret historical change positively instead of as discontinuity and decline. Foxe in the sixteenth century uses his apocalypticism for the sake of historical consolidation, reinterpreting the break with the religious past as a restoration of tradition. A century later Milton uses his apocalypticism to emphasize the nation's break from the past, to free it from stultifying traditions, embracing the novelty of the future. Milton thus "solves" the national problem of historical loss in the way some eighteenth-and nineteenth-century nationalists would, by postulating a narrative of historical progress. Yet I also qualify this interpretation by arguing that Milton often registers, as, for example, with the dismembered body of Truth in *Areopagitica*, a sense of the cost of modern temporality: a national history so utterly susceptible to human manipulation is also a history from which God has to some degree withdrawn.

I describe chapter 1 last because it does not explain a single mode of historical recovery but rather offers a preliminary example of the interplay between recovery and loss from Foxe's *Acts and Monuments*. In taking up the Protestant defense of Sir John Oldcastle, the early-fifteenth-century Lollard executed during the reign of Henry V, Foxe must face a fundamental difficulty that the Reformation created for national history. Medieval men and women who resisted Catholic doctrine in England certainly qualified as members of the true church of Christ, but could the Tudor Reformers also consider them patriots? That is, did not the Lollards' disobedience of English authorities make them national traitors, albeit godly ones? Was it possible for Foxe to represent a figure like Oldcastle as an exemplar of both the true church and the nation, or did an unavoidable discontinuity mark England's religious history, a discontinuity that the Reformation might compensate for but never erase? I suggest in chapter 1 that the Reformation did not so much compensate for a discontinuity as create it, forcing the Tudors to see their nation in terms of a *now* and *then* in an unprecedented manner. That I choose *Acts and Monuments* as my preliminary example of the problems of national time suggests how important the religious dimension of Renaissance culture is to this study. This is not a book only about the Reformation, nor do I argue that the Reformation made national consciousness inevitable (indeed, I argue in chap. 1 that it both encouraged and impeded national consciousness). Yet the Reformation institutes a new relation between past and present, one that foregrounds the issue of historical difference, and this relation resonates crucially with the strategies of antiquarian, apocalyptic, and fictional history that I examine in chapters 2, 3, and 4. By returning to Foxe's traditionalism in chapter 5 and contrasting it with Milton's sense of innovation, I establish the break with Rome in the 1530s and the Civil War in the 1640s as two moments between which the nation emerges as a community rooted in history, to be sure, but in a history now conceived as profoundly limited.

1 TRAITOROUS MARTYRS, OR A HISTORY TO FORGET?

Did the Reformation encourage the development of a national consciousness in sixteenth-century England? In several obvious ways it did, and these have been well documented. It stimulated, at least to some degree, an English-reading public.[1] It aligned ecclesiastical administration with state bureaucracy, creating an English church different from those of most nations in Europe. England's reformed distinctiveness encouraged some writers to ascribe a special, though it seems not elect, status for their nation in the eyes of God.[2] Mary I's reign gave rise to a flood of Protestant propaganda arguing that "men ought to have more respect to their country than to their prince," creating at least the potential for thinking about England as a community of citizens rather than only as subjects of the monarch.[3] The

---

[1] Adrian Hastings discusses the printing of the English Bible as encouraging "a common language," in *The Construction of Nationhood: Ethnicity, Religion, and Nationalism* (Cambridge: Cambridge University Press, 1997), 58.

[2] The classic study of this phenomenon is William Haller, *Foxe's Book of Martyrs and the Elect Nation* (London: J. Cape, 1963). Subsequent scholarship has of course questioned Haller's specific claim about England's "election" in the eyes of Elizabethan Protestants, but his more general assertions about English exceptionalism remain influential.

[3] John Poynet, *A Short Treatise of Politic Power* (Strasbourg, 1556), D7r. For a thorough review of this Protestant propaganda during Mary's reign, see Herbert Grabes, "England or the Queen?" in *Writing the Early Modern English Nation: The Transformation of National Identity in Sixteenth-and Seventeenth-Century England*, ed. Herbert Grabes (Amsterdam: Rodopi, 2001), 47–87.

break with the Roman Church produced a radically revised sense of annual festival and celebration, leading to the adoption of "a new national, secular and dynastic calendar centering on the anniversaries of the Protestant monarch."[4] Important for my interests, the Reformation spurred a concerted effort to expose and correct a Catholic "bias" in previous national historiography, instituting a new picture of the past that revealed how foreign interests had interfered with the domestic affairs of England. Such a picture made it easier to see English history as a story of national resistance to alien invaders rather than a series of self-destructive civil conflicts. Thus, although we should stop short of seeing the nation as an inevitable consequence of the break with Rome, it is hard in retrospect to conceive of how England could have achieved the relative insularity and uniformity it eventually did without the help of these foregoing developments.

Yet recent research has persuasively offered another side of the Reformation and its effects on national consciousness. Scholars such as Christopher Haigh have sought to redescribe early English Protestantism as a series of uneven starts and stops rather than as a single shift to a new faith that created public uniformity.[5] Tony Claydon and Ian McBride have noted how Protestantism's reactive quality fueled internal disputes with divisive charges of popery.[6] Peter Lake, examining the tendency of Reformers to describe themselves as a persecuted and scattered flock of faithful believers, concludes that Protestantism was a poor basis for a national church.[7] Others have demonstrated how deeply the Reformers saw their church as an international community, one that little respected the contingencies of state borders. In a recent examination of early modern drama, Jeffrey Knapp convincingly argues that the history plays, rather than promoting a national community, look forward to "the *supranational*

---

[4] David Cressy, *Bonfires and Bells: National Memory and the Protestant Calendar in Elizabethan England and Stuart England* (Berkeley: University of California Press, 1989), xii.

[5] Christopher Haigh, *English Reformations: Reform, Politics, and Society under the Tudors* (Oxford: Clarendon Press, 1993).

[6] Tony Clayton and Ian McBride, "The Trials of the Chosen Peoples: Recent Interpretations of Protestantism and National Identity in Britain and Ireland," in *Protestantism and National Identity: Britain and Ireland, c. 1650–c. 1850*, ed. Tony Clayton and Ian McBride (Cambridge: Cambridge University Press, 1998).

[7] Peter Lake, "Presbyterianism, the Idea of a National Church and the Argument from Divine Right," in *Protestantism and the National Church in Sixteenth-Century England*, ed. Peter Lake and Maria Dowling (New York: Croom Helm, 1987).

Christian society that should follow upon English 'reformation'."[8] According to Knapp, this transnational ideal follows in part from Reformation England's painful sense of its division from the world. Given these effects of uneven development, internal divisiveness, ecclesiastical isolation, and universalist aspiration, the Reformation appears to sound the death knell of English national consciousness rather than giving birth to it.

This debate has yielded tremendously useful insights into English Renaissance culture, but it also convinces me that we must acknowledge the heterogeneity of the Reformation, recognizing that many Elizabethan phenomena can have opposite effects and yet still be called "Protestant." The evidence suggests that the various aspects of Reformation thinking and practice interacted variously with national consciousness. Yet in this chapter I do not wish, in the name of ecumenical broadmindedness, to dull the recent sharp polemic that opposes church to nation; rather, I want to embrace it, extending the point about England's divided place in the world to its divided place in time. The Reformation cut England off from its religious past as much as it separated England from its fellow nations in Europe. My interest here, however, is to show that the nation does indeed persist despite this temporal isolation, an isolation that in fact contributed immensely to the conception of the English nation as a historically contingent and recent community. I have chosen John Foxe's account of Sir John Oldcastle as a brief, preliminary example of this effect because it reveals the degree to which the nation, rather than neatly contributing to the defense of the reformed church, often awkwardly threatened to associate the church with its own novelty. That is, although recent scholarship has focused on how the church impedes the nation, it has paid less attention to the nation as a disadvantage for the church. The investment in Englishness in fact makes Foxe's goal of religious continuity more difficult, compelling him to draw on the discourses of antiquarian, apocalyptic, and fictional history as a means of overcoming this difficulty—modes of historical recovery that chapters 2, 3, and 4 examine at length. Foxe achieves limited success, which ought to lead us to question why he bothers to defend the nation so persistently. In this interest I follow Paul Stevens, who, in his searching article about Milton's nationalism, has asked "why

---

[8] Jeffrey Knapp, *Shakespeare's Tribe: Church, Nation, and Theater in Renaissance England* (Chicago: University of Chicago Press, 2002), 86 (emphasis in original).

would someone as poetic and religious as Milton, so absorbed in universals, in the contemplation of the absolute and eternal, invest so heavily in a concept as contingent and ephemeral as the nation?"[9] This question can be applied as relevantly to Foxe, who, trying to construct a continuity for the true church of Christ, has everything to lose and little to gain from investing in a nation whose past is so obviously "papist."

No phenomenon in Renaissance England impinged on the question of national history as keenly as did the break with the Roman Church. Although the English community did, in the course of the sixteenth century, become primarily Protestant, we must not underestimate how deeply this development divorced the religious present from the national past. The "English" Church had been Catholic for centuries, as English Catholics loved to point out. When Thomas Stapleton, the religious controversialist who left England soon after the accession of Elizabeth, set out to criticize the reformed church by distinguishing "between the ancient faith of England and the upstart news of protestants,"[10] he was touching on an issue that created considerable anxiety for English Reformers: their church's conspicuous lack of antiquity. Many Protestant writers attempted to mitigate the sense of novelty by insisting that the reformed church had in fact restored the primitive, true church of Christ from which Rome had swerved.[11] Yet this formulation still left a wide (Catholic) gap in English religious history, a gap that many English writers found uncomfortable. Even John Bale, a stalwart defender of both the Reformation and England, was forced to acknowledge that in his nation's medieval period, "the more part of writers were wholly given to serve Antichrist's affects in the perilous ages of the Church."[12] Such a perception inevitably linked England to the corruption and cruelty of the Church of Rome, forcing some Protestants to concede Stapleton's point that Catholicism was indeed "the ancient faith of England."

[9] Paul Stevens, "Milton's Janus-Faced Nationalism: Soliloquy, Subject, and the Modern Nation State," *Journal of English and Germanic Philology* 100, 2 (2001): 256.
[10] Thomas Stapleton, *A Fortress of the Faith First Planted among Us Englishmen* (Antwerp, 1565), Ee1v.
[11] See, e.g., John Jewel, "An Apology of the Church of England," in *The Works of John Jewel, Bishop of Salisbury*, 4 vols., ed. Rev. J. Ayre (Cambridge: Parker Society, 1845), vol. 3, esp. 92, 100.
[12] John Bale, *The New Year's Gift* (London, 1546); reprinted in *John Leland's Itinerary*, ed. John Chandler (Dover, N.H.: Alan Sutton, 1993), 2.

Thus, for Reformers who wished to invest in some kind of national community, the rift between England's religious past and present was also the fault line between church and nation.

The Protestant demand for the truth of history made this fault line all the more difficult to cross. Jennifer Summit has recently argued that the Reformation fundamentally changed the process of historical interpretation because the suspect nature of pre-Reformation histories forced Protestant historians into a seemingly endless process of untangling true claims from false (Catholic) distortions, what Summit calls "a *lectio* of suspicion": "While allegoresis enabled medieval readers to reconcile apparently unorthodox texts with orthodox aims, post-Reformation readers attempted to bring texts into alignment through a process of selective chastening."[13] In part, the new emphasis on "chastening"—in editing, marginal commentary, and prefaces—in the name of historical and religious truth served as a powerful rhetorical advantage. It gave the Reformers a justification for "taking over enemy territory, and using enemy ammunition," as Margaret Aston describes the Protestant appropriation of medieval Catholic writing.[14] Yet what if, despite selective chastening, the truth of history offers exempla inappropriate to or incommensurate with the present? John Foxe's *Acts and Monuments*, the most sustained narrative of English ecclesiastical history in the Renaissance, engages this possibility more thoroughly than any text in the period. The polemical context of his writing, ostensibly correcting past Catholic inaccuracies with a more precise account, requires him to thematize repeatedly the truth of his narrative. Regarding the potential tension between spiritual and historical truth, Patrick Collinson has argued that "John Foxe's huge enterprise in its entirety depended upon a denial of any such conflict."[15] Yet Foxe's "denial" involved both a confident dismissal and uneasy repression. At a basic level, the truth that *Acts and Monuments* offers involves a portrait of English men and

[13] Jennifer Summit, "Monuments and Ruins: Spenser and the Problem of the English Library," *English Literary History* 70, 1 (2003): 1–34; at 15. My thanks to Prof. Summit for kindly sharing her manuscript with me before its publication.

[14] Margaret Aston, *Lollards and Reformers: Images and Literacy in Late Medieval Religion* (London: Hambledon Press, 1984), 235–36.

[15] Patrick Collinson, "Truth, Lies, and Fiction in Sixteenth-Century Protestant Historiography," in *The Historical Imagination in Early Modern Britain: History, Rhetoric, and Fiction, 1500–1800*, ed. Donald R. Kelley and David Harris Sacks (Cambridge: Cambridge University Press, 1997), 41.

women suffering through history—commoners, tradesmen, divines, and aristocrats—a portrait that comes very close to Benedict Anderson's description of national feeling as a "horizontal comradeship." Yet for Foxe, which comradeship do we mean—that of the nation, or that of the "true" church? This question has been asked many times before,[16] but I focus my answer on the manner in which the two communities sometimes split off into past and present in *Acts and Monuments*, the true church vying for historical precedent with the Church of Rome, whereas the English nation seems to reach back only to the recent accession of Elizabeth.

Foxe writes, like Dee, Spenser, and Milton, with a latecomer's perspective, seeing his generation at the end of series of struggles between the true church and the false one, awaiting the final coming of Christ in "these latter and perilous days."[17] This sense of an imminent reckoning fuels the impulse to recall the past, an impulse that governs Foxe's entire project. According to him, there is "nothing more lacking in the church than a full and complete story" (1570, ☞2v), and the lack of such a story has left the English people "wrapped in blindness . . . for wanting the light of history" (1570, *2r). One of Foxe's goals in providing the "light of history" was to reveal the continuity that ran through England's religious history, to demonstrate "the continual descent of the church till this present time" (1570, ☞4v). The reformed church did not simply represent a restoration of the truth for Foxe, but also the triumphant culmination of a long-beleaguered (but always extant) tradition. The medieval martyrs transform, under his pen, from a heretical minority in history to the heroic representatives of Christ's unbroken community. Yet, to some degree, Foxe establishes a religious link to the past at the expense of a national one. When he announces that he will write of "what sides and sorts of men, of princes, kings, monarchs, governors,

---

[16] Influential answers have been offered by Haller, *Foxe's Book of Martyrs and the Elect Nation;* Richard Helgerson, *Forms of Nationhood: The Elizabethan Writing of England* (Chicago: University of Chicago Press, 1992), esp. 247–94; and, more recently, Patrick Collinson, "John Foxe and National Consciousness," in *John Foxe and His World*, ed. Christopher Highley and John N. King (Aldershot, U.K.: Ashgate, 2002), 10–34.

[17] The quotation is from the title page of the 1563 edition. There were four English editions of *Acts and Monuments* published during Foxe's lifetime, in 1563, 1570, 1576, and 1583. I make subsequent parenthetical references to Foxe by means of edition date and signature. When the edition is obvious from the context, I do not bother to include the date.

and rulers of the world, with their subjects, publicly and privately, with all their strength and cunning, have bent themselves against this church" (1576, A1r), his own narrative forces him to acknowledge that many of these princes, subjects, and officials were English. As a result, at certain moments in *Acts and Monuments* Foxe implies that any member of the true church, faced with such hostility, would be forced to oppose his country: "For where it is so proved by the laws, that the sincere worshipping of Christ is counted for heresy, and a heretic counted a traitor, what citizen can, in that commonwealth, live in safety, without sin and wickedness, or be godly, without peril and danger?" (1563, R3r). Foxe at times backtracks on his commitment to the national community, giving priority instead to the universal church: "I have addressed this present history, intending . . . not so much to delight the ears of my country in reading of news, as most specially to profit the hearts of the godly, in perusing antiquities of ancient times" (1576, A1r). Here we have the language of Stapleton and his account of the reformed church as merely "upstart news"; yet Foxe's formulation displaces novelty from the church onto the nation ("my country . . . reading of news"). The nation repeatedly emerges in *Acts and Monuments* as a community only of the recent present, unfit for representation in history, where it participated in the "barbarousness of those days" (1570, a1r).

Foxe of course might have chosen to abandon or at least marginalize his defense of the national community, embracing instead a fully international conception of Protestantism. Yet he refuses to give up the attempt to offer a positive account of specifically English history, striving to represent his nation's past as an exemplary narrative for the present, offering many of his martyrs as exemplars of both church and nation. Much of the exemplarity of the narrative draws on the discourse of *imitatio Christi*, and most of Foxe's martyrs become Christlike at their deaths.[18] Yet Foxe also relies on the more recent humanist model of exemplarity, which, unlike the typical conception of *imitatio Christi*, emphasized the value of historical knowledge for moral action in the present. In effect, humanist exemplarity exploits the contingencies of specific historical contexts in order to draw from them transhistorical values, linking now and then through a relation-

---

[18] On the role of *imitatio Christi* in Protestant devotionality, see Elizabeth K. Hudson, "English Protestants and the *imitatio Christi*, 1580–1620," *Sixteenth Century Journal* 19, 4 (1988): 541–58.

ship of similarity.[19] Foxe seizes on exemplarity's power to liken past
and present when he engages his own nation's potentially alienated
history, hoping that the martyrs' courage and faith, as universal values, can bridge any historical distance. In one of his 1570 prefaces,
"To the true Christian reader, what utility is to be taken by reading of
these histories," Foxe discusses the spiritual value of reading about
the martyrs, asking rhetorically, "what man, reading the misery of
these godly persons may not therein, as in glass, behold his own
case?" (*3r). Foxe invites his readers to identify with the martyrs' suffering, hoping that they will see his history as a synchronic reflection
("as in a glass") of the present.

It is precisely this kind of reflection that Foxe hoped to offer his
readers when in the 1563 edition of his book he tells of "the history
of the most valiant and worthy Martyr of Christ, Sir John Oldcastle,
knight, Lord Cobham" (Bb5r). Annabel Patterson has written about
this knight as a "symbol of Reformation historiography," and his textual lineage more than confirms this characterization.[20] Oldcastle, a
lord during Henry V's reign, was accused of heresy and treason in
1417 and eventually was hanged and burned. Fifteenth-century historical accounts record that around 1414, Oldcastle, having escaped
from the Tower of London, raised an army with the intention of over-
throwing Henry's reign and assuming control of England. Revisionist
accounts of Oldcastle's life by Protestants such as Tyndale, Bale, and
Foxe disputed this claim, arguing that it was unlikely Oldcastle was
the leader or even that such an army existed. Instead, Foxe offers Oldcastle's steadfastness in the face of Catholic persecution as an exem-
plum for English readers. However, although Oldcastle is an exemplary servant of Christ, his status as an English subject is ambiguous.
To maintain his faith to the true church, Oldcastle must defy the au-

---

[19] The best recent work on exemplarity and its paradoxes is Timothy Hampton,
Writing from History: The Rhetoric of Exemplarity in Renaissance Literature
(Ithaca: Cornell University Press, 1990).

[20] Annabel Patterson, "Sir John Oldcastle as Symbol of Reformation Historiography," in *Religion, Literature, and Politics in Post-Reformation England, 1540–1688,*
ed. Donna B. Hamilton and Richard Strier (Cambridge: Cambridge University Press,
1996), 6–26. This essay follows upon and extends some of Patterson's comments
about Oldcastle in *Reading Holinshed's "Chronicles"* (Chicago: University of Chicago Press, 1994), 128–53. I have benefited immensely from Patterson's impressive research on this matter.

thority of his king. Following Bale's 1544 account almost to the word, Foxe handles this potential conflict between church and nation cautiously. When describing Oldcastle's resistance to Henry V's personal request that the knight recant his heresy, Foxe reports Oldcastle saying, "most worthy prince . . . unto you, next my eternal God, owe I my whole obedience, and submit me thereunto, as I have done ever, all that I have, either fortune or nature, ready at all times to fulfill whatsoever ye shall in the Lord command me" (Bb5v). This response almost offers absolute service to the king ("whatsoever ye shall . . . command me"), but is carefully qualified by "in the lord." Foxe goes as far as he can to maintain Oldcastle's national loyalties without compromising his commitment to the true church.

Of course, because Foxe's account follows Bale's so closely, it is slightly misleading to ascribe the strategies employed in the narrative to the martyrologist himself. Yet these strategies are representative of Reformation polemical tactics that emerged in the 1530s and flourished through the Civil War. When the same tactic appears in a new context, we have to be alert to what degree its resonance may change. For example, Bale's use of apocalyptic language creates a particular effect in 1544, one slightly different from the effect created by Foxe in 1563. Bale wrote his account of Oldcastle in the early 1540s in the Netherlands, having fled England upon the death of Cromwell. In 1542, Bale's books were proscribed by royal proclamation.[21] When Bale published his *Oldcastle* in 1544, he did so in the context of England's growing hostility to reformed theology, a sense that things were going from bad to worse. We cannot be certain to what degree he altered or elaborated on his fifteenth-century sources in order to suit the context of his writing, but the apocalyptic rhetoric of his account recalls tropes he employs elsewhere.[22] Describing the second exchange between Oldcastle and Henry V, Bale comments in a marginal note that "[t]he king here worshippeth the beast" and that "Cobham

[21] J. S. Brewer, Robert Henry Brodie, and James Gairdner, eds., *Letters and Papers, Foreign and Domestic, of the Reign of Henry VIII,* 21 vols. (London: Longman, Green, Longman, and Roberts, 1862–1932), 17:177.

[22] John N. King discusses Bale's interest in Joachim de Fiore's apocalyptic interpretation of church history, noting that "the Joachimist extracts that Bale appended to his life of Sir John Oldcastle set the suffering of the Lollard martyr in an apocalyptic context." See King, *English Reformation Literature: The Tudor Origins of the Protestant Tradition* (Princeton: Princeton University Press, 1982), 199.

would not obey the beast." Bale uses this apocalyptic rhetoric to thematize the struggle between the churches of Christ and Antichrist
throughout history, a struggle he would describe in detail a year later
in *The Image of Both Churches* (1545). In his account of Oldcastle's
second examination, Bale has the knight expand on this apocalyptic
theme in his reply to his inquisitors:

> Both Daniel and Christ prophesied that such a troublous time should
> come, as hath not been yet since the world's beginning. And this
> prophecy is partly fulfilled in your days and doings. For many have ye
> slain already, and more will ye slay hereafter, if God fulfill not his
> promise. Christ saith also, if those days of yours were not shortened,
> scarcely should any flesh be saved. Therefore look for it justly, for God
> will shorten your days.[23]

Not only do the Catholic clergy serve Antichrist, but their participation was foretold as part of God's eschatological plan. Yet how were
Bale's Protestant readers, in 1544, likely to understand Christ's promise in Matthew 24 to "shorten your days"? The poor state of the English Church probably inclined them to take it as a prophecy of
Christ's victory over the false church at the last day, when Christ
would return to judge and destroy the world. A triumph of the universal church but a loss of the nation. The context of Bale's *Oldcastle*
offers little apocalyptic hope for England.

In chapter 3 I discuss how Reformation writers came to adopt
Bale's language of apocalyptic inevitability as a means to impose continuity on their nation's history. Yet for the moment, I want to point
out how the effect of this language may have differed between 1544
and 1563. Foxe follows Bale's details precisely, including the marginal
glosses about the Beast (Bb6v) and Oldcastle's apocalyptic prophecy
(Cc3r). These details now appear, however, in a larger ecclesiastical
history peppered with apocalyptic references. The effect of a large-
scale apocalyptic continuity in English history was probably magnified for Foxe's audience in 1563, who could now see Oldcastle in a
line of English heroes—John Wyclif, Anne Askew, Jane Gray, the
bishops Ridley and Latimer—who resisted Catholic authorities in the

---

[23] John Bale, *A Brief Chronicle concerning the Examination and Death of the
Blessed Martyr of Christ, Sir John Oldcastle* (Antwerp, 1544); reprinted in *Select
Works of John Bale*, 36 vols. (Cambridge: Parker Society, 1849), 1:23, 36–37.

name of the Christ's church. Furthermore, Elizabeth's formal reestab-lishment of this church in England would have mitigated the pes-simistic implications of "shorten your days," at least to the degree that the prophecy may have put readers in mind of not only the final destruction of the earth but also of victory in England. In other words, these references to Revelation, though taken from Bale, assist Foxe's specific purposes in presenting an exemplar of both the true church and the English nation.

With this particular story, however, Foxe was not able simply to gloss over the tension between church and nation. In 1566, Nicholas Harpsfield, the biographer of Thomas More and ejected archdeacon of St. Paul's Church, published in Antwerp an attack on Foxe's 1563 edi-tion of *Acts and Monuments*.[24] Writing under the pseudonym Alan Cope, Harpsfield questioned the accuracy of Foxe's martyr stories, aiming his most vehement assault at the story of Oldcastle, whom Harpsfield described as a traitor to his king and his country. Harps-field focuses his attack on the Protestant claim that Oldcastle did not participate in the 1414 rebellion. However, he also makes the more general criticism that Oldcastle betrayed his nation by directly dis-obeying Henry in the first place and by escaping from the Tower. Harpsfield took the problems in the Oldcastle story as paradigmatic of all the martyrs: Foxe's own narrative, representing the martyrs' dis-obedience to English authorities, condemned them as traitors. Harps-field based his critique of Foxe on fifteenth- and early-sixteenth-century accounts of Oldcastle, which he argued were closer to the events described and so more reliable. Patterson observes that "[t]he question that Bale and his successors in the Protestant tradition wished to bring to the attention of later readers was whether Oldcastle and his followers were . . . to put it sharply, vicious traitors or unjustly martyred religious reformers."[25] Yet Bale and Foxe had to confront a third possibility as well—that Oldcastle was *both* a traitor and martyr.

Again attending to context, it is instructive to compare the manner in which Bale and Foxe respond to the accusation that Oldcastle led the 1414 rebellion and was thus a traitor. What we find is that al-though Bale in 1544 is generally willing to sacrifice Oldcastle's na-tional attachments for the sake of his religion commitments, Foxe

[24] Nicholas Harpsfield, *Dialogi Sex contra Summi Pontificatus, Monasticae Vitae, Sanctorum, Sacrarum Imaginum Oppugnatores, et Psudomartyres* (Antwerp, 1566).
[25] Patterson, "Sir John Oldcastle," 8.

tries much longer and harder in 1570 to reconcile the two. When Bale was preparing to publish his account of Oldcastle's life, his version of the story had already received criticism regarding the knight's participation in the uprising. Bale responded by attaching a short preface defending his position, but interestingly spends little time actually going through the historical evidence that might exonerate Oldcastle and more time implying that service to God trumps service to the nation. He begins the preface by insisting on the superior heroism of spiritual over secular warriors, observing that although "[i]n the profane histories of old . . . they are much commended . . . which have . . . died for their country," the greater glory belongs to martyrs: "what then is to be thought of those godly and valiant warriors which have not spared to bestow their most dear lives for the verity of Jesus Christ." Bale also remarks that although men have commonly faced secular battle without fear—"many thousands have had in that great courage"—these same men usually lose their nerve during spiritual trials: in "the defense of Christ's verity" they "have been most faint-hearted cowards and very desperate dastards." Finally, the moral that Bale draws from Oldcastle's story is not the dignity of English resistance to papal interference but rather the just punishment England received, in the form of a century of political chaos, for its treatment of Sir John Oldcastle.[26] Bale, for all his commitment to the English nation throughout his career, sees the rhetorical difficulty of defending it in the past and willingly privileges Oldcastle's religious over his national identity.

Foxe, in contrast, is not so quick to jettison the nationalist potential of the Oldcastle story. Whereas Bale writes a five-page preface to defend Oldcastle from the charge of treason, in the 1570 edition of his book Foxe adds a twenty-five-page, double-columned, response to Harpsfield's attack (the original story's length is only ten pages). Foxe brings up the question of patriotism involved in the Oldcastle controversy, referring repeatedly to the monstrousness of Harpsfield's own disloyalty to his native England. Foxe's perception of the national stakes of the controversy itself has perhaps been underestimated by recent commentary. Foxe affects a sense of hurt upon receiving an attack from one who ought to help him: "I . . . think myself ungently dealt withal at Master Cope's hand . . . being mine own countryman, an Englishman" (Oo4r). "If he had not, in the front of his book," Foxe

[26] Bale, *Works* 1:5, 6, 7, 11–12.

writes, "entitled himself to be 'an Englishman', by his writing I would have judged him rather some wild Irishman" (Oo3v). He also puns on Harpsfield's nom du plume: "I here briefly answer Master Cope again (or what Dutch body else soever lieth covered under this English Cope)" (Oo6r). These comments suggest that to attack the loyalty of past English martyrs risks divorcing oneself from the contemporary national community, to expel oneself beyond the borders ("wild Irishman"), or to lose one's authentic Englishness by wearing foreign vestments. Foxe's demand that true Englishmen treat their history properly may well reflect his own heartfelt English identity, but it is also a rhetorical demand, an attempt to make his readers think about national history in a certain way.

Along with this rhetorical framing, Foxe examines and offers comprehensive refutations for each objection Harpsfield makes. Foxe responds to the contention that Oldcastle raised the 1414 rebellion by casting doubt on the details Harpsfield offers and claiming that the scanty evidence makes it impossible to say for certain what really happened. Foxe uses this lack of definite proof to ease the tension between Oldcastle's national and religious commitments, arguing that the knight is "neither traitor to his country, nor rebel to his prince" (Nn2v) and repeatedly insisting on the knight's loyalty to the king, "whom God and [his] conscience taught to obey" (Nn3r). However, when it comes to the most basic sense of the knight's disobedience to his monarch, Foxe has a difficult time mounting a coherent defense. I offer a typical example early in the defense:

> sent for by the king, [Lord Cobham] obeyed and came. Being come, what lowly subjection he showed there to the king, the page 664 declareth. Afterwards he yielded an obedient confession of his faith: it would not be received. Then did he appeal to the bishop of Rome, for which the king took great displeasure with him, and so he was . . . committed to the Tower: which also he did obey. (Nn2v)

Foxe piles on a multitude of "obedient" acts, even directing the reader back to the original account, to cover up the basic fact of Oldcastle's disobedience. In truth, Oldcastle's "obedient confession of his faith" is disobedient in that it opposes the king's will; it must be disobedient in order to stay true to the church of Christ. Against obvious contrary evidence, Foxe resists acknowledging that the knight

is a traitor at any level, attempting to present Oldcastle as a specifically English as well as a Christian exemplar.

Foxe's account of Oldcastle exemplifies the problem of historical
loss that concerns us throughout this book. Foxe writes his narrative
in order to restore his nation's history, but the gesture of filling in the
details of the truth of the past exposes this past as a complicated one.
Foxe would like to remember certain aspects of national history and
deemphasize others, occasionally appealing to the name of martyrdom itself as the figure that will somehow resolve the tensions in
Oldcastle's story: "what lacketh now, or what should let to the contrary, but that he, declaring himself such a martyr, that is, a witness
to the verity (for which also at last he suffered the fire) may therefore
worthily be adorned with the title of martyr, which is in Greek as
much as witness-bearer?" (Nn3r). We should recall here Timothy
Hampton's account of Renaissance exemplarity in which the exemplar's name functions as a conflict-resolving mechanism, "a single
sign which contains folded within it the entire history of the hero's
deeds."[27] Like his humanist contemporaries, Foxe turns to his hero's
name, hoping that the title "Oldcastle, martyr," armed with its
Greek etymology, might in itself persuade readers of Oldcastle's
virtue and inspire them to imitate that virtue. Yet as the title "Oldcastle, martyr" is unfolded in the course of the historical narrative,
certain elements of his story begin to contest the quality of that
virtue. This is precisely the problem Hampton identifies with exemplary narratives, the ambiguous details of which may come into conflict with the exemplar's name.[28] The tension between Oldcastle's
duty to England and his duty to the true church becomes evident
when the narrative actually depicts him disobeying the king and escaping from the Tower—no matter how strongly Foxe might wish the
title "Oldcastle, martyr" to communicate an unproblematic and in-
contestable exemplarity. Foxe sets out to recover an exemplary past

[27] Hampton, *Writing from History*, 25.
[28] Hampton writes, "the life of the hero can easily be sliced into a multitude of discrete metonymically related segments or moments. Some of these may connote
virtue, but some may suggest vice, and their interaction always produces conflict and
moral dialectics, with the potential to turn back and subvert the pedagogical intention of the humanist who evoked the exemplar as a model for his student or reader in
the first place. In other words the persuasive function of the name may be under-
mined by the ambiguity of certain of the hero's acts" (ibid., 26–27).

with narrative, but his own historicizing impulse ("history . . . without the knowledge whereof man's life is blind" [1570, ☞2v]) uncovers an unfamiliar and hostile culture.

Yet the Oldcastle episode, beyond illustrating the humanist double bind of example and alienation, shows us to what degree the commitment to the nation creates the effect of historical discontinuity in the first place. It is Oldcastle as a *national* figure that produces such a problem in representation. If Foxe would simply give up on (or at least minimize, as did Bale) his defense of Oldcastle's national credentials, if he would accept a caesura in national history for the sake of maintaining the continuity of the *universal* true church of Christ, he could reduce his rhetorical difficulties considerably. Yet Foxe remains committed to the national story, despite the inconveniences it raises for his ecclesiastical narrative. In the 1563 edition of his book, he had declaimed against the erroneous opinion that "this religion now generally used hath sprung up and risen but of late and few years, even by the space (as many do think) of 20 or 30 years" (1563, Ii6r). His goal in writing *Acts and Monuments*, he tells his readers, is to "declare that this profession of Christ's religion hath been spread abroad *in England* by the space almost of 200 years, and before that time, and hath oftentimes sparkled although the flames thereof have never so perfectly burnt out" (my emphasis). England has, as it were, continued to carry the torch for the true church throughout the centuries; the martyrs, rather than simply enduring English wickedness for the sake of the church, in fact truly represent England in the past. This is a tough claim to sustain, but the alternative would be to acknowledge the traitorous status of these figures and admit that England as a nation did not come into a godly consciousness until "the space . . . of 20 or 30 years." A godly England, in this view, would be a novelty. Foxe resists this conclusion as much as he can because he has no historical framework in which a novel community could be desirable. Nonetheless, it is a point he sometimes comes close to conceding.

In 1570 Foxe tries to forestall this concession in part by opposing his own responsible use of primary documents to Harpsfield's reliance on hearsay and fable. Although we see this tension between archival rigor and poetic license at work in the narratives of Dee, Spenser, and Milton, Foxe is perhaps the least willing of all four to grant the value of fiction to historical narrative. This is not to deny the "artful literary hand" that John N. King has discerned at work in many of the martyr death scenes in *Acts and Monuments*.[29] Yet unlike Spenser and Milton, Foxe never offers as history events he also concedes to be fictional. In his controversy with Harpsfield, he emphasizes the need for physical evidence from the past to determine the truth about Oldcastle's patriotic credentials. Foxe condemns the Catholic writer's reliance on Robert Fabian, Polydore Vergil, and Edward Hall to prove Oldcastle's traitorous intentions, since these historians offer no documentary evidence to support their claims. In his attacks we find Summit's "*lectio* of suspicion" at work: "what authority do they avouch? what acts, what registers, what records, or out of what court do they show? Or what demonstration do they make? And do you think it sufficient, because these men do only affirm it, without any further probation, with your αυτοσ εφη, therefore we are bound to believe it?" (Oo1v). Foxe repeatedly associates their unsubstantiated narratives with "Sinon's art" (Nn3r), accusing Harpsfield and his predecessors of "only following bare rumors, or else such words as they see in such fabling prefaces or indictments expressed" (Nn5v). Foxe contradicts Harpsfield's use of Hall in particular by claiming that the historian, once he read John Bale's account of Oldcastle, crossed out his own negative assessment of the knight and produced a more fair-minded reckoning: "the very selfsame first copy of Hall, rased and crossed with his own pen, remaineth in my hands to be shown and seen, as need shall require" (Oo2v). "The very selfsame first copy": Foxe invokes the authenticity of the antiquarian monument, its physical immediacy and its originality. (That this authentic monument is also a ruined one will be relevant to our discussion in chap. 2.)

With these gestures we see how Protestant historiography dovetails with the growing antiquarian interest in the material remains of the past. Reformation writers regularly linked their intention to offer a

---

[29] John N. King, "Fact and Fiction in Foxe's *Book of Martyrs*," in *John Foxe and the English Reformation*, ed. David Loades (Aldershot, U.K.: Scholar Press, 1997), 12–35; quotation, 24. On the basis of this literary shaping, King argues that "Foxe subscribes to a historical standard whereby invented fiction may conform to moral and religious truth" (14–15). Similarly, D. R. Woolf has shown us the variety of literary models Foxe relies on to report a history he nonetheless believes to be true; Woolf, "The Rhetoric of Martyrdom: Generic Contradiction and Narrative Strategy in John Foxe's *Acts and Monuments*," in *The Rhetorics of Life-Writing in Early Modern Europe: Forms of Biography from Cassandra Fedele to Louis XIV*, ed. Thomas F. Mayer and D. R. Woolf (Ann Arbor: University of Michigan Press, 1995), 243–82.

chastened account of the English past with the claimed methodological rigor of antiquarian inquiry. The friendship between Bale and John Leland, the most noted antiquary of his generation, represents an explicit instance of a pervasive general assumption in the sixteenth century. Foxe in fact derives from the specific examples of material evidence that he cites a general principle about historiographical method:

> You must consider, Master Cope, if you will be a controller in story-matters, it is not enough for you to bring a railing spirit, or a mind disposed to carp and cavil where any matter may be picked: diligence is required, and great searching out of books and authors, not only of our time, but of all ages. And especially where matters of religion are touched pertaining to the church: it is not sufficient to see what Fabian or what Hall saith, but the records must be sought, the registers must be turned over, letters also and ancient instruments ought to be perused, and authors with the same compared, finally the writers among themselves one to be conferred with another. (Oo2v)

Such a sentiment makes clear how fully Foxe imagines the "monuments" of his book's title to refer to the physical records that he preserves and makes known by reproducing them in print. Indeed, for all the importance Foxe and his contemporaries placed on the value of printing, they continued to see print as a second phase in the process of historical writing. The truth lay with the primary material records, without which printed histories would derive from the same Catholic fabling that produced Oldcastle's alleged armed followers: "If they came out of [no English counties], as none are named," Foxe sneers, "then let them come out of Utopia, where, belike, this figment was first forged and invented" (Nn5r).

Foxe uses this opposition between archive and fiction in 1570 much as he employs the apocalyptic rhetoric in his 1563 account, as a means of producing a convincing historical continuity for both his nation and the true church. Patterson is right to note that "Foxe scored some points in his battle with Harpsfield."[30] Yet for all Foxe's narrative success and rhetorical confidence, the basic fact of Oldcastle's disobedience, as well as the uncertainty about the alleged insurrection, continues to gnaw at Foxe throughout his account. The evi-

---

[30] Patterson, *Reading Holinshed's "Chronicles,"* 147.

dence of his irresolution comes at the end of his reply to Harpsfield,
when, after almost twenty pages of detailed refutation, Foxe grants
that Oldcastle and his friends may have been traitors:

> And admit this (as granted unto you, Master Cope) that these men had
> been traitors, which ye are not able to prove. Well, they had their pun-
> ishment therefore; the world can go no further, and what would you
> have more? and if they repented, why may they not have as good a part
> in Christ's kingdom as yourself? Now, forsomuch as the said persons
> also suffering a double punishment were so constant in the way of
> truth, and most principally for the same were persecuted, and chiefly
> therefore brought to their death: that part of example, because I saw it
> pertain to the profit of the Church, why might I not insert it with other
> church stories in my book? Let the church take that which belongeth
> to the church. Let the world take that which to the world pertaineth,
> and go no further. . . . And what if I should also call the thief and mur-
> derer, hanging on the right side of the Lord, by the name of a holy saint
> and confessor, for his witnessing of the Lord, what can Master Cope say
> against it? (Oo5v)

Foxe keeps this concession hypothetical, but it goes to the heart of
his narrative difficulty. The choice here is no longer that of martyr *or*
traitor; Oldcastle is now both. His exemplary value now resides in
"that part of example" that Foxe finds useful to the present; the other
parts of the example he disowns. Foxe replaces his earlier attempt to
negotiate Oldcastle's conflicting loyalties to the true church and to
England with the quite conventional conviction that "the church"
and "the world" each have their legitimate (though not equally legitimate) claims on human society.

Foxe does not try to excuse or deny the fact of the martyr's civic
transgression; the martyr may truly be a "thief" or a "murderer" according to the perspective of the world. Yet now that traditional
Christian duality governs the discussion, Foxe can shift registers
without contradiction by invoking the power of the exemplar's name:
"And what if I should also call the thief and murderer, hanging on the
right side of the Lord, by the name of a holy saint and confessor, for
his witnessing of the Lord?" Just as Foxe revises the worldly punishment for crime, "hanging," as "hanging on the right side of the Lord,"
so he is able to absorb the criminal status of a man by assuming the
perspective of the "church." In this perspective, England's religious

past maintains its continuity, if at the cost of Oldcastle's national meaning.

My goal in this book is not to decide whether writers succeed or fail in recovering the past but to describe the effects of the historical absence that motivates their projects and inhabits their narratives. Foxe's (hypothetical) concession would seem to lend credence to recent views that the Reformation impeded national sentiment as much as it encouraged such sentiment. Indeed, Foxe's "decision" to admit Oldcastle's traitorous status was overdetermined from the start: no Tudor Protestant would privilege the nation over Christ's church, if it came to a choice. This is true of Dee, Spenser, and Milton as well. Yet this overdetermination does not simply negate the national investment of *Acts and Monuments*, nor the effects of Foxe's anxiety that national and religious history come into conflict. If the passage quoted earlier represents Foxe's inevitable subordination of nation to Christ, then the twenty pages preceding this passage represent the nation's resistance to this subordination. Why does Foxe bother to defend the nation as well as the church? Why, to borrow again Paul Stevens's question about Milton, would someone as religious as Foxe, so absorbed in universals and in the universal dimension of the true church, invest so heavily in a concept as contingent and ephemeral as the nation? Part of the answer is that Foxe, like Dee, Spenser, and Milton, has a *feeling* for his Englishness, a vague but persistent sense of kinship with fellow citizens–subjects,[31] more than he has an overt national program. That nationalism is not yet an explicit principle like republicanism or presbyterianism does not mean that these writers lack a sense of a national community. Their repeated invocation of England is "real" in the sense that it does not merely function as a rhetorical tool for defending the reformed church—a defense, as we have seen, that creates as many problems as it solves. They maintain the legitimacy of English history even when it places them at a rhetorical disadvantage. This sense of English kinship, like all kinships, is a mystification, and by no means innocuous,

[31] I maintain the citizen–subject split to leave open the question in recent scholarship about the degree of political autonomy experienced by Elizabethans. Patrick Collinson has suggestively argued that "when it came to a crunch, the realm took precedence over the ruler. So citizens were concealed within subjects"; Collinson, *De Republica Anglorum, or History with the Politics Put Back* (Cambridge: Cambridge University Press, 1990), 24. Revisionist scholarship would of course find this assessment anachronistic.

sometimes coming at the terrible expense of the other nations surrounding England ("wild Irishman"). And in its interface with religion, the universalist demands of the true church sometimes super-
sede it. Yet Foxe continues to be fascinated and disturbed by the
national community, which represents for him both a desired consequence of the break with Rome and the historical loss that makes it
so difficult to establish the church's continuity.

In Foxe's narrative, the church extends back into history and forward toward the Apocalypse, whereas the nation often balances on
the promontory of the present. England persists throughout the narrative, but does so by means of a rhetoric that reinscribes it as recent
community. The nation's recentness exposes its historical contingency, creating a space for Foxe and his colleagues to acknowledge
their impression of historical difference, an acknowledgment they
cannot make regarding the church. Yet Foxe remains uneasy with
this state of affairs, because he and his contemporaries usually saw a
community as legitimate to the degree that it was authorized by tradition. Repeatedly, in *Acts and Monuments,* Foxe associates the nation, which he elsewhere tries to describe as historically continuous,
with the ephemeral, the unrooted, the merely new: "as naturally as
we love our country, so fondly we favor the present fashions, wherein
we be trained and educated" (1563, Oo5v). To love such a contingent
community is both natural and foolish. This complex double bind of
tradition and novelty was not unique to *Acts and Monuments;* it embraced all accounts of English religious history in the early Reformation period. Foxe perhaps feels it more keenly than other writers as a
result of the uncompromising continuity he tries to impose between
past and present. He is deeply caught in the paradox that Debora
Shuger suggests gripped nearly all early Protestant historiography:
"its own methodology, designed to retrieve the exemplary past from
the ravages of time, unearthed alien cultures fixed in time . . . but the
estrangement of the past did not destroy the longing for it."[32] This
conflicted attitude toward history—playing on the axis between exemplarity and estrangement—also determines the ambivalent approaches of Dee, Spenser, and Milton to recalling their nation's past.

[32] Debora Shuger, *The Renaissance Bible: Scholarship, Sacrifice, and Subjectivity*
(Berkeley: University of California Press, 1994), 53.

2 ANTIQUARIAN HISTORY
Dee, Spenser, and the Tudor Search for Arthur

Spenser's Prince Arthur, reading a history of Britain from its founding to the reign of his father, finds himself deeply disappointed to discover that the narrative suddenly ends, as we have seen. Spenser makes a point of noting the physical nature of this interruption:

> After him Vther, which Pendragon hight,
> Succeding There abruptly it did end,
> Without full point, or other Cesure right,
> As if the rest some wicked hand did rend,
> Or th'Authour selfe could not at least attend
> To finish it. . . . [1]

The paradoxes of "Succeding" followed by "end," and of "Cesure," which implies both a cessation or conclusion ("cessure," *OED*) but also a caesura or interruption, call attention to the manner in which the narrative's ending leaves Arthur high and dry, without a British identity, cut from history. Yet the material locator "There" also briefly juxtaposes the imaginary page of *Briton moniments* and the physical page of *The Faerie Queene*, giving the reader a sense of what it feels like to have a book physically fail you. The two possible

---

[1] Edmund Spenser, *The Faerie Queene*, ed. A. C. Hamilton (New York: Longman, 2001), II.x.68.1–7. All subsequent references to the poem are from this edition. In-text citations of *The Faerie Queene* refer to the work as *FQ*.

causes for this narrative rupture that Spenser offers—the raging of a biblioclast or the negligence of a historiographer—both highlight the vulnerability of texts, their material limitations. The unreliability of the physical text *Briton moniments*, found after all in a chamber filled with old books and manuscripts "[t]hat were all worme-eaten, and full of canker holes" (ix.57.9), threatens to impede the knowledge of history and the completion of Arthur's national identity.

This episode's combination of Arthur's presence and imperfect ancient records keenly reflects the Elizabethan attempt to formulate a national history out of the Arthurian narratives, especially to the degree that Spenser imagines such a history emerging from the material remains of ancient Britain. Many historical writers saw in Arthur (and in the entire account of Britain's founding as set down by Geoffrey of Monmouth in 1136) a means of undoing their sense of historical embarrassment. This embarrassment had grown, ironically enough, partly as a result of increasing sophistication in historiographical method. The sixteenth-century advances of humanist and antiquarian research on national history, while shedding new light on the English medieval past, also awkwardly revealed England's isolation from classical civilization.[2] Lacking a connection to the Greek and Roman heroic dispensation, many writers concluded that England had simply not taken sufficient care of the historical records that might have established this connection. Such carelessness led antiquaries such as John Bale to feel a sense of national inadequacy: "for so little esteeming our true Antiquities, the proud Italians have always held us for a Barbarous nation."[3] Bale and his fellow Protestant antiquaries John Leland and John Prise numbered King Arthur's ancient realm among those "true Antiquities" that the English ought to esteem. The Galfridian narrative seemed to offer the Tudors an ideal solution to their seemingly barbarous history: it provided a historical continuity from antiquity through the seventh century C.E., describing the founding of Britain by Aeneas's great grandson Brutus, and representing in Arthur's realm a thriving native civilization independent of Catholic Rome.

I argue, however, that the Tudor effort to resurrect the Arthur nar-

---

[2] On this point see Joseph M. Levine, *Humanism and History: Origins of Modern English Historiography* (Ithaca: Cornell University Press, 1987), 80.

[3] John Bale, *The New Year's Gift* (London, 1546); reprinted in John Chandler, *John Leland's Itinerary* (Dover, N.H.: Alan Sutton, 1993), 5.

rative followed what Michel de Certeau explains as the paradox of historical loss and recovery that accompanied early national consciousness, whereby a culture is able to pursue its past insofar as it already perceives this past to be missing. We have looked at Certeau's notion that this paradoxical combination functions as the defining characteristic of Renaissance historiography. The Tudor search for Arthur very much participated in what Certeau describes as the "return to origins," which always "states the contrary of what it believes, at least in the sense that it presupposes a *distancing* in respect to a past . . . and a will to *recover* what in one fashion or another seems lost in a received language."[4] The Tudors thus began to re-create Arthurian history most urgently at the moment their historical inquiries started to make them suspect that this history was either fictitious or simply lost. As with John Foxe's attempt to represent the medieval martyrs as historical antecedents of a specifically *English* Reformation, the antiquarian demand for *national* continuity in the Arthur narrative made Certeau's paradox all the more difficult to avoid. Foxe himself saw little value in the Arthurian stories ("more fabulous, than that any credit should be given to them" [1570, n5r]), but many English Reformers tried to use this period of ancient British Christianity as the answer to the Roman Church's alleged anteriority. At first glance, then, Arthur recovered the past of both church and nation, his heroic resistance to Roman incursions setting a precedent for contemporary England's anti-Catholicism. Yet, as John E. Curran, Jr., has recently shown, this reliance on Arthur as anti-Roman precedent risked exposing the English Church's past as barbarous, obscure, or both.[5] The poverty of historical evidence for the British prince's existence often painfully reminded the antiquaries of their nation's lack of a glorious (and well-documented) history, which had forced them to turn to Arthur in the first place.

We noted in chapter 1 that Foxe, in his polemic with Nicholas Harpsfield, appealed to a specifically antiquarian sense of history, one in which the truth of the past emerged in the past's material remains. This chapter focuses more directly on the antiquarian effort to forge a link between the English past and present by means of such remains.

[4] Michel de Certeau, *The Writing of History,* trans. Tom Conley (New York: Columbia University Press, 1988), 136.

[5] John E. Curran, Jr., *Roman Invasions: The British History, Protestant Anti-Romanism, and the Historical Imagination in England, 1530–1660* (Newark, Del.: University of Delaware Press, 2002).

In particular, it is concerned with the manner in which the anxious search for Arthur took the form of a dialectic between two opposite notions of historical knowledge: a sense of the material remains of the past (monumental history), on the one hand, and a prophetic, spiritual access to the past (prophetic history) on the other. The first centers on the figure of the "monument" (stemming from *monēre*, "to remind"), a term that Tudor antiquarians often used to refer to the physical remains of the past, such as old statues, artifacts, and manuscripts. Many historiographers seized upon such remains, and upon the idea of the monument itself, as a primary link to the English past. As Antonia Gransden has demonstrated, one of the primary developments in sixteenth-century English historiography was the critical treatment of physical evidence, examining documents for traces of forgery and constructing narratives around material remains: "the humanist historians exploited the evidence of topography and antiquities, including ancient buildings, archaeological remains, and coins."[6]

However, the fate of Arthur's *Briton moniments* hints at the limitation of this figure. The monument's materiality, inevitably subject to decay in time, assured that it, like the past it signified, would some day be gone.[7] Camden, writing about the scarcity of evidence about the nation's ancient past, notes that even if the early Britons did create records, "in so long continuance of time, in so many and so great turnings and overturnings of States, doubtless of the same had been utterly lost, seeing that the very stones, pyramids, obelisks, and other memorable monuments, thought to be more durable than brass, have yielded long ago to the iniquity of time."[8] The antiquary's emphasis on physical remains, the source of his capacity to know history, also represented his limitation. Even worse, many English historical writ-

[6] Antonia Gransden, *Historical Writing in England*, 2 vols. (Ithaca: Cornell University Press, 1974, 1982), 2:428.

[7] In the sixteenth century the term *monument* could signify any enduring object. In *Titus Andronicus* (ca. 1588), Titus boasts to the tribunes about the antiquity of his family's sepulcher: "This monument five hundreth years hath stood, / Which I have sumptuously re-edified" (1.1.354–55); *The Complete Works of Shakespeare*, ed. David Bevington (Glenview, Ill.: Scott, Foresman, 1980). At the same time, *monument* could signify "any damaged or ruined object"; in his *Microcosmographie* (London, 1628), John Earle ridicules the figure of the antiquary and his monuments: "A great admirer he is of the rust of old Monuments, and reads only those Characters, whose time hath eaten out the letter" (C2r).

[8] William Camden, *Britain*, trans. Philemon Holland (London, 1610), 4.

ers felt that their nation treated its monuments especially poorly, as evidenced by the Reformation spoliation of the monastic libraries. This concern developed into a major theme of English historical writing over the course of the sixteenth century. The early Stuart antiquary John Weever complained that whereas "in other kingdoms, the Monuments of the dead are preserved," the English fail to exercise this kind of care: "barbarously within these his Majesty's Dominions, they are (to the shame of our time) broken down, and utterly almost all ruinated."[9] Like so many of his contemporaries, Weever believes his countrymen have done an especially poor job, compared to other nations, of preserving the remains of the national past. The monument transmitted the past to the present, but it was a fragile vehicle of transmission, symbolizing both the Tudors' confidence that they could recover their nation's history and their simultaneous fear that this history was dead and buried.

In contrast, the second mode of historical knowledge, prophecy, did not rely on material remains but rather divine inspiration, thus avoiding the ravaging effects of time. The "prophetic" knowledge of the past encompassed both the inspired understanding of history—such as John Foxe's claim that he was "suddenly" struck, "as with a majesty" (1576, J3r), by an insight into a difficult passage in Revelation—and also encompassed the conception of the past as Providential, patterned, ordered, and inevitable. Many of the writers who appealed to ancient British prophecies about the future, or who themselves claimed prophetic insight into the past, believed that they were pulling their nation's past and future into its present without any gap or loss. Prophecy could accomplish this link by transcending the material register. For example, Michael Drayton, in his *Poly-Olbion* (1612), has the river Dee complain that doubters of Brutus and Arthur base their skepticism on the fact that "we shewe no Booke our Brutus to approve."[10] Drayton responds to this lack by arguing that "th'ancient British Priests, the fearlesse Druides" committed historical events to memory and transmitted them to the present, prophetically, in an unbroken oral tradition (10.264). He elaborates in the superiority of prophetic memory to monuments with a logic that rather perversely resembles Camden's:

[9] John Weever, *Ancient Funeral Monuments* (London, 1631), 1.
[10] *The Works of Michael Drayton*, 4 vols., ed. J. William Hebel (Oxford: Shakespeare Head Press, 1933), 4:10.261.

> For, when of Ages past wee looke in bookes to read,
> Wee retchlesly discharge our memory of those.
> So when injurious Time, such Monuments doth lose
> (As what so great a Work, by Time that is not wrackt?)
> Wee utterly foregoe that memorable act:
> But when we lay it up within the minds of men,
> They leave it their next Age; that, leaves it hers agen.
>
> (10.270–76)

Ideally, prophecy avoids the effects of "injurious Time" on the material monument by allowing history to travel unimpeded through the minds of men. Drayton goes on to explain that prophetic knowledge is ultimately divine, a form of inspiration that began with Moses (10.283–90). This link between prophecy and divinity was a commonplace. However, as we shall see, historical prophecy itself found its self-consuming limit in eschatology: relying on a divine vision to preserve the national past risked losing this past to the Apocalypse.

Although some scholars argue that Tudor writers treat the prophetic and apocalyptic as distinct modes,[11] I locate them both over against the materiality of the monument, conceiving the Apocalypse as the implicit telos of Renaissance prophecy. The Book of Revelation was the primary model for prophetic discourse in the Renaissance, and prophecy's typological structure of figure and fulfillment marked it as both etiological and eschatological, as Howard Dobin has observed: "Prophecy offered a double promise: first, the correct . . . interpretation of history and, second, the better anticipation of that final glorious fulfillment at the end of time."[12] Dobin's account of prophecy could equally describe early Protestant apocalyptic writing,

---

[11] Kenneth Gross is especially lucid in his distinction between prophecy's disruptive, antideterministic effects on historical patterns, on the one hand, and the tendency of apocalyptic writing to impose cosmic uniformity on history, on the other hand. Yet even he acknowledges that "the two modes overlap and may completely merge in postbiblical writings"; Gross, *Spenserian Poetics: Idolatry, Iconoclasm, and Magic* (Ithaca: Cornell University Press, 1985), 82 n. 2. Bart van Es has recently insisted on the non-Providential nature of "political" prophecy, which "reads very much like history written in the future tense" (9). He observes, however, that the term *prophecy* in general referred to a variety of discourses in the sixteenth century, some of them apocalyptic (8); Es, " 'Priuie to his Counsell and Secret Meaning': Spenser and Political Prophecy," *English Literary Renaissance* 30, 1 (2000): 3–31.

[12] Howard Dobin, *Merlin's Disciples: Prophecy, Poetry, and Power in Renaissance England* (Stanford: Stanford University Press, 1990), 79.

which identified the narrative of Revelation with events that had already occurred in history. John Foxe and Richard Harvey, as well as Dee and Spenser, were all nationalist writers who imagined that their prophetic articulations of history would lead, directly or indirectly, to the end of time, an end they believed to be imminent.[13] Tudor writers also took advantage of the link, in place since the Middle Ages, between the Merlinic prophecies and the predictions of Saint John the Divine; for example, John Bale, who claimed in his *First Two Parts of the Acts or Unchaste Examples of the English Votaries*, that Merlin had foretold the break with Rome in Geoffrey's *Historia*, likewise interpreted the Reformation as the historical manifestation of the cosmic tumult prophesied in Revelation.[14] Apocalyptic discourse, then, is the prophetic mode at its most Providential and totalizing; at the same time, as I suggest later, it marks the limits of prophecy's capacity to recall history *as history*—as heterogeneous, contiguous, and emergent.

Historical Evidence and Geoffrey's Ancient Welsh Book

The Tudor debate over the validity of Geoffrey of Monmouth's *Historia Regum Britanniae* (ca. 1136), initiated by Polydore Vergil's 1534 denial of the text's veracity and extended in intensely nationalist terms by the antiquarian defenses of John Leland and others, has been ably described in several forms.[15] My concern here does not center on the conflict between believers and nonbelievers but rather on the as-

[13] See, for an example I have already cited, Foxe's *Acts and Monuments* (1576, J3r), and Richard Harvey's *An Astrological Discourse upon the great and notable Conjunction of the two superior Planets Saturn and Jupiter* (London, 1583), 44.

[14] On Bale's comments about Merlin, see Keith Thomas, *Religion and the Decline of Magic* (New York: Charles Scribner's, 1971), 408. On the medieval link between biblical and Galfridian prophecy, see Susan Martha Schwarz, "The Prophecies of Merlin and Medieval Political Propaganda in England," Ph.D. diss., Harvard University, 1977, 83.

[15] See T. D. Kendrick, *British Antiquity* (London: Methuen, 1950), esp. 78–98; Christopher Dean, *Arthur of England: English Attitudes to King Arthur and the Knights of the Round Table in the Middle Ages and the Renaissance* (Toronto: University of Toronto Press, 1987), chaps. 1, 6, and 7; Arthur B. Ferguson, *Utter Antiquity: Perceptions of Prehistory in Renaissance England* (Durham, N.C.: Duke University Press, 1993), esp. chap. 5; and James P. Carley, "Polydor Vergil and John Leland on King Arthur: The Battle of the Books," in *King Arthur: A Casebook*, ed. Edward Donald Kennedy (New York: Garland, 1996), 185–204.

sumptions the believers made about their national past and historical knowledge. The Tudor antiquarians who wanted to defend the Arthur narrative found themselves in a difficult position: their historical enthusiasm stemmed in part from a slowly emerging sense of methodological rigor, yet this new rigor made them painfully aware of the material, historiographical shortcomings of the *Historia.* They had to acknowledge that Geoffrey wrote a full six centuries after the events he describes. His narrative included many improbable elements, such as sea monsters, giants, and British victories in Europe against seemingly impossible odds. Further, no foreign histories corroborated Geoffrey's claims about Arthur's international exploits. In fact, the *Historia Regum Britanniae,* a text many antiquarians wanted to proffer as the material evidence for their understanding of their nation's past, itself highlighted how little evidence they after all possessed. Hence, some Arthur-defenders shifted their focus from Geoffrey's book and concentrated instead on its source, "the very ancient book" from Wales that Geoffrey claimed to have received from a friend and translated.[16] Although no one had ever found this book, they argued that it contained the true account of Arthur's reign, free from the absurdities and contradictions that troubled Geoffrey's imperfect translation. This anterior text, paradoxically by virtue of its absence, potentially skirted the difficult question of material evidence.

John Leland, one of the most prominent historical writers of Henry VIII's reign, employed this shift from material to absent evidence early in the Arthur debate. Ironically enough, he began his career by reminding his colleagues of the need to preserve material evidence. Alarmed by the destruction of manuscripts and books during the spoliation of the libraries, he took it upon himself in 1533 to inform Henry VIII of his resolve "to peruse and diligently to search all the libraries of monasteries and colleges of this your noble realm, to the intent that the monuments of ancient writers . . . might be brought out of *deadly* darkness to *lively* light."[17] We see in Leland's statement the fear, voiced so many times during the sixteenth century, that the "monuments" needed to know England's past were fragile items, always on the verge of decay—even despite the new writing technology

[16] Geoffrey of Monmouth, *The History of the Kings of Britain,* trans. Lewis Thorpe (New York: Penguin, 1966), I.1.

[17] This letter was printed in Bale, *New Year's Gift,* 1–2. This text, written by both Leland and John Bale, is an account of Leland's findings and their implications.

of the printing press.[18] We can also see that he regards these documents as constitutive of the national past, a matter of life and death ("deadly darkness" versus "lively light").

Two years after Polydore Vergil's 1534 attack on Geoffrey's *Historia*, however, Leland wrote and circulated a pamphlet that defended not the existing narrative but rather Geoffrey's Welsh source, even though Leland could not claim to have actually seen this original document. Although "patriotism" can partly explain Leland's acceptance of this absent source, James P. Carley has suggested that the antiquary's credulity stemmed also from his experience with and desire to protect the manuscript remains of the medieval past.[19] Expanding and publishing this pamphlet under the title *Assertio Inclytissimi Arturii Regis Britanniae* in 1544, Leland expresses confidence that historians will eventually find the material remains to prove Arthur's existence. For example, he describes with delight his discovery at Westminster of an artifact he believes to be Arthur's royal seal:

> the sight of the Antiquity pleased me at full, and for a long time the Majesty thereof not only drew away but also detained mine eyes from me to the beholding thereof. . . . Certes Reader, I pray God I be dead but thou wouldest desire to see the same, such and so great is both the antiquity and also the majesty of the thing.[20]

Leland's expression of awe at the presence of the historical artifact resonates with John Foxe's pride in possessing "the very selfsame first

[18] The Tudor historians and antiquaries knew that the great volume of chronicles and chorographies they were churning out depended on anterior physical evidence, such as medieval manuscripts, maps, and ancient inscriptions—all objects the historiographers feared could be damaged, tampered with, or eventually lost. They also felt that printed books themselves shared in this fragile materiality, as John Bale indicated when recounting his friend Leland's travels through England in 1549, reporting with disgust the uses to which book owners were putting books in Reformation England: "some [books] to serve their jakes, some to scour their candlesticks, and some to rub their boots. Some they sold to grocers and sopesellers, and some they sent overseas to the bookbinders, and not in small number, but at times whole ships full, to the wondering of the foreign nations" (*New Year's Gift*, 10). Even the proliferation of printing, with its powerful advantage for Protestant propaganda, does not compensate for the self-consuming materiality of the historical monument.

[19] Carley, "Polydor Vergil and Leland on King Arthur," 198 n.12.

[20] John Leland, *A Learned and True Assertion of the Original Life, Acts, and Death of the Most Noble, Valiant, and Renowned Prince Arthur, King of Great Britain*, trans. Richard Robinson (London, 1582), fols. 12v–13r.

copy" of Edward Hall's manuscript account of Sir John Oldcastle. It also speaks to the antiquarian sense of expertise that we see in a letter by John Bale to Matthew Parker, describing the loss of "the oldest book that I ever saw yet, and most strangely written, but yet legible to him that was acquainted with that kind of writing. . . . A very pitiful case, that our countrymen are so uncircumspect and, as it were, unnatural to the old monuments of their nation."[21] In other words, Leland's delight in Arthur's seal conforms in part to an emerging genre of antiquarian writing, in which historical knowledge, authority, and authenticity result from valuing the physical artifact.

Yet, as Bale's lament suggests, the loss of such artifacts limits the capacity of antiquarian knowledge. Leland implicitly contradicts his passionate emphasis on the material monuments of the past by defending the *Historia* in terms of its absent Welsh source. He again refers to Geoffrey only as the "interpreter" (that is, translator) of the original account,[22] and we can see in his retort to William Paruus (who insisted that the *Historia* was a fable) the double bind of the Arthur-defender who needs Geoffrey's narrative but finds it inadequate as it stands:

> Well I know, and that too well, many fables and vanities are dispersed throughout the whole History of Britain. Yet, therein are matters (if a man behold the same more thoroughly) *such as might not be desired*[23] *without great hindrance of ancient knowledge,* and which being rather read than understood by William Paruus bear not any show at all of commodity. Again, I will also here set down another honorable testimony, namely not only touching the Interpreter of the history, but also concerning Arthur himself.[24]

The rhetorical work of this passage consists in neutralizing the "fables and vanities" of the *Historia* with the almost parenthetical reminder

---

[21] Bale, "John Bale's Letter to Matthew Parker," July 30, 1560; printed in *The Recovery of the Past in Renaissance England: Documents by John Bale and John Joscelyn from the Circle of Matthew Parker,* ed. Timothy Graham and Andrew G. Watson (Cambridge: Cambridge Bibliographical Society, 1998), 20–21.

[22] Leland, *Learned and True Assertion,* fol. 22r.

[23] I.e., "such as might not be omitted." Leland's original is *desiderarentur,* from *desiderare,* "to lack"; John Leland, *Assertio Inclytissimi Arturii Regis Britanniae* (London, 1544), fol. 35v.

[24] Leland, *Learned and True Assertion,* fol. 37r (my emphasis).

that Geoffrey is only "the Interpreter of the history." By implication, the Welsh source of this translation remains pure, free of the corrupting fictions that Geoffrey may have included. This implication is, of course, rather paradoxical: in a tract that emphasizes the importance of physical evidence, how can an absent text represent the appropriate form of that evidence? Although Leland does not explicitly embrace the notion of absent evidence, he reveals the need for at least suggesting it when he insists that the *Historia* possesses information the lack of which would lead to "great hindrance of ancient knowledge." Leland here gives an early voice to the dilemma of the national historian: he needs this ancient knowledge, but the available physical evidence may be an inadequate vehicle. The implicit shift to the original though absent source attempts to resolve this dilemma.

Leland's approach to the problems of Geoffrey's *Historia* in many ways sets the tone for subsequent Arthur-defenders. Four years later we find in Edward Hall's preface to his chronicle an even more pointed use of the absent Welsh book to avoid the problem of the material monument. Although writing about more recent English history, Hall begins his chronicle by lamenting the ancient historiographical problem of "Oblivion, the cankered enemy to Fame and renown, the sucking serpent of ancient memory."[25] The antidote to oblivion, according to Hall, is historical writing. He celebrates the fact that Moses

> in the third age invented letters, the treasure of memory, and set forth five notable books, to the great comfort of all people living at this day. . . . So every nation was desirous to enhance lady Fame, and to suppress that deadly beast Oblivion . . . although they [princes and heroes] be dead by mortal death, yet they by writing and Fame live and be continually present. . . . Thus, memory maketh men dead many a thousand year still to live as though they were present; Thus, Fame triumpheth upon death, and renown upon Oblivion, and all by reason of writing and history. (v–vi)

Hall emphasizes the importance of *physical* records—"letters" and "books"—as a means to resist death, recalling the past for the pres-

[25] Edward Hall, *The Union of the two noble and illustre famelies of Lancastre & Yorke,* in *Hall's Chronicle* (London: J. Johnson et al., 1809; reprint, New York: AMS Press, 1965), v.

ent, so that even if the heroes of the past "be dead by mortal death," writing makes them "live and be continually present."

Yet when Hall turns to the early periods of his own nation's history, he finds it more difficult simply to put his faith in material records because Britain lacks adequate physical remains:

> my heart lamenteth to know and remember what rule this tyrant Oblivion bare in this realm, in the time of the Britons. For from the first habitation of this land, no man of the Britons either set forth histories of their beginning, or wrote the whole lives of their princes & kings. . . . But one Geoffrey of Monmouth a thousand year and more after Julius Caesar, translated a certain British or Welsh book, containing the coming of Brute with the sequel of his lineage, till the time of Cadwallader, which British book if it had slept a little longer, Brute with all his posterity had been buried in the poke of Oblivion, for lack of writing. (vi)

Hall seems about to identify Geoffrey as the figure who finally "set forth histories" of the British past: "But one Geoffrey of Monmouth a thousand year and more after Julius Caesar." But Hall, like Leland, names Geoffrey merely as the one who "translated a certain British or Welsh book" and identifies the Welsh book itself as the text that saves the British past from "the poke of Oblivion" and from a "lack of writing." Of course, there is nothing odd about identifying the Welsh book as the true source of knowledge about Britain's past; Geoffrey himself claimed as much. Yet, in a discussion about the lack of *physical* records on Britain's early history, it is strange that Hall emphasizes the ancient book as the "writing" that preserves the memory of Brutus and his progeny, because this writing is in fact absent. It cannot actually serve as the physical evidence of Brutus's story. This passage reveals Hall's attempt to circumvent the problematic figure of the monument as the vehicle of England's story; instead, he appeals to an absent, materially unproblematic authority. The ancient Welsh book defends against both the "lack of writing" (it provides—in Hall's imagination—a record of British history) and, if you will, the "lack *in* writing" (it avoids the potential loss of the past entailed in the transience of physical documents). The past "slept" but has awakened, and so escapes the corporealizing fate of being "buried."

We might pause at this point and ask what exactly Tudor defenders of the Arthur narrative thought they would gain if they recovered Ge-

offrey's ancient Welsh source. Would not the lack of supporting physical evidence dog this text as well? Would not this text, predating Geoffrey by at least several centuries, be in worse physical shape than
the manuscripts of the *Historia* that antiquarians possessed? The answer is that they did not really expect the ancient Welsh book to materially resolve the problem of monumental history; the absent book
transcended the problem, shifting the register of historical knowledge
to a nonmaterial certainty. Although such a formulation comforted
those who believed in Arthur, it did little to convince skeptics.
William Paruus, Leland's old foe, cheerfully admitted that Geoffrey's
Historia was a translation, the original of which consisted of "fabulous dreams" to which Geoffrey "hath also added many things after
the device and imagination of this own brain."[26] John Twyne, the
headmaster of King's School at Canterbury, saw the lack of the ancient Welsh book as a reason to discount rather accept much of what
Geoffrey asserted.[27] Overleaping the problem of the material monument did not make the problem go away.

John Dee and the Prophecy of Nationhood

In his discussion of John Dee's *General and Rare Memorials Pertaining to the Perfect Art of Navigation,* William Sherman acutely observes that in the treatise "Dee struggles with the appropriate *tense*
of the imperial outlook,"[28] evidencing Dee's stated intention to represent Britain "as it hath been; Yea, as it yet is; or, rather, as it may &
(of right) ought to be."[29] I begin my brief consideration of Dee's antiquarian efforts with this phrase, because it serves as an excellent emblem for the sense of temporal isolation many English historical writers felt. The tentative, provisional quality of the syntax ("yea . . .
rather . . . may . . . ought") suggests not so much a stable vision of the

[26] Leland reports Paruus's opinion, in *Learned and True Assertion,* fol. 36v.

[27] Thomas Twyne, *De Rebus Albionicis Britannicis atque Anglicis* (written ca.
1550; printed in London, 1590), 13, 39.

[28] William Sherman, *John Dee: The Politics of Reading and Writing in the English
Renaissance* (Amherst: University of Massachusetts Press, 1995), 151. Prof. Sherman's research on Dee's manuscript writings, as well as his private advice to me, has
been invaluable to this chapter.

[29] John Dee, *General and Rare Memorials Pertaining to the Perfect Art of Navigation* (London: John Daye, 1577), 3.

nation's past, present, and future, but rather the feeling that focusing on one tense potentially obliterates the others. For Dee, as for many of his colleagues, this temporal provisionality manifests itself as a dialectic between the material and nonmaterial bases of historical knowledge. Dee seeks to recall his nation's past by relying on the figure of the monument but finds that the monument's self-consuming materiality assures the loss of history rather than its resurrection. Just as Leland and Hall attempt to transcend the inadequacy of the physical evidence at hand by appealing to its nonmaterial source, Dee appeals to his self-proclaimed status as a national prophet to recover history through spiritual, metaphysical knowledge, gathering together England's alienated past and future into a single, present, prophetic moment. However, the price of prophetic knowledge is eschatology, and Dee's treatise risks losing England's history in a vision of the coming Apocalypse. *General and Rare Memorials* is in fact ideal for exploring the Tudor problem of historical loss because it vacillates with such extremity between resignation to the materiality of history and the fervent attempt to imagine a pure, dematerialized form of historical knowledge.

Dee's *General and Rare Memorials*, published in 1577, recommends the establishment of a small English naval force, explaining the economic advantage of doing so and elaborating on the aspects of navigation relevant to such a project. In the last seven pages of the treatise, Dee turns to the issue of English history to remind his readers of the exploits of the tenth-century ruler of England, King Edgar, and his royal navy, using the example of the past to motivate the English in the present; in this respect Dee also refers to King Arthur. The significance of the title of Dee's treatise becomes most clear in this final historical section: the term "memorial" (almost a synonym for "monument" in the sixteenth century) refers to the testimony from ancient documents on the greatness of King Edgar's (and Arthur's) realm that Dee adduces. He includes substantial English and Latin passages from these documents within his own prose, consistently emphasizing their memorializing nature: "as by ancient records it may appear" (56); "as Matheus Westmonastariensis, of [Edgar], to his Immortal Commendation, hath left us a Remembrance" (57); "as many Monuments, yet to our days, remaining, do of [Edgar] undoubtedly Testify" (58); "in another Monument" (59); "with memorial whereof . . . to commit to perpetual Memory" (60).

Dee seems to strive to overwhelm his readers with the sheer bulk of manuscript evidence of Edgar's greatness and his glorious navy.

Dee spent much of his intriguing career marshaling the material remains of the past, which, he felt, would lead to a clear understanding of his nation's history. He himself amassed the largest private library in Tudor England, collecting and preserving many valuable documents from medieval England. Twenty years before the publication of the *Memorials*, in 1556, he supplicated Queen Mary to halt the destruction of library collections being carried out by Catholic commissioners in the universities, lamenting "the spoil and destruction of so many and so notable libraries, wherein lay the treasures of all Antiquity, and the everlasting seeds of continual excellency in this your grace's realm."[30] Dee sees in these libraries the double value of the monument, because the books curiously seem to defy materiality and time as "everlasting seeds" and yet fall pray to "spoil and destruction." The simultaneous promise and fragility of material evidence motivate much of Dee's rhetoric in his subsequent manuscript writings, especially *Of Famous and Rich Discoveries* (1577) and *Brytanici Imperii Limites* (1576), in which he devotes a significant amount of time and energy to defending the historical existence of Brutus, the Trojan founder of Britain, and King Arthur. Like Leland, Dee expresses confidence that the physical evidence required to prove the historical validity of Geoffrey's narrative will eventually be found: "at an other apter time and in more apt pla[ce] marvelous agreement of the histories of Antiquity and great unlooked for light and credit will be restored to the Originals of Brutus' fir[st] conquest here."[31] He promises the same for Arthur: "many good and credible Authors have written of king Arthur's arts and conquests: which books . . . lie either uncome by, or unexamined yet."[32] Yet in these

---

[30] This letter, titled *De conservandis et recuperandis antiquis monumentis et scriptoribus supplicatio*, was included in a Renaissance compilation of Dee's manuscripts, now held at the British Library: MS Cotton Vitellius C.VII, fol. 310r. It is reprinted in R. J. Roberts and A. G. Watson, *John Dee's Library Catalogue* (London: Bibliographical Society, 1990), 194.

[31] John Dee, *Of Famous and Rich Discoveries* (BL MS Cotton Vitellius C.VII), fol. 206v. (cited hereafter in the text as *Discoveries*). Ironically enough, this text about the fragility of the material remains of the past is badly burned and in some places unreadable.

[32] John Dee, *Brytanici Imperii Limites* (BL Add. MS 59681), fol. 18r. (cited hereafter in the text as *Limites*).

passages we can see that Dee feels less than complete confidence about Arthur's historical status. The *Memorials* argues for Edgar's royal navy by means of copious documentary evidence; the *Discoveries* and the *Limites*, however, can defend Arthur for the most part only with physical evidence yet to be discovered.

Dee feels the need for material substantiation of Arthur's existence perhaps even more keenly than does Leland. Indeed, as far as I am able to determine, Dee is the only Tudor antiquary who actually claims to have seen the ancient Welsh book that Geoffrey supposedly translated: "the British ancient monument of [Geoffrey's] translating . . . which sundry times I have seen, though some Englishmen think that book not to be extant" (*Limites*, fol. 18r). It is hard to believe that Dee is telling the truth at this point: surely he would have shared this crucial discovery with his colleagues after having seen it "sundry times," ensuring the preservation of (or at least a description of) this monument.[33] Yet, beyond the biographical issue of Dee's veracity, we need to ask *why* a respected antiquary and scholar would make a claim about historical evidence that he could not expect even his fellow Arthur-defenders to take seriously. Dee's claim in fact speaks to a development in the Tudor search for Arthur: the implicit strategy of Hall and others—to treat the absent, nonmaterial Welsh book as the true source of historical knowledge—no longer serves as an adequate response to the pressure Tudor writers felt to discover the physical remains of their nation's past. Dee's commitment to the material monument is such that he would rather make up evidence, so it seems, than accept an absent book in lieu of a present one.

We can thus understand Dee's rather scandalous claim as a result of his need, expressed throughout much of his career, for the physical evidence of Arthur's existence. Yet Dee finds the very category of physical evidence, subject to physical decay or destruction in time, problematic in itself. As much as he voices confidence in the eventual discovery of the material remains of Brutus's and Arthur's reigns, Dee also acknowledges that material remains are always a dubious vehicle for the transmission of the past to the present. Discussing an-

---

[33] I do not wish to suggest that Dee was alone among Tudor antiquaries in possibly fabricating or exaggerating evidence. John Bale, for example, may have done the same in his account of the library he possessed while living in Ireland. See the comments in Graham and Watson, *Recovery of the Past*, 2–3.

cient evidence of Brutus's original founding of Britain, Dee focuses on Ethicus's assertion that

> these Isles of Albion and Ireland sho[uld] be called Brutannicae and not Britannicae, a good confirmation . . . that the text is not c[or]rupt . . . (whereof likewise in ma[ny] . . . places are agreeable copies). . . . But to reform the untrue orthography and pronounciation of that work Ethicus thought it good: and of so notable and ancient a discourse and conquest, well known to him by [a] wrong pronounciation to bring the [ori]ginal Discoverer and conquerer, and the first absolute king of these septentional British Islands to be forgotten: or some wrong person, in undue Chronology, with repugnant circumstances, to be nominated in our Brutus the Italian Trojan's stead. (*Discoveries*, fols. 202r–202v)

For Dee, textual decay leads to historical decay: one mistake in manuscript orthography creates "undue Chronology" and ousts Brutus from his rightful place in history. He writes hopefully that Ethicus's "text is not c[or]rupt," but goes on to admit that textual corruption caused the obscurity under which Brutus's heritage now labors. Arthur's place in national history has suffered equally from the vulnerability of the physical remains of the past. Dee cites the "ancient monuments" that might have proved the British king's existence, "which willfully and wickedly . . . Polydore [Vergil] burnt; yea a whole cart load almost" (*Limites*, fol. 18v). As unlikely as this accusation of Italian malevolence may be, it reveals Dee's fear that the monument as a means to historical knowledge leads as often to the loss of the past as to its recovery. Dee thus feels the double bind of historical knowledge even more intensely than do most Tudor antiquarians: he is torn between an intense commitment to empirical evidence and a pervasive anxiety about this evidence's transience.

Returning to the "memorial" section of Dee's *General and Rare Memorials*, we can start to understand the manner in which Dee voices his reservations about the material monument in a treatise that otherwise relies heavily on physical evidence about the past. Dee begins by asserting that "[t]his Peaceable KING EDGAR was one of the perfect Imperiall Monarchs of this Brytish Impire: and therefore, thus, his Fame remayneth (for ever) Recorded" (56). What follows is a passage in Latin enclosed in a decorative design, with a Coat of Arms on top (see illustration). The passage compares Edgar to famous rulers

This Peaceable KING EDGAR, was one of the perfect Imperiall
Monarchs of this Brytiſh Impire: and therfore, thus, his Fame
remayneth (for euer) Recorded:

ANGLICI ORBIS BASILEVS,
FLOS, ET DECVS ÆDGARVS,
non minus Memorabilis Anglis quàm Cyrus Perſis : Romu-
lus Romanis : Alexander Macedonibus : Arſaces Parthis:
* *Carolus Francis : Anno vitæ 37.ma Regni ſui, cum*
Fratre, & póſt, 21.mo Jdibus Julij, obijt: &
apud GLASCON. Sepelitur.

O Glaſtonbury, Glaſtonbury : the Threaſory of the Carcaſſes
of ſo famous, and ſo many rare Perſons, (* *Quæ olim MATER SANC-*
TORVM dictæ es : &, ab alijs, TVMVLVS SANCTORVM: quam, ab
ipſis DISCIPVLIS DOMINI, ædificatam fuiſſe, Venerabilis habet An-
tiquorum Authoritas.) How Lamentable, is thy caſe, now ? How hath
Hypocriſie and Pride, wrought thy Deſolation ? Though I omit (here)
the names of very many other, both excellent holy Men, and Mighty
Princes (whoſe Carcaſſes are committed to thy Cuſtody,) yet, that A-
poſtlelike Ioſeph, That Triumphant *BRYTISH ARTHVR*, And
now, this Peaceable, and Prouident Saxon, King Edgar, do force me,
with a certayn ſorrowfull Reuerence, here, to Celebrate thy Memory.

This Peaceable King Edgar, (as by Ancient Records may ap-
pere:) His Sommer Progreſſes, and Yerely chief paſtymes, were, The
Sayling rownd about this Whole Ile of Albion : Garded with hys
Grand Nauy of 4000 Sayle, at the leaſt : parted into 4 Equall
Partes, of Pety Nauies : eche, being of a Thowſand Ships. For, ſo it
is Anciently Recorded. *Idem quoq, ÆDGARVS, 4000 NAVES CON-*
GREGAVIT: ex quibus, omni Anno, poſt feſtum Paſchale, 1000 Naues ad
quamlibet Angliæ partem * *Statuit : Sic, Æſtate Inſulam* * *Circumnauigauit, Hy-*
eme verò, Iudicia in Prouincia exercuit . Et hæc omnia, ad ſui Exercitium, & ad
Hoſtium fecit Terrorem.

Could, and would that Peaceable, and wiſe King Edgar, before nede
(as being in Peace, and Quiet, with all Nations, about hym) And Not-
withſtanding, miſtruſting his poſſible Enemies, make his Paſtymes, ſo Roy-
ally, Politically, and Triumphantly: with ſo many Thowſand Ships: And
at the leaſt, with ten tymes ſo many Men, as Ships: And that, yerely ?
And ſhall we, being not aſſured of ſuch Neighbours ſrendeſhips, as may
                                                                              become

John Dee, *General and Rare Memorials* (1577), p. 56. Reproduced by
permission of the Huntington Library, San Marino, California.

throughout history, implying the ability of England to compete with any nation in the world:

> Anglici Orbis Basileus, Flos, et Decus Aedgarus, non minus Memorabilis Anglis quam Cyrus Persis : Romulus Romanis : Alexander Macedonibus : Arsaces Parthis : * Carolus Francis : Anno vitae 37. mo Regni sui, cum Fratre, & post, 21.mo Idibus Julii, obiit: & apud Glascon. Sepelitur. (56)

> The king of England, that flower and glory, Edgar, not less memorable to the English than Cyrus was to the Persians, Romulus to the Romans, Alexander to the Macedonians, Arsaces to the Parthians, * , or Charlemagne to the French: in the 37th year of his reign, with his brother, on the 21st of July, he died: he is buried near Glastonbury. (My translation)

Both in its content and iconographic presentation, the passage is strikingly reminiscent of an inscription on a tombstone. This impression is confirmed by Dee's lament, immediately following this passage, addressed to the cemetery at Glastonbury where Leland and other antiquarians believed King Arthur to be buried. I quote from only the beginning and end of the passage:

> O Glastonbury, Glastonbury: the Treasury of the Carcasses of so famous and so many rare Persons (* *Que olim* MATER SANCTORUM dicta es: &, ab aliis, TUMULUS SANCTORUM. . . .). . . . That Triumphant British Arthur, And now, this Peaceable, and Provident Saxon, King Edgar, do force me, with a certain sorrowful Reverence, here, to Celebrate thy Memory. (56)

In the celebratory "monuments" appearing in the pages that follow, Dee, as we have seen, invokes Edgar's name with a triumphant tone. But in these two passages, a curious sort of ambivalence creeps into Dee's prose. Dee suggests here that Edgar and Arthur are glorious—"That flower and glory, Edgar," "That Triumphant British Arthur"—and insists that the memory of their glory is secure: "for ever Recorded," "Memorable." However, although elsewhere the "monuments" that link Edgar and Arthur to the present are passages from manuscripts, here the monument is a tombstone in a cemetery. The image calls into immediate presence the metaphor of the past as dead. The tombstone itself visually confronts the reader, and the

great figures of England's past are "carcasses." The monument, elsewhere the bridge to the past, is here the sign of the rupture that exiles
Edgar from the present. As he puts it, the monument is both the
"Mater Sanctorum" and the "Tumulus Sanctorum," both the womb
and grave of the holy ones.

Worse still, the "monument" that Dee offers to his readers does not
preserve the memory of Arthur but rather *leaves him out of history.*
Dee notes this absence with an asterisk that he places between "Ar-
saces" and "Carolus," noting in the margins: "And why not ARTURUS
BRITANIS? Because King ARTHUR his Name seen was a thorn in the
Saxons' eyes, of those Days: and his Name rehearsed was Odible to
their Ears: Whose ancestors were by that British Arthur 12 times
overcome in Battle" (56). With this marginal indicator of textual absence, Dee suddenly exposes the monument as Saxon, ideologically
slanted and selective, calculated to reconstruct the past incom-
pletely. Dee makes this complaint about the post-Arthurian neglect
of British monuments even more explicitly and furiously in the *Limites:* "the Saxons, Scots, Picts, Danes, Normans, and others (who felt
the force and dint of his sword) did what they could to deface or utterly to raze out the memories of that incomparable Britain" (fol.
14v). Such a statement gives the impression that the entire world set
out to annihilate the British past, an act of aggression that should
unite English antiquarians in the present. However, in the context of
Dee's exaltation of the Saxon Edgar, the marginal note exacerbates
the lack of homogeneity in England's past, underscoring the antago-
nism rather than accord between national figures such as Arthur and
Edgar. Although elsewhere in the *Memorials* Dee maintains an ecumenical stance toward the issue of national origin ("this English or
British State" [D3v], "the selfsame British and English Commons"
[34]), Dee's note here almost forces the reader to choose: is the nation's heritage Saxon or British? If it is truly British, then what does it
mean that Dee must rely on Saxon remains to produce a national
past? Dee's asterisk visually reminds us of the material gaps that
trouble the human-made memorial.

Although deeply committed to the search for empirical evidence
about Edgar's and Arthur's reigns, Dee attempts to avoid (and sublate)
the self-limiting condition of the monument by appealing to the
power of prophecy. English Renaissance prophecy, as Keith Thomas
has pointed out, primarily served to impose the appearance of conti-

nuity over historical novelty.[34] Its structure of prediction and fulfillment, as well as its ability to confer a retrospective inevitability on
past events, allowed many "prophetic" writers and interpreters to
find uniformity in the English past. One thinks of the anonymous
verse that hailed Henry VII as the fulfillment of the prophecy in Geoffrey's *Historia* (xii.17), that the line of Cadwallader (the last Welsh
king before the Saxon occupation) would be renewed one day: "if that
I shall not lye, / This same is the fulfiller of the prophecy."[35]
Prophetic knowledge here includes both the ancient prediction and
the sixteenth-century inspired interpretation ("if that I shall not lye")
of that prediction. Prophetic insight linked the modern interpreter's
mind with the consciousness of the original prophesier, and Dee finds
this disembodied, nonmaterial connection a powerful alternative to
the more ambiguous figure of the monument.

In the *Memorials*, after again reminding his readers of England's potential to become an naval power, Dee explains that this idea has in
fact come to him prophetically from Edgar himself:

> This peaceable King Edgar (about 600 years ago) had in his mind the
> notion of a great part of the same *Idea* which (from above only and by
> no man's advice) has graciously streamed down into my imagination;
> being (as it becomes me, a subject) careful for the Godly prosperity of
> this British Empire under our most peaceable Queen Elizabeth.
>
> O wisdom Imperial: most diligently, to be Imitated. *Videlicet,
> Prospicere:* to Foresee: O Charitable Kingly Parent, that was touched
> with Ardent Zeale, for Procuring the Public-Profit, of his Kingdom. (54)

This passage offers an understanding of Edgar and the link to the past
that is rather different from the sections we considered previously.
Here, the value of Edgar as an example ("most diligently, to be Imi-
tated") is guaranteed not by the testimony of monuments but rather
Dee's prophetic understanding of English history. Dee describes
Edgar's own wisdom in prophetic terms: "*Prospicere:* to Foresee."
This knowledge of the past, then, springs from a spiritual commun-

---

[34] Thomas, *Religion and the Decline of Magic*, 422–32.
[35] Quoted in Sidney Anglo, "The British History in Early Tudor Propaganda," *Bul-
letin of the John Rylands Library* 44 (1962): 17.

ion of two minds, and not from the survival of physical artifacts.[36]
Edgar's "Idea"—of nationhood and a royal navy—travels through time
unhindered; history is transmitted without interruption to the present. Dee claims that this idea comes "from above only and by no
man's advice," and here we can see how prophecy functions in part as
a dialectical alternative to the tombstone monument, transcending
the material and deriving "from above only" rather than from a
buried "treasury of carcasses." Dee's appeal to prophecy parallels the
earlier appeal of Tudor antiquarians to Geoffrey's absent Welsh
source, but Dee raises the stakes: unlike the Welsh source, which
still holds out the promise of an eventual material confirmation of
Arthur's existence, prophecy confirms the value of Edgar's reign by
transcending the material altogether.

As in the case of Leland and Hall, I am less interested in the level of
belief Dee's prophetic claim might have compelled from his audience—though Dee's mixed reputation makes this a difficult and interesting issue[37]—than in the modes of historical knowledge Dee
finds natural to employ, as well as his sense of the limits of those
modes. But, in Dee's *Memorials*, what are the limits of prophecy?
They emerge, ironically enough, in relation to the most sacred form
of prophecy—apocalyptic discourse. I have already discussed the Renaissance link between the prophetic and apocalyptic modes, especially regarding the dual retrospective and proleptic tendencies of
both—their concern to gather up the past with reference to the future. It remains to observe that prophecy's affiliation with apocalyptic rhetoric in fact compromised its ability to recover national history, even as prophets such as Dee derived a sacred legitimacy from
the biblical narrative. Apocalyptic writing's totalizing effects, its tendency to observe human affairs from a God's-eye view, inclined it to
reformulate and simplify history in the process of recovering it. Kenneth Gross, examining the apocalyptic rhetoric in Spenser's *A View
of the State of Ireland*, notes an anxiety about "too ungoverned an appeal to the ideal, the atemporal, the providential." Interpreting the

---

[36] Peter French observes that Dee wrote in the *Monas Hieroglyphica* that he believed he had discovered within himself the secrets of the ancient magi and that this
union of minds gave him his special insights. See French, *John Dee: The World of an
Elizabethan Magus* (London: Routledge and Kegan Paul, 1972), 76–78.

[37] The Tudor reception of Dee was often extreme, ranging from Queen Elizabeth's
polite audiences with him to John Foxe's contemptuous dismissal of Dee as "the
great conjurer" (quoted in French, *John Dee*, 8–9).

apocalyptic imagination as a flight from rather than to history, Gross suggestively concludes that its "universalizing, deterministic cosmologies" make the Apocalypse "a liability for any prophetic author who refuses to exclude either man or God from *the ongoing process of choice and change.*"[38] Nationalist historians such as Leland, Hall, and Dee want very much to include "choice and change" in their histories, to represent the circuitous successes and failures of the past so as to derive exemplary models for the future.

Yet Dee's appeal to prophecy stems from a desire not only to testify to the ongoing process of history but also to prevent this history from slipping away, depriving his nation of the exemplarity of its past (Edgar's navy and the Arthurian kingdom). Prophecy responds to the precariousness of the material monument by sublating it, clarifying the past and promising a direct link to history, "from above only and by no man's advice." In this context Dee can hardly avoid trying to legitimize his prophetic interpretation of history by appealing to the Ur-prophecy of Revelation. As Dee insists on the divine nature of his retrospective link to King Edgar, the anticipation of end time creeps into his sense of prophetic knowledge.[39] After confirming his own status as a national prophet, Dee meditates on the nature of England's future opportunities:

> a perfect cosmographer [must] . . . meditate on the Cosmopolitical Government thereof, under the King Almighty: passing on, very swiftly, toward the most Dreadful, and most Comfortable Term Prefixed.
>
> And I find . . . that if this British Monarchy, would heretofore, have followed the Advantages, which they have had, onward, they might, very well, ere this, have surpassed (By Justice and Godly, sort) any particular Monarchy, else, that ever was on Earth, since Mans Creation.
>
> But yet . . . there is a little lock of Lady Occasion's hair flickering in the air for our hand to catch hold of, whereby we may, yet once more (before all be utterly past and gone forever), discreetly and valiantly recover and enjoy . . . our Ancient and due appurtenances to this Imperial British Monarchy. (54–55)

[38] Gross, *Spenserian Poetics*, 84, 54 (my emphasis).

[39] Sherman does us a great service by pointing out that in the work of many twentieth-century critics, the historical writings of Dee "have all too often taken on mystical coloring" (*John Dee*, 150). Yet, his insistence that Dee's historical-nationalist vision "was by no means apocalyptic" (150), while generally true, does not apply to a passage such as the one we are considering here.

Dee notes England's potential to become the greatest nation on earth and regain what in his view are its past imperial holdings. He invokes a cosmic, universal community in order to highlight England's special status as a particular nation, mentioning the coming Apocalypse to indicate England's importance in the divine scheme of things, linking the glory of the past to the promise of the future. However, Dee's own reference to the imminent end of time betrays its questionable advantage for the English nation: "the most Dreadful, and most comfortable Term Prefixed." Is the Apocalypse something England should look forward to or dread? Dee's striking ambivalence stems from a contradiction, which I discuss at length in chapter 3, between the early Reformation hope for a glorious national future and the apocalyptic (rather than millenarian) expectation of the imminent end of time.

The cosmic conclusion of worldly existence thus forecloses the possibility of any kind of earthly future. The point here is not primarily that the apocalyptic prophecy "defers" national fulfillment but rather that prophecy—as a compensatory sublation of monumental history—recovers the national past by swallowing it up, reformulating its temporality so that it is scarcely recognizable as history. The shift from the material to apocalyptic register, reducing "the ongoing process of choice and change" to cosmic hypostasis, brings with it a new possibility of historical loss, and for this reason Dee's statements about England that follow in the next paragraph focus on the English past ("have followed," "have surpassed") and occur in the conditional ("would," "might"). And in the final paragraph, which offers the most optimistic view for England's future, Dee acknowledges, almost as if under his breath, in a parenthesis, the limiting condition of apocalyptic temporality: "before all be utterly past and gone forever." Dee's prophetic eschatology, trying to forge a spiritual link to English history, also threatens to displace that history absolutely.[40]

Dee, like many of his fellow Tudor historiographers, finds the monument an unstable figure of historical knowledge but is unable or unwilling to ignore the potential cost of a dematerialized, prophetic link

---

[40] As Jeffrey Knapp has suggestively observed of this passage, "Dee cannot decide whether he sees a door opening or closing . . . the source of indecisiveness would appear . . . to be the theological trickiness, the potentially heretical superstitiousness, of basing an imperialist hope on an apocalyptic one." See Knapp, *An Empire Nowhere: England, America, and Literature from "Utopia" to "The Tempest"* (Berkeley: University of California Press, 1992), 102.

to the past. He finds that the materiality of history is a problem from which he cannot simply turn away. When he looks back to his nation's past, he sees crumbling monuments; when he looks forward to the future, he sees the apocalyptic term prefixed. He thus finds himself engaged in a kind of ongoing temporal revision, filling in the gaps that his own representation creates, searching unsuccessfully for that divine temporality that suffers from no loss and is never alien to itself.

Spenser's Poetic Monuments

Elizabethan writers often celebrated poetry's ability to memorialize the past and teach virtue in terms that recall the opposing modes of monumental and prophetic history that we have been considering. Sir Philip Sidney noted with satisfaction that the Romans called the poet *vates* and suggested poetry's transcendence of the earthly register: "Only the poet, disdaining to be tied to any such subjection, lifted up with the vigor of his own invention, doth grow in effect another nature, in making things . . . better than nature."[41] Yet Renaissance writers did not view poetry as simply the opposite of the physical. Although they saw poetry as superior to the material monument, poetry is monumental nonetheless, and even possesses a complicated materiality. Horace's claim to artistic immortality in his *Odes*, endlessly referenced by Renaissance thinkers, reveals poetry's affiliation with and distance from the physical monument: "I have finished a monument more lasting than bronze and loftier than the Pyramid's royal pile, one that no wasting rain, no furious north wind can destroy, or the countless chain of years and the ages' flight."[42] Renaissance writers often took Horace's assertion of poetry's extra-material durability—"more lasting than bronze"—as sign of its peculiar duality. On the one hand, poetry was more lasting than bronze because it did not rely on the physical register for its existence: it possessed a spiritual essence, escaping material dissolution in time. On the other hand, the fact that poetry could be compared to bronze at all linked it to the physical register, and in such a register poetry was a paltry

[41] Philip Sidney, *An Apology for Poetry*, ed. Forrest G. Robinson (New York: Macmillan, 1985), 11, 14.

[42] Horace, *Odes* (23 B.C.E.), III.30, in *Horace: The Odes and Epodes*, trans. C. E. Bennett, Loeb Classical Library (Cambridge: Harvard University Press, 1978), 278–79.

thing indeed. This sense of poetry's duality sometimes placed it between the materiality of the monument and the spirituality of the past object it was saving—the soul, a memory, an image, fame, and so forth. For the Renaissance, poetry possessed a spiritual essence that pyramids and statues did not, but it was also, in fact, paper and ink. We can see a humorous expression of this duality in a passage by George Chapman, who explains that the soul, disgusted with the body, created "another fruitless, dead and despised receptacle to reserve her appearance with unspeakable profit, comfort and life to all posterities—and that is this poor scribbling, this toy, this too living a preservative for the deathful tombs of nobility."[43] Chapman implies that poetry is less material than the body but still more so than the soul; poetry memorializes by giving "life to all posterities" but is a "dead and despised receptacle."

Edmund Spenser makes crucial use of poetry's ambivalent identity when he turns to the matter of Arthur. Through much of his career, Spenser's interest in English national identity takes the form of historical contemplation. In *A View of the State of Ireland,* the inquiry into Irish and English nationhood takes the form of "many sweet remembrances of antiquity," revealing a remarkable interest in historiographical method. Irenius claims that, while he relies on Irish chronicles and oral traditions for Irish history,

> unto them besides I add mine own reading; and out of them both together, with comparison of times, likewise of manner and customs, affinity of words and names, properties of natures, and uses, resemblances of rites and ceremonies, monuments of churches and tombs, and many other like circumstances, I do gather a likelihood of truth.[44]

This attention to comparative traditions and conventions, as well as to physical evidence, attests to Spenser's engagement in antiquarian discourse and perhaps controversy. Yet both in the *View* and in his other writing, he sometimes emphasizes the precariousness of historical posterity. Consider the effect of Spenser's translation of Du Bellay's *Les antiquitez du Rome* as *Ruines of Rome*—"antiquities"

---

[43] George Chapman, *Chapman's Homer,* 2 vols., ed. Allardyce Nicoll (Princeton: Princeton University Press, 1967), 1:503.

[44] Edmund Spenser, *A View of the State of Ireland,* ed. Andrew Hadfield and Willy Maley (Oxford: Blackwell, 1997), 43, 46.

translated into "ruins." This sense of precariousness persists in the "historical" sections of *The Faerie Queene* (II.x and III.iii). Spenser would like to give his nation the epic past that Virgil and, to some degree, Ariosto and Tasso gave their nations, but he finds his narrative in Certeau's double bind of historical loss and recovery, registering his sense of the gap between past and present even as he tries to forge a bridge. This is the ontology of early national consciousness, especially in England, when a new sense of historical novelty and anachronism highlighted the insufficiency of the nation's past, but before any notion of historical progress allowed Tudor writers to interpret historical difference positively. The dialectic between the material and nonmaterial bases of historical knowledge thus takes on a special urgency for antiquarians such as Leland, Hall, and Dee as they struggle to find the appropriate link to England's past. Spenser takes the antiquarian concepts of the monument and prophecy and turns them into monumental and prophetic *poetry*, giving himself a degree of distance from them in order to play seriously with the idea of national history and historical loss. His poetry is prophetic in that it attempts to initiate a dialectical movement "from ground . . . unto the highest skies," as Spenser puts it in the introductory stanza to the *Briton moniments* canto (II.x)—a movement launched by what David Lee Miller has called "an initial refusal of the literal facts of the flesh."[45] Yet his poetry also thematizes the elusiveness of the posterity it is supposed to celebrate. His verse both enacts and represents the self-limiting functions of monumental and prophetic history, keenly registering the need for historical origins and mourning their inevitable loss.

Returning to the textual moment where we began this discussion (*FQ* II.x.69), we are in a position to bring into a specific historical perspective the evocative image of Arthur hunched over the ancient tome containing his nation's history. First, I want to suggest that

---

[45] David Lee Miller, *The Poem's Two Bodies: The Poetics of the 1590 "Faerie Queene"* (Princeton: Princeton University Press, 1988), 191. The comments that follow owe much to Miller's splendid Hegelian–Lacanian reading of the entire *Briton moniments* episode (183–214). However, Miller is too optimistic when he asserts that "if Spenser does not explicitly complete the dialectical elevation of British history into British glory, he nevertheless structures the chronicle so as to *anticipate* its sublation without remainder in the act of reading—Arthur's reading and ours insofar as we allow the text to identify us with Arthur" (200). Arthur's reading and subsequent nationalist apostrophe are not so much a sublation without remainder as a compensation for an imperfect sublation, both blind to and resigned to its alienation from history.

Briton moniments is Geoffrey's ancient Welsh source, the absent text coveted by Leland and Dee, provided that we understand the Welsh book as not merely a literal identification but also as an emblem of the antiquarian optimism and pessimism about the nation's Arthurian past, entailing the problematics of monumental history that we have been discussing. After all, literally speaking, a fifth-century Arthur cannot be reading an eighth- or ninth-century Welsh chronicle that describes Arthur's death. Yet the text does *seem* like the Welsh source, closely following Geoffrey's *Historia Regum Britanniae* while predating Geoffrey by at least six centuries. To the degree that Spenser wants to suggest a connection between the Welsh source and *Briton moniments,* he also suggests how vulnerable historical knowledge is to material decay in time. Even the Welsh source, the anterior, nonmaterial evidence of England's Arthurian past for many nationalist antiquarians, is here represented as physically damaged and incomplete, the victim of material decay. As such, *Briton moniments* intervenes in Spenser's Arthurian fable in order to highlight the historical crisis confronting English nationhood, perhaps even to underscore why a national figure like Arthur can appear only in fables, not in history. The interruption at the end of the narrative, resulting from physical decay, seems to confirm the archival unavailability of England's Arthurian heritage. Like Dee's marginal note about the Saxon monument that excludes Arthur, Spenser represents Arthur's exclusion from *Briton moniments* as a material gap: "There abruptly did it end" (II.x.69.2). As we have noted, the word "there" indicates the point of interruption in the narrative but also indicates the space on the page—right "there" in the physical book that Arthur (and, at another remove, we) read. Spenser is unwilling to treat the ancient Welsh source as the nonmaterial confirmation of Arthur's existence. The Welsh source itself is all too material, perhaps Spenser's wry suggestion of what the antiquarians would get if they actually found this book.

This "materialization" of Geoffrey's Welsh book, the reduction of the absent, anterior source to decaying monument, effectively establishes Spenser's Prince Arthur as a "virtual" figure—almost part of history, but not quite. Indeed, recent critics have argued that Arthur's historical identity does not fully coalesce in Spenser's account, that he stands awkwardly between past and future, *quondam et futurus* only in the most liminal manner. Several of these readings suggest that Spenser in fact predicates Arthur's identity on the cut that excludes him from history. Elizabeth Bellamy interprets Arthur's limi-

nality as a function of Lacanian misrecognition in which his historical existence depends on his failure to "read" himself, and W. A. Sessions has recently proposed, in an analysis that takes into account
the epic genre's reliance on a protagonist figure, that Arthur functions as the symbol of a historical absence that makes possible an imperial future.[46] Likewise, Kenneth Gross suggests that *Briton moniments*'s concluding break makes possible Arthur's activity in the
poem in the first place, avoiding the idolatrous "overidentification of
a self with its genealogical origins" that characterizes a figure like
Orgoglio.[47] Yet I wish to place such exemplary interpretations within
the cultural context that Spenser seems to invoke with his description of Eumnestes' chamber: the virtual nature of Arthur's identity is
symptomatic of the Tudor anxiety about national history. Spenser derives his Arthur not so much from Chrétien, Mallory, or Tasso as
from Leland, Dee, and (despite his skepticism) Camden. Crucially,
Arthur's "historiographic" identity is circumscribed by his apparent
inability to play a part in British history and give his nation the posterity it needs; he is an *almost* historical Arthur whose selfhood is
both enabled and blocked by the precariousness of material remains.
The "wicked hand" (II.x.68.4) that may divide Arthur from the narrative he reads stems from the same anxiety that imagines a Polydore
Vergil who (according to Dee) "willfully and wickedly" has destroyed
Arthurian monuments, "yea a whole cart load almost."

By identifying *Briton moniments* as the "materialization" of Geoffrey's Welsh source, I also wish to qualify earlier interpretations of
the chronicle as a fully or positively achieved historical vision. Jerry
Leath Mills has identified intriguing numerological patterns in the
narrative, and Joan Warchol Rossi has argued that the episode offers a

[46] Elizabeth Bellamy suggests that Arthur's subjectivity is determined by a "just-
missed encounter" with his past: "Arthur has simply come to Eumnestes' chamber
too early (or too late) to 'read' himself, almost as if he can be represented in the
Briton moniments only under the condition that he fails to 'read' himself"; Bellamy,
Translations of Power: Narcissism and the Unconscious in Epic History (Ithaca: Cornell University Press, 1992), 227. In a paper given at the Spenser Society session at
Kalamazoo, Mich., W. A. Sessions argues that Arthur's generic anachronism imbues
him with a kind of virtual presence in *The Faerie Queene*, an "ellipsis" out of which
can be fashioned an epic future: "Arthur, as ironically present and distant at the same
time, can bring old history forward but, through a method of ellipsis, Spenser can
focus the center of his epic elsewhere, on disparate georgic labors. So, in a phrase that
begins to sound like rap music, ellipsis is prolepsis, and prolepsis is ellipsis—at least
in *The Faerie Queene*"; Sessions, "Spenser's Anachronism," Spenser at Kalamazoo,
May 2000. My thanks to Prof. Sessions for kindly giving me a copy of his paper.

[47] Gross, *Spenserian Poetics*, 123.

conception of aggressive temperance.[48] Yet their conclusions run too much against the grain of the overriding chaos and discontinuity that marks the narrative of *Briton moniments.* The best overall description of the tone of the canto is still Harry Berger, Jr.'s assertion that the chronicle dramatizes "the intransigence of real facts to meaning."[49] This "intransigence" results, I argue, from Spenser's pessimistic conception of national history and historical knowledge as materially transient. Yet he does not foreclose the possibility of a more positive historical vision: *Briton moniments* acquires its "materialized" quality in part from its contrasting relation to a prophetic conception of the past. We must remember that Spenser associates Arthur and the Arthurian past with an interruption ("There abruptly did it end") that occurs precisely between two segments of national history: *Briton moniments*'s account of the narrative from Brutus to Uther Pendragon, and Merlin's prophecy of British history from King Conan to Queen Elizabeth (III.iii). In representing these two modes of historical narrative, Spenser engages the dialectic between the monumental and the prophetic link to the past that we have been tracking in Tudor antiquarian writing. Indeed, we must interpret these two episodes together, seeing Merlin's prophecy as a *second* try at recovering the national past, the sublation of a failed material vision to a purer prophetic one. The few positive aspects of *Briton moniments,* rather than hinting at an underlying optimism, signify the text's anticipation of its sublation by prophecy in Merlin's narrative (III.iii).[50]

We can see this anticipation in Spenser's depiction of Eumnestes,

[48] See Jerry Leath Mills, "Spenser and the Numbers of History: A Note on the British and Elfin Chronicles in *The Faerie Queene," Philological Quarterly* 55 (1976): 281–86; and see Joan Warchol Rossi, "*Briton moniments:* Spenser's Definition of Temperance in History," *ELR* 15 (1985): 42–58. Rossi, for example, argues against the interpretation of *Briton moniments* as morally ambiguous and pessimistic, insisting that "this is an untenable position for an epic poet creating a national vision for the Age of Elizabeth" (43). The problem from my point of view, however, involves the lack of unambiguous origins from which to derive a "national vision."

[49] Harry Berger, Jr., *The Allegorical Temper: Vision and Reality in Book II of Spenser's "Faerie Queene"* (New Haven: Yale University Press, 1957), 103.

[50] It may be objected that this sublation occurs in the Fairy History that Guyon reads (II.x.70–76). Yet if we are talking about a sublation *by and as history,* we must regard the Fairy genealogy as a separate genre or paradigm. Indeed, as I argue in chap. 4, it represents fictional history. It is not so much Providentialized history (exemplified by Merlin's prophecy) as it is ahistorical, a continuity pushed to the point of eternity. As David Lee Miller has shrewdly observed, "such an ahistorical 'history' is the only kind the sovereignty proper should have" (*Poem's Two Bodies,* 206).

the keeper of the chamber in which Arthur finds the tome, a depiction that explicitly raises the problem of preserving the past with material means. At first, Spenser suggests that Eumnestes can recall the past with no loss:

> The man of infinite remembrance was,
> And things foregone through many ages held,
> Which he recorded still, as they did pas,
> Ne suffred them to perish through long eld,
> As all things else, the which this world doth weld,
> But laid them up in his immortal scrine,
> Where they for ever incorrupted dweld.
> (II.ix.56.1–7)

"Remembrance" is an entirely nonmaterial faculty here, opposed to the wasteful transience of "this world." The stanza occludes or transforms writing itself: it tells us that Eumnestes "recorded" past events but does not specify by what means. "Recorded" seems here to play up its etymology in "*cor*," suggesting that the inscription of the past occurs only as spiritualized writing—on the heart itself. But this spiritualized writing, this memory without loss, is revised in the next stanza:

> His chamber all was hangd about with rolles,
> And old records from auncient times deriv'd,
> Some made in books, some in long parchment scrolles,
> That were all worme-eaten, and full of canker holes.
> (ix.57.6–9)

Eumnestes now looks more like an overworked Tudor antiquary than a reservoir of pure memory. Spenser uses the word "records" again, but the repetition calls attention to the difference between the two uses: here, the "old records" are the actual, physical documents that lie around Eumnestes' chamber. The material documents that now preserve history are unreliable because they decay in time: the "canker holes" in Eumnestes' scrolls threaten corresponding gaps in history itself. The possibility of loss through material decay requires the compensatory appearance of Anamnestes in the next stanza—a figure whose presence is puzzling if Eumnestes truly is a "man of infinite remembrance." The physical monument creates the possibility of forgetting and thus the compensatory need for the mechanism of Anamnestes—an anti-amnesia—to prevent such a forgetting.[51]

Continuing the opposition between spiritual and physical writing, the opening stanzas of II.x seek to define the threat of the materiality by contrasting it with a prophetic vision of the past. They essentially translate *Orlando Furioso* 3.1–3, with the notable exception of 3.2.6–7. Whereas at this point Ariosto cautiously invokes the prophetic inspiration behind his poem—"if I be not deceived in my prophetic sight"[52]—Spenser excludes this phrase and instead calls attention to his inability to represent Elizabeth's ancestry:

> A labour huge, exceeding farre my might:
> How shall fraile pen, with feare disparaged,
> Conceive such soveraine glory, and great bountihed?
>
> (x.10.7–9)

Spenser conceives of his artistic inadequacy to recall the past as a "frail pen," linking the loss of the past with physical inscription, as he did in Eumnestes' chamber. The stanza thus suggests that the upcoming chronicle functions as writing, as a monument, rather than as prophecy. The fourth stanza reiterates both possibilities: Spenser praises Elizabeth's ancestors,

> Whose noble deedes above the Northerne starre
> Immortal fame for ever hath enrold;
> As in that old mans booke they were in order told.
>
> (4.7–9)

Once again, Spenser contrasts heavenly vision ("immortal fame") with physical writing ("that old mans book"). In the *Briton moni-*

---

[51] Mary Carruthers has observed that "all accounts of the workings of memory written after Aristotle separate its activity into two basic processes: that of storage (in a strictly defined context, the activity to which the words *memoria* and *mnesis* are applied); and that of recollection (*reminiscentia* and *anamnesis*)." See Carruthers, *The Book of Memory: A Study of Memory in Medieval Culture* (Cambridge: Cambridge University Press, 1990), 46. The dual presence of Eumnestes and Anamnestes clearly follows this tradition closely. Nonetheless, Spenser uses the compensatory figure of Anamnestes to emphasize the material failings of Eumnestes rather than to supplement his activities.

[52] Ludovico Ariosto, *Orlando Furioso*, trans. Guido Waldman (Oxford: Oxford University Press, 1974), p. 20.

ments canto, history is finally inscribed in the material book rather than above the North Star.

The instances of material insufficiency in *Briton moniments* thus function as negative moments in a dialectic that yields a positive vision in Merlin's prophecy. The disappointment of "that old mans book" is redeemed by Spenser's promise that the second narrative derives from the heavenly muse Clio and her "great volume of Eternity" (III.iii.4.5). *Briton moniments* tends to thematize the material fact of historical loss—"in the end was left no moniment / Of *Brutus*, nor of Britons glory auncient" (II.x.36.8–9)—and historical discontinuity: when King Morgan dies, "[h]is son Rivallo his dead room did supply" (x.34.1), a succession that rhetorically reveals the death or gap that underlies all successions. In precise contrast, Spenser emphasizes the link rather than the gap between rulers in Merlin's prophecy, making King Malgo the son of Vortipore rather than merely his successor (III.iii.31.7)—despite what Geoffrey reports—and similarly upgrading King Careticus from successor to son (iii.33.1). There is no authority in Spenser's sources for these changes: he invents them, deliberately strengthening the ties within the English royal lineage.[53] *Briton moniments* often calls attention to the transience of earthly life, commenting on the end of King Donwallo's magnificent reign with the rhetorical question "what may live for ay?" (II.x.40.1). In contrast, Spenser suggests that a heavenly Providence guides Merlin's entire (prophetic) historical narrative: "universall peace [shall] compound all civill iarre" (iii.23.6–9). I have more to say about the implications of this "universal peace," but meanwhile we should note that Merlin from the outset promises a harmonious conclusion to any conflict we may hear of in the narrative. Although *Briton moniments* never recuperates its gaps and setbacks in any fully realized manner, Merlin's prophecy always foregrounds the immanence of destiny. For example, Spenser attributes the most substantial setback in Merlin's prophecy—the loss of British rule after Cadwallader—to "the full time prefixt by destiny" (iii.40.5). This is a heavy sentence against the British, but because destiny, rather than chance, brings about this loss, destiny can restore it as well:

> Tho when the terme is full accomplishid,
> There shall a sparke of fire, which hath long-while

[53] See Carrie Anne Harper, *The Sources of "The British Chronicle History" in Spenser's "Faerie Queene"* (Philadelphia: John C. Winston Co., 1910), 148–52.

> Bene in his ashes raked up, and hid,
> Be freshly kindled. . . .
>
> (iii.48.1)

Abandoning the material basis of historical vision, Spenser can subordinate the contingency of history to the continuity of destiny,
prophetically ensuring that England's past will eventually find its
way to the present.

The very condition of prophecy's success also limits that success,
however, because, to subordinate history to destiny, Spenser appeals
to eschatology. In turning to prophecy as a dialectical solution to the
self-consuming monument, he runs into the same end-time problematic that Dee encounters in *General and Rare Memorials,* in which
the totalizing tendency of eschatology displaces rather than confirms
history's provenance.

Thomas Betteridge has recently suggested that a tension between
earthly temporality and apocalypticism characterized a great deal of
Reformation historiography, in which eschatology and history are
often fundamentally opposed:

> the appearance of apocalyptic imagery in a work of history radically
> undermines the truthfulness of the historical text by introducing an in-
> herently ahistorical, if not anti-historical, truth into its midst. In other
> words, once an event becomes apocalyptic it implicitly becomes not of
> history and, in a sense, drops out of historical discourse; it becomes
> scriptural.[54]

Likewise for Spenser, the displacement of history is the cost of
prophetic knowledge. The apocalyptic register creeps into Merlin's
discourse of destiny, as when the prophet's lament for the defeated
Britons pointedly echoes the lament of Revelation 8:13: "Then woe,
and woe, and everlasting woe, / Be to the Briton babe, that shalbe
borne, / To live in thraldome of his fathers foe" (iii.42.1–3). In this
case, the British defeat does not in fact turn out to be final, as Spenser
assures us two stanzas later: "Nay but the terme (said he) is limited, /
That in this thraldome Britons shall abide" (iii.44.1–2). However,
Spenser's references to the Apocalypse elsewhere in the narrative cre-

---

[54] Thomas Betteridge, *Tudor Histories of the English Reformations, 1530–83*
(Brookfield, Vt.: Ashgate, 1999), 16.

ate a cumulative effect of eschatological displacement. Consider the passage, which we looked at earlier, that expresses the prophetic inevitability of Merlin's narrative:

> The feeble Britons, broken with long warre,
> They shall upreare, and mightily defend
> Against their forrein foe, that comes from farre,
> Till universall peace compound all civill iarre.
>
> (iii.23.6–9)

Harry Berger has observed that the last line of this passage too glibly fixes the serious problems that have come before it ("feeble," "broken," "defend," "foe").[55] Indeed, to extend Berger's comment, the final line is inappropriate because it too quickly changes registers from a national, earthly setting to a universal, heavenly setting: England's historical problems are not resolved but rather displaced. This "universal peace" significantly echoes the "eternal peace" of the apocalyptic New Jerusalem that Redcross Knight sees in a vision (I.x.55.9), a heavenly city that "dims" the mere earthly glory of Cleopolis (I.x.58.9). Likewise emphasizing the disparity between earthly and heavenly registers, the millennial-sounding "universal peace" not only subordinates history to destiny but also threatens to lose history in eschatology.

Why does Spenser, like Dee, feel obliged to reveal the apocalyptic limit of prophetic discourse, given that, within certain bounds, they have a choice in the matter? In part, as I have suggested, they are resigned to the conception of national history as material, as discontinuous and heterogeneous; indeed, Spenser's gesture of poetically splitting national history into two parts stems from this resignation. The emerging novelty of national consciousness requires, to some degree, an oblique rather than direct connection to the distant past, reformulating the nation's temporality as "a limited history," to borrow Foucault's phrase again. The powerful temptation to sublate the imperfect, material basis of historical knowledge to prophetic continuity thus carries with it an awareness of what is lost in this sublation—namely, history itself as a contiguous, polyvalent register for articu-

[55] Harry Berger, Jr., *Revisionary Play: Studies in the Spenserian Dynamic* (Berkeley: University of California Press, 1988), 121. Berger's chapter on Merlin's prophecy originally appeared as "The Structure of Merlin's Chronicle in *The Faerie Queene* III (iii)," *Studies in English Literature* 9 (1969): 38–51.

lating national identity. Thus the famously problematic conclusion of Merlin's otherwise optimistic prophecy:

> But yet the end is not. There *Merlin* stayd,
> As overcomen of the sprites powre,
> Or other ghastly spectacle dismayd,
> That secretly he saw, yet note discoure.
>   (iii.50.1–4)

Because Spenser presents so many elements in Merlin's prophecy as improved versions of negative moments in *Briton moniments*, we might reasonably expect the climax of Merlin's prophecy, the celebration of Elizabeth, to both parallel and improve upon Arthur's interruption in the first narrative.[56] Yet rather than sublating the transient material to a lasting prophetic vision, Merlin's "ghastly spectacle" instead reaffirms the temporal precariousness of national history. The prophet's final phrase echoes Christ's phrase when he warns of the Last Judgment and the eventual end of the world: "for all these things must come to pass, but the end is not yet" (Matt. 24:6). Like Dee, Spenser explicitly refers to the expectation of an imminent end, recalling and exacerbating the troubling intimations of Merlin's "universal peace" (iii.23.9). Even more completely than before, England's earthly triumph is displaced to heavenly eternity, and this eschatological fate results from the narrative's earlier reliance on a prophetic destiny marked with apocalyptic undertones (iii.42, 44). The prophetic moment of national history slips into an apocalyptic moment. Spenser thus chooses to link his two historical narratives most fully in terms of their respective *failures* to recall the past, suggesting how fragile he imagines his grasp of national history to be.

---

[56] It has not often been noted how thoroughly Spenser makes these two moments parallel, interrupting both narratives with the word "there" ("There abruptly did it end" [II.x.68.2] and "There Merlin stayd" [III.iii.50.1]). He offers two interpretations of each interruption (II.x.68.4–6 and III.iii.50.2–4), and each time he depicts the reader's/listener's response (II.x.68.7–9 and III.iii.50.6–7). These two stanzas embody the most verbally precise similarity between the two historical narratives.

3 APOCALYPTIC HISTORY AND ENGLISH DEFERRALS

If, as I suggested in the previous chapter, eschatology emerges as the antihistorical limit of national prophecy in Dee and Spenser, then what is the relationship between nation and apocalyptic theology in the Elizabethan period? We are obliged to ask this question because many English Protestants used the Book of Revelation to interpret both the past and the near future. Unlike national prophets who, in the process of sacralizing English history, risked losing their past in an ahistorical eternity, other Elizabethan writers attempted to turn the divine prophecy of Revelation into history, making it available as a source of national articulation. As John Pocock has shrewdly observed, "apocalyptic, which sacralizes secular time, must always in an opposite sense secularize the sacred, by drawing the processes of salvation into that time which is known as *saeculum*."[1] In the sixteenth century, perhaps more than in any earlier period in English thought, English Protestants broke with the idealist, Augustinian interpretation of Revelation in favor of a historical interpretation, trying to match up the continuity of the divine apocalyptic narrative with their own seemingly fractured history.

Apocalyptic thinking, to the degree that it remains historically elaborated, represents a structural contrast to the effects of eschato-

[1] John Pocock, "England," in *National Consciousness, History, and Political Culture in Early Modern Europe*, ed. Orest Ranum (Baltimore: Johns Hopkins University Press, 1975), 109.

logical displacement that we discussed in chapter 2. Rather than ab-
sorbing the national past into a prophetic *nunc stans*, apocalyptic interpretation sought to reveal how English history itself bore the
marks of God's divine plan. This mode of interpretation took events
of the national past as the fulfillment of things prophesied in the
Book of Revelation. Apocalyptic history helped Bale and Foxe, as we
saw in chapter 1, to represent Oldcastle's resistance to Catholic officials in 1414 as a meaningful and inevitable moment in a larger, divine story. Crucially, it allowed English Reformers to describe the
break with Rome as an event prophesied fifteen centuries earlier.
They could thus think about this break both as a restoration of a lost,
pristine church and as the prophetic confirmation that this church
was never entirely lost, that it continued to reveal itself to the faithful throughout history. This happy continuity was still remote from
the Enlightenment notion of historical progress, in which the narrative of improvement proceeds *immanently*, event by event. The apocalyptic story was eschatological, not progressive; Christ's return
loomed closer and closer, but the world did not necessarily improve
in the meantime. The expectation of a foreshortening eschaton created the tricky matter of articulating the nation's future vis-à-vis
Christ's imminent return. The Book of Revelation helped consolidate
England's past, but its prediction of the destruction of the world
seemed to leave little room for an English future.

The problem with the national future often led to a rhetoric of eschatological postponement in the Tudor period. Recent critical commentary on apocalyptic nationalism has often centered on the idea of
deferral. Indeed, no recent idea about apocalyptic thinking is more
common than the observation that eschatology relies on the deferral
of the end even as it anticipates this end.[2] The Apocalypse is always
about to arrive, but not yet. The impossibility of an "Apocalypse
now" seems built into the genre, perhaps built into the text of Revelation itself, as Richard Bauckham has recently suggested:

---

[2] The humanist Frank Kermode, the deconstructionist Hillis Miller, and the post-
modernist Jean Baudrillard all demonstrate, from quite different perspectives, the in-
evitable deferral or displacement of the end. See Frank Kermode, *The Sense of an
Ending: Studies in the Theory of Fiction* (New York: Oxford University Press, 1967);
J. Hillis Miller, "*Heart of Darkness* Revisted," in *Fiction and Repetition: Seven En-
glish Novels* (Cambridge: Harvard University Press, 1982); and Jean Baudrillard,
"Apocalypse Now," in *Simulacra and Simulation*, trans. Sheila Faria Glaser (Ann
Arbor: University of Michigan Press, 1994), esp. 59–60.

Eschatological delay is as much a feature of Revelation as eschatological imminence. It is written into the structure of the book. From the moment the martyrs cry, "How long?" and are told to wait a little while longer (6:10–11), the reader . . . becomes conscious of the tension of imminence and delay, as the End is constantly approached but not definitively reached.[3]

I do not wish to deny this observation but rather to question its historical specificity: assuming that not all deferrals mean the same thing, what is important about the differences? This is an important question underexamined in current studies of Renaissance apocalyptic nationalism. Too often have scholars lumped together the heterogeneous and shifting patterns of sixteenth-century eschatology under the category of "Tudor apocalypse," content to contrast it simply with the more radical apocalyptic theology of the 1640s and 1650s.

I propose, when considering the relation between apocalyptic and national temporality, that we identify at least four fairly distinct phases: (1) Marian apocalyptic, (2) early-Elizabethan apocalyptic, (3) post-Armada apocalyptic,[4] and (4) Civil War apocalyptic. In making these distinctions, we are able to account for the differences between the apocalyptic vision of writers such as Foxe, on the one hand, and Spenser on the other, especially regarding their sense of what the gesture of apocalyptic deferral means for their nation. Foxe appeals to deferral for the sake of national *existence,* whereas Spenser appeals to it for the sake of national *achievement.* Foxe uses narrative to delay the Apocalypse in order to forestall the absolute destruction of the earth and earthly distinctions (such as national identity). Spenser, though committed to the historical apocalyptic vision he inherits from Foxe, nonetheless imagines apocalyptic delay as creating a *future* space

---

[3] Richard Bauckham, *The Theology of the Book of Revelation* (New York: Cambridge University Press, 1993), 157.

[4] I borrow this phrase from Richard Mallette's fine chapter on book V of *The Faerie Queene.* See Mallette, "Post-Armada Apocalyptic Discourse," in *Spenser and the Discourses of Reformation England* (Lincoln: University of Nebraska Press, 1997), 143–68. Although Mallette and I disagree on many of the effects of the Armada victory on apocalyptic thinking in the 1590s, he is one the few critics who has been willing to focus on the differences between early- and late-Elizabethan eschatology. Furthermore, as will become clear in my discussion of Spenser, I find the term "post-Armada" preferable to "late-Elizabethan" because it encompasses the first several decades of seventeenth-century apocalyptic writing, which maintains a continuity with apocalyptic writing in the 1590s.

wherein England might perform some final earthly acts that would create the proper conditions for Christ's return. Another way we might put the distinction is to say that Foxe and his early-Elizabethan contemporaries see Christ's return only as the *judgment* of history, whereas Spenser and his fellow post-Armada writers start to think about this return also as the *culmination* of history. Book I of Spenser's poem thus begins tentatively to conceive of a commensurability between the national and apocalyptic futures, a commensurability that would hallmark the nationalist discourse of many Civil War apocalyptic writers.

In proposing this dynamic of continuity and deferral in Foxe and Spenser, I seek to demonstrate that the Tudor and Stuart language of apocalyptic delay itself has a history, signifying different things at different times. I wish to revise the frequent assumption that apocalyptic rhetoric in this period functions simply as either inflated propaganda for England or universalist indifference to England. On the contrary, it provided the Tudors not so much with cant or critique as with a means to imagine their nation moving through time historically while linked to a divine plan outside of history. To some degree, it supplied a "theory" of national temporality for a community trying to place itself within historicity yet lacking an explicit model of history as progressive. This is not at all to say that apocalyptic history represents merely the inchoate prototype of a soon-to-emerge progressive, secular history but rather to suggest that the Tudors used the conceptual tools at hand to describe the continuity they so dearly wished to find in the English Church. The apocalyptic view of national time came with a drawback, as I have suggested, radically foreshortening the English future. The gestures of deferral in Foxe and Spenser represent an attempt to carve out a negotiation between a foreshortening eschaton and a forward-looking national expectation. *Acts and Monuments* and *The Faerie Queene* (especially book I) attempt to work out the relationship between national and divine temporality, to articulate—according to the dictates of two different historical moments—a link between the apocalyptic narrative of God and the English narrative.

Historical Continuity and the Apocalyptic Future

Throughout the sixteenth century, the Book of Revelation provided Renaissance English writers with a sense of historical continuity.

The English Reformers reinvigorated the tradition of historical interpretation pioneered by Joachim de Fiore and Nicholas of Lyra in a
radical manner.[5] Despite Luther's initial rejection of Revelation as
authentic Scripture, and despite Tyndale's resistance to the idea of
an imminent Apocalypse, the 1540s and 1550s saw the growth of
three interrelated ideas: first, that the papacy was the historical
manifestation of Revelation's Antichrist; second, that the break from
the Church of Rome signaled the approaching end of the world; and
third, that the various "events" prophesied by John had been historically fulfilled in English history.[6] Identifying the pope with Antichrist provided an apparent scriptural authenticity for the Reformers' polemics against Rome, and apocalyptic imminence lent moral
urgency to this polemic. Perhaps most importantly for Tudor religious historians, reading Revelation as a prophecy of recent national
history imbued this history with a divine continuity. As John N.
King has suggested, the Reformers found in John's prophecy "an
apocalyptic revelation of truth, which had endured despite the 'distortions' of late medieval devotion."[7] In 1545 Bale was perhaps the
first Reformer to insist that the Book of the Apocalypse, while primary in itself as Scripture, required application to history: "It is a
full clearance to all the chronicles and most notable histories which
hath been wrote since Christ's ascension, opening the true natures of
their ages, times, and seasons."[8] Revelation revealed the entire history of the Christian world, a history in which England played a crucial role, and the text made it possible to understand the past as a
complete story in a way that antiquarian study alone could not do.
As Thomas Brightman insisted, the apocalyptic prophecy "min-
istreth Histories of the world itself from the first beginning unto the

---

[5] Joachim of Fiore was a twelfth-century Calabrian abbot who advanced a progres-
sive-historical and millenarian interpretation of the Apocalypse, whereas Nicholas of
Lyra was a fourteenth-century Franciscan monk who advanced a linear-historical but
antimillenarian interpretation. Both writers were read with interest by Tudor Reformers. For a brief discussion of Joachim and Nicholas, and their interpretations, see
Robert Alter, "Revelation," in *The Literary Guide to the Bible*, ed. Robert Alter and
Frank Kermode (Cambridge: Harvard University Press, 1987), 525–34.

[6] On the shift in thinking from early to later Reformers, see Katharine R. Firth,
The Apocalyptic Tradition in Reformation Britain, 1530–1645 (New York: Oxford
University Press, 1979), 23–35.

[7] John N. King, *Spenser's Poetry and the Reformation Tradition* (Princeton:
Princeton University Press, 1990), 142.

[8] John Bale, *Image of Both Churches*, in *Select Works of John Bale* (Cambridge:
Parker Society, 1849), 253.

latter end thereof: for which cause this unestimable treasure ought
to be to every one most dear."[9]

The apocalyptic interpretation of history also crucially helped the
Reformers to think of the English break from Rome as a restoration
of the "true" church rather than as an innovation. George Giffard, in
the dedicatory letter for his 1573 translation of William Fulke's exposition of the Apocalypse, saw in Revelation's continuity a polemical
resource for the struggle against Catholic propaganda:

> They say that this Church of ours was not anywhere to be found within
> a hundred or two hundred years past, and therefore cannot be the true
> Catholic Church of Christ. But let the diligent reader judge of these
> things when he hath perused this book: for herein he shall find even
> painted out before his eyes the form and shape both of the true Church,
> and also of the false, which is the Synagogue of Satan.[10]

The apocalyptic prophecy makes clear the constant opposition between
the true and false churches throughout history, dispelling, in Giffard's
view, the specious appearance of Reformation novelty. Richard Mallette's recent claim that "Tudor apocalypticism had a huge political task
before it, to renounce centuries of tradition and institute a new religion,"[11] while describing the function of the phenomenon *in fact*, mis-
represents the way the Tudors thought about apocalyptic interpretation.
They almost never claim to renounce tradition or engage in "historical
overturning"; on the contrary, they turn to Revelation for confirmation
of the tradition and continuity they deeply desire to find in their past.

Foxe himself produced one of the most thorough and detailed historical applications of the Apocalypse, in the four English editions of
Acts and Monuments published in his lifetime as well as in his apocalyptic commentary written primarily in the 1580s, *Eicasmi seu
meditationes in sacram Apocalypsin*. Revelation's prophetic narrative allowed him, as it did Giffard, to interpret the seeming absence of
the true church in history as a continuity rather than as an interruption, a sustained struggle between Antichrist and the faithful. God's

---

[9] Thomas Brightman, *Revelation of the Apocalypse* (Amsterdam, 1611), A4r.

[10] George Giffard, dedicatory letter, in *Praelections upon the Sacred and Holy
Revelation of S. John*, by William Fulke and trans. George Giffard (London, 1573),
A2r. Although modern scholars usually prefer the spelling "Gifford," I retain the
spelling as it appears on the title pages of the author's tracts.

[11] Mallette, *Spenser and the Discourses of Reformation England*, 47.

apocalyptic plan, Foxe insists, has shaped human history in a detailed, profound, and discernable manner. Foxe divides all history into apocalyptic ages—four ages in the 1563 edition (C4r), revised to five ages in 1570 (e1r)—each revolving around the activity of Antichrist and the true church's attempt to resist him. The first book of the 1570 edition concludes with a numerological interpretation of the Book of Revelation and of recent events in European history (m3v–m4v). The 1576 edition expands this discussion and gives it a separate heading, "The mystical numbers of the Apocalypse opened" (J3v). The Book of Revelation functioned as God's warning to the faithful about the persecution by Antichrist throughout history:

> he had premonished them sufficiently by special revelation in the Apocalypse of John his servant. In the which Apocalypse, he declared to his church before, not only what troubles were coming at hand toward them, where, and by whom they should come, but also in plain number (if the words of prophecy be well understood) assigneth the true time, how long the said persecutions should continue, and when they should cease. (1570, m4r)

Foxe differentiates his sentiment from the common and orthodox conviction of God's providential control of history by insisting that humans can know the divine plan. The Book of Revelation is not an inscrutable mystery but rather a map by which we can understand the course of human history and the future.

Foxe's interpretation of Revelation grants England a prominent place in history, framing his history of the English nation, its martyrs, and the Church of England within an eschatological view of an apocalyptic end. In 1570 he identifies the thousand-year period of Satan's captivity (mentioned in Rev. 20) as beginning with the fourth-century Donation of Constantine ("born in Britain," Foxe informs us [m4r]) and ending with the rise of Wyclif's teaching in the fourteenth century (m4r)—thus giving England an important place in the apocalyptic scheme. Book 5 of the 1570 edition begins with a further extended commentary on the release of Satan around 1360 (U1r), in preparation for the story of Wyclif's life shortly afterward (Y4r–Bb6v). In his *Eicasmi*, the seven trumpets of Revelation all refer to specific moments in history, the sixth trumpet corresponding to, among other things, the Reformation in which England has played an impor-

tant part.[12] Foxe thus derives from Revelation a providential understanding of English history. Even more than Bale, he conceives of the
Apocalypse as an unbroken, pre-scripted story, a continuity allowing
him to "set forth the acts and proceedings of the whole church of
Christ, namely, of the church of England . . . from the first primitive
age of Christ's gospel, to the end of queen Mary, and the beginning of
our gracious queen Elizabeth" (1576, TTTTt4v).

In mapping out the links between English history and John's
prophecy, Foxe and his colleagues made clear their belief that Christ's
Second Advent, coming *after* the millennium of Revelation 20 that
had already occurred in history, would bring a sudden and absolute
end to earthly existence. In emphasizing the historical implications
of the Book of Revelation for national continuity, the Tudors rejected
the futurist interpretation that their Civil War successors cultivated.
They maintained, in the technical language of theological scholarship, antimillenarian and postmillennial positions. The concept of
millenarianism has remained somewhat obscure in modern studies,
tangled up in questions about the elect nation, utopian thought, and
political radicalism.[13] Yet if we look at how most Tudor apocalyptic
commentators actually use the terms "chiliast" and "millenary,"
two primary ideas emerge: (1) the return of Christ will inaugurate not
the destruction of the world but rather a thousand years of bliss, and
(2) this future period will be *earthly*. As is well known, nearly all
Tudor commentators distance themselves from this interpretation.
Foxe's friend William Fulke insists on a historical rather than futurist
dating of the millennium: "we fall into the dotage of the Chiliasts, if
we think these thousand years of which S. John speaketh to be begun
and counted from the time that Antichrist was overcome."[14] Arthur
Dent writes contemptuously of the millenarian expectation of an
earthly paradise:

> The Chiliasts or Millenaries do fondly gather from this scripture [Rev.
> 20] that after the overthrow of Antichrist the Lord Jesus would come

[12] John Foxe, *Eicasmi seu meditationes in sacram Apocalypsin* (London, 1587),
107–11.

[13] The Reformers did in fact oscillate between seeing England as a besieged faithful
remnant and as a triumphant godly nation. See, for a brief, lucid, and recent discussion, Crawford Gribben, *The Puritan Millennium: Literature and Theology,
1550–1682* (Dublin: Four Courts, 2000), 63–64.

[14] Fulke, *Praelections upon the Sacred and Holy Revelation of S. John*, R8v.

and reign with the faithful, here a thousand years upon the earth, as a great and glorious king upon the earth, [and that] his subjects should enjoy all manner of earthly pleasures and delights. This foolish error is confuted by the words that follow in the texts as we shall see afterward.[15]

Foxe himself, who places the millennium of Revelation 20 in the past, decries the revolutionary quality of early Protestant millenarians as Satanic: "[Satan] laboureth all he can to inflame and stir up mischievous instruments and seditious spirits to sow sedition, as Monetarius [i.e., Munzer] and his like" (1563, Oo5r). Foxe's *Eicasmi* and other Tudor commentaries make clear that Christ's return will end earthly existence and that this end will arrive soon, while they firmly reject the millenarian interpretation.[16] They hold, by contrast, a "postmillennial" position, locating Christ's Second Advent "post" of the historical millennium. Although the Tudors do not call themselves "postmillennial" (they do not call themselves anything, in this respect), they understand their interpretive scheme as the opposite of the millenarian expectation of a future, earthly paradise.[17] The thou-

[15] Arthur Dent, *The Ruin of Rome, or An Exposition upon the Whole Revelation* (London, 1603), Nn3v.

[16] Foxe's *Eicasmi* does quietly postulate a short period of earthly peace between Antichrist's overthrow and Christ's final return (148), where Foxe differentiates between the destruction of "Babylon" and the end of the world. Palle J. Olsen offers some thoughtful comments about this slight shift from Foxe's earlier theology in "Was John Foxe a Millenarian?" *Journal of Ecclesiastical History* 45, 4 (1994): 600–24, esp. 618–24. This is a fascinating development in Foxe's thinking that nearly all commentators in the 1590s come to accept. I return to this development in my discussion of Spenser.

[17] The traditional distinctions in theological scholarship include amillennialism (which denies any future or historical millennium), premillennialism (which expects Christ's return to inaugurate a future millennium), and postmillennialism (which expects Christ's return to follow shortly upon a millennium). The latter two categories are sometimes taken to encompass forms of millenarianism, in contrast to nonmillenarian amillennialism (see Gribben, *Puritan Millennium*, 16). Yet to call the nonmillenarian Tudors "amillennial" misleadingly groups them with the idealist interpretation of Augustine, who reads Revelation 20 as spiritual symbolism bearing no link to earthly time. Foxe and his contemporaries *do* firmly believe that the millennium refers to earthly time—to the historical past. Furthermore, although seventeenth-century millenarians are sometimes of the postmillennial variety, the Tudor commentators nearly always conceive of any futurist interpretation as premillennial, as a heretical error that imagines Christ's return inaugurating his personal reign on earth for a thousand years. For three examples out of many, see John Napier, *A Plaine Discovery of the Whole Revelation of Saint John* (London, 1593), 240; George Giffard,

sand years of Satan's captivity lie in the past, and the apocalyptic judgment of God approaches closer each day.

I rehearse these rather well-known facts in order to foreground more clearly the problems that sixteenth-century apocalyptic theology created for conceptualizing national temporality. Unlike the millenarians of the 1640s, the postmillennial Tudors assumed the imminent destruction of the earth, which left little room conceptually for an earthly, English future. The impact of this assumption varied importantly as the sixteenth century progressed. For example, the prospect of a world-destroying Apocalypse seemed like a virtue to some Protestants during the 1550s, when the true church of Christ appeared to have a limited chance of worldly success. Indeed, during Mary I's reign, many Protestant theologians conceived of the Apocalypse as a comforting end that would soon free the persecuted from their pain. Rudolph Gualter, a French Protestant theologian who was popular among the English Marian exiles, spoke of the Marian persecutions as the final assault of Antichrist.[18] Bishop Ridley, imprisoned in the Tower in 1555 and seeing little hope for the Reformation in England, attributed his nation's betrayal of the true church to the work of "Antichrist and his brood," yet he comforted his followers by assuring them that "the world without doubt . . . draweth toward an end," urging them to "be not afraid, and remember the end."[19] The Second Advent of Christ would deal divine justice to the papist oppressors and stop the sufferings of the congregation of the true church, giving its members their reward in heaven. The very fact that the true church lacked political, earthly power proved that it was on God's side, because the preaching of God's word, rather than the temporal sword, would overcome Antichrist at the apocalyptic end of the world.[20]

Sermons upon the Whole Book of Revelation (London, 1596), Cc4r; and (again) Dent, *Ruin of Rome,* Nn3v. Given their sense of their own theological position, then, it makes the most sense to call the Tudor commentators postmillennialists.

[18] Rudolph Gualter, *The Sermons upon the Prophet Zephaniah,* trans. Moses Wilton (London, 1580). For a discussion of Gualter's influence on the Marian exiles, see Richard Bauckham, *Tudor Apocalypse* (Oxford: Sutton Courtenay Press, 1978), 7–8.

[19] Ridley's prison speech was printed after his death in *A Piteous Lamentation* (London, 1566); these quoted passages are from Nicholas Ridley, *Works* (Cambridge: Parker Society, 1841), 53, 75, 79.

[20] As Bauckham notes, the Tudors begin to consider victory over Antichrist by the sword as well as by preaching as the century progressed (*Tudor Apocalypse,* 173–80). Yet the Marian exiles never express this view.

Foxe's *Christus Triumphans,* an apocalyptic drama he wrote during his exile in the Netherlands, confirms the interpretation of the end of the world as a release from earthly pain. He probably finished the play in 1556, a year after the burning of Protestants had begun in England.[21] This drama is his first major foray into apocalyptic theology, as the *Commentarii rerum in ecclesia gestarum,* which he had composed some time before 1553, relied little on the Book of Revelation. As with other Protestant writers, Foxe imagines Christ's return as imminent:

> it seems that all the parts of the play have been acted out and that the scene of this world is rushing to that final "Farewell, and applaud." Thus, with the catastrophe of everything imminent and the prophecies completely fulfilled, nothing seems to remain except that apocalyptic voice soon to be heard from heaven, "It is finished."[22]

With his theater metaphor, Foxe appears to imply that his ability to represent the entire apocalyptic drama derives from history's near completion—very little earthly time remains before the end. Foxe also offers his apocalyptic narrative as a revelation of history. The character Pseudamnus represents the pope and the papal corruption of the true church. Adopylus (servant of Satan) is called Catholicus in act 5, referring to the papal title of Phillip II. Dynastes is Mary I. The preacher Hierologus partly represents Martin Luther, though when he is arrested with Theosobes in act 5 the pair probably stand for Latimer and Ridley, arrested in March 1554. Indeed, as the play progresses, Foxe begins to identify Christ's bride Ecclesia as the English Church, suffering through history and now afflicted most acutely by Mary's reign.

Yet with this identification we need to note Foxe's emphasis in *Christus Triumphans* on national history rather than the future. The future will come, Christ will return, but this return will not fulfill England *as a nation;* rather, it will free England and the rest of the world from its earthly condition. In the last scene of the play, when Ecclesia prays for the arrival of her bridegroom, she is flanked by the

[21] On the contested date of Foxe's play, see John Hazel Smith, ed., *Two Latin Comedies by John Foxe the Martyrologist* (Ithaca: Cornell University Press, 1973), 31–33.

[22] Foxe, *Christus Triumphans,* in *Two Latin Comedies by John Foxe the Martyrologist,* 207. In-text citations in parentheses refer to *Christus Triumphans* as *CT* if needed for clarity.

international company of Africus and Europus: the Apocalypse will have a universal rather than national effect. Foxe called his play a "comoedia apocalyptica" (*CT* 200), and England participates in this happy ending to the degree that it identifies itself with the universal true church of Christ, which has nothing to lose in earthly terms except suffering. Even in the play's prefatory letters, in which Foxe and fellow exile Laurence Humphrey exchange comments about the plight of their nation, Foxe still speaks of the end as a judgment rather than fulfillment of England: "If too strong a following wind carry you away, let a stronger one bring you back, o Briton, that you may become a vineyard pleasing to your husbandman the Lord. But, Laurence, I hope the vengeful anger of our father's rod will not wait long" (225). England should attempt to improve its sinful condition, but nonetheless the Apocalypse will come to the English, as to the rest of the sinful world, as a final reckoning.

Christus Triumphans also exemplifies how the meaning of eschatological deferral varies according to historical context. In the case of Foxe's drama, deferral does not take on a national significance, as it will later in the sixteenth century. Like so many apocalyptic texts, *Christus Triumphans* counterpoises the conviction of apocalyptic imminence with the repeated gesture to delay of the end. Ecclesia herself calls attention to the deferral by pleading for its removal: "End the delays, you who are called; come quickly, bridegroom" (369). As the last scene ends with the expectant bride on stage, the Chorus of Virgins announces that "[n]othing remains except the bridegroom himself, who will bring the final catastrophe to our stage. When that will happen none will say for sure" (371). What do these gestures of deferral mean, beyond the idea—present in almost all apocalyptic writing—that Christ's actual return exceeds human representation? The context of Foxe's exile and the sorry condition of the true church in England are illuminating. Since human activity cannot make the world better, deferral creates a space for repentance before the final judgment, both for the faithful and even for those who currently cooperate with Antichrist. In his dedicatory epistle, Foxe acknowledges the possibility of a delay in Christ's return: "Perhaps it will not be long delayed, though how quickly he will come is not for us a matter of certitude . . . let us for now attend sedulously to that which is within our competence, so that each of us may prepare himself for that day lest the bridegroom burst in suddenly and accost us snoring on our backs or abandoned to dissoluteness" (207). Delay offers sinners a chance to become ready, to repent and prepare themselves for judgment and the destruction of the world. Delay does not, however, function as a space for England to develop itself as a national community. Foxe cares about England and keenly represents its suffering in history and in the present, but in 1556 he firmly conceives of the apocalyptic future as an erasure rather than fulfillment of nationhood.

Early Elizabethan Apocalyptic and Postmillennial Foreclosure

The nonmillenarian interpretation—anticipating the Apocalypse as the judgment and destruction of a sinful world rather than the beginning of earthly paradise—persisted even after Elizabeth's accession radically improved the true church's standing in England. After all, as many scholars have noted, Elizabethan Protestants were still inclined to see their nation in the context of international Catholicism, where Antichrist continued to rage unabated.[23] Commentaries such as John Jewel's sermon on Thessalonians (1569) make clear the continued expectation of future judgment rather than a future earthly paradise.[24]

---

[23] See Firth, *Apocalyptic Tradition in Reformation Britain*, 109ff.; and Bauckham, *Tudor Apocalypse*, 128–35.

[24] John Jewel's sermon on Thessalonians was composed shortly after the Northern Rebellion in 1569, and it offers a good example of the characteristics of much early Elizabethan apocalyptic writing. Like Marian apocalyptic writers, Jewel advances an imminent and nonmillenarian interpretation of the end. Christ will arrive soon and without warning: "He shall come as a thief, suddenly, when no man looketh for his coming"; *Works of John Jewel* (Cambridge: Parker Society, 1847), 24:869. The Apocalypse will entail the absolute destruction of the physical world, analogous to Noah's flood but this time permanent: "the rain came upon them, and the floods grew so great that it destroyed the whole world . . . so shall it be in the coming of Christ" (868). Although Jewel gives thanks for the protective presence of Elizabeth—"Save, O Lord, queen Elizabeth thy servant"—in the same paragraph he immediately makes clear that Christ, not the godly magistrate, will ultimately defeat Antichrist, with no special fulfillment for England as a nation: "Let us comfort ourselves with these words, that 'God hath not appointed us to wrath, but to obtain salvation by the means of our Lord Jesus Christ.' He hath overcome the world: let us be of good cheer" (874). Like his Marian predecessors, Jewel sees the Apocalypse as God's judgment of earthly sin, a sinfulness repeatedly exemplified by anti-Christian acts such as the Northern Rebellion. Christ will not bring a paradise to earth, but rather the inhabitants of the earth will be snatched up to the sky: "stand in readiness," he instructs, "and watch, and pray, that we may be caught up into the clouds to meet our Redeemer" (873).

Nevertheless, despite the tone of religious caution that most early Elizabethan Protestants strike, their outlook on the English Church is more hopeful than that prior to Elizabeth. After all, with the new queen's accession, the true church was suddenly supported by a temporal, national power. Christ's agent Elizabeth, rather than the apocalyptic Christ himself, had delivered the persecuted out of Mary's hands. This fact created a rhetorical difficulty for some English apocalyptic writers: how could they celebrate England's apparent contribution to the defeat of Antichrist while at the same time acknowledging the imminent end of the world that would make English identity irrelevant? No one believed that Elizabeth was the literal figure of the Redeemer or that her kingdom was a millenarian paradise on earth. Yet it could not be denied that her triumph had occurred close to "the end of days," and therefore early in her reign some writers make an optimistic connection between the English Elizabeth and the Apocalypse. That is, they praise the queen not only as a glorious sign of the approaching return of Christ but also as a figure of apocalyptic agency, implying (in a way the Marian exiles did not) a commensurability between the apocalyptic and English futures.

The occasional though vehement association of Elizabeth with eschatological expectation subtly shifted the focus of the apocalyptic story from the past to the future. In 1564 Thomas Becon calls Elizabeth "a noble conqueror of antichrist and of his wicked kingdom."[25] John Aylmer's *A Harbor for faithful and true subjects* (1559), a timely defense of the legitimacy of female rulers, speaks of Elizabeth as a Hebrew type of apocalyptic agent in the final days of the world: "I trust [that God] will now in the latter age of the world show his might in cutting of this proud Holofernes' head [Antichrist], by the hand of our Judith." He ends his treatise with another anticipated decapitation, hoping that Elizabeth "may many years carry the sword of our defense, and therewith cut off the head of that Hydra, the Antichrist of Rome." The summary formulation of the national issue that he writes in the margin, so often quoted by modern scholars, is striking: "God is English."[26] These enthusiastic comments no doubt owe part of their force to the local circumstances of political rhetoric. After all, Aylmer writes his tract to counter John Knox's polemic against fe-

---

[25] Quoted in Bauckham, *Tudor Apocalypse,* 128.
[26] The quoted passages are from John Aylmer, *A Harbor for faithful and true subjects* (London, 1559), Q1r, R3r, and P4r.

male rulers.[27] Yet Aylmer's apocalypticism is not "just" rhetoric—he could certainly have made his case for Elizabeth without it. The same holds true for the link between Elizabeth and the apocalyptic future made in an edition of Bale's *King John* revised shortly after 1558, in which the characters Nobility and Clergy speak of Elizabeth as the apocalyptic angel of Revelation 7:2–4, who at the end of time will place the seal of God on the 144,000 elect to protect them from harm:

> NOBILITY: She is that Angel, as Saint John doth him call,
> That with the lord's seal doth mark out his true servants,
> Printing in their hearts his holy words and Covenants.
> CLERGY: In Daniel's spirit she hath subdued the Papists,
> With all the offspring of Antichrist's generation.[28]

Bale here appears to encourage an at least oblique connection between the English community under Elizabeth and the elect who are saved from God's apocalyptic wrath in Revelation. Unlike Marian apocalyptic writers, Aylmer and Bale refuse to imagine a relation between England and Revelation only in history. Elizabeth's accession inclines them to experiment with imagining some kind of affiliation between their nation and Christ's return *at the Apocalypse*. Their language differs substantially from earlier apocalyptic writers, and they seem to be trying to clear a space for English participation in the cosmic future.

If we stopped at this point in the analysis, we might be tempted to revisit the now infamous elect-nation thesis of William Haller, who argued for the widespread presence of a nationalist millenarianism in Elizabethan England, suggesting that in *Acts and Monuments* Foxe expected an earthly, English paradise in the future.[29] One of the initial attractions of Haller's work, I think, lay in its presentation of an early modern nation, with its incipient sense of horizontal comrade-

---

[27] John Knox, *First Blast of the Trumpet against the monstrous regiment of women* (London, 1558).

[28] *John Bale's "King Johan,"* ed. Barry B. Adams (San Marino, Calif.: Huntington Library, 1969), 147.

[29] William Haller, *Foxe's Book of Martyrs and the Elect Nation* (London: J. Cape, 1963). Haller makes his millenarian claim in effect but does not use the term. However, William Lamont, elaborating Haller's thesis in *Godly Rule: Politics and Religion, 1603–60* (New York: St. Martin's Press, 1969), applies this term to Foxe and his contemporaries.

ship, yet one still tied to a premodern, theocentric cosmology—an England with one foot in the past and one foot in the future. Three scholars in the 1970s—Norskov Olsen, Richard Bauckham, and Katherine Firth—discredited Haller's thesis by noting, among other things, the nonmillenarian slant of Elizabethan apocalyptic writing, especially when compared to the seventeenth-century expectation of a future English paradise.[30] These historians thus claimed that Elizabethan Protestants, Foxe among them, produced their apocalyptic discourse in the context of an international rather than national struggle against Antichrist. Most subsequent scholars have agreed with their conclusions. They are surely right, to a large degree. The early Elizabethans have no expectation of a future rule of English saints on earth, and they occasionally go out of their way to distance themselves from the millenarian interpretation, as we have seen. Nonetheless, the anti-Haller position underestimates the genuine strain of nationalism in much early Elizabethan apocalyptic writing.[31] Bauckham's claim that "by and large patriotism was tempered rather than aggravated by the apocalyptic element in contemporary religious thought"—while accurate for many texts—oversimplifies the rhetoric we see in writers such as Bale and Aylmer; nor is it ulti-

---

[30] Norskov Olsen, *John Foxe and the Elizabethan Church* (Berkeley: University of California Press, 1973); Bauckham, *Tudor Apocalypse;* and Firth, *Apocalyptic Tradition in Reformation Britain.* In their studies these historians point out that Foxe never actually claims in *Acts and Monuments* that England is the elect nation of God, suggesting that Foxe simply relied on his conviction that Foxe assumes this idea in his book (Firth, 107; Olsen, 43–44). They also note that Haller makes the remarkable omission of not referring to Foxe's own unfinished commentary on the Book of Revelation, the *Eicasmi,* which expresses an unwavering belief in the universal, international nature of the Apocalypse (Bauckham, 74, 85). Firth (108) quotes the following passage from the *Eicasmi:* "Non Romae, non Angliae, non Franciae, regnum Christi divinaque obstringitur promissio. Ubicunque spiritus viget veritis, ubi vera pietas, ubi evangelicae nullis fermentata erroribus institutio . . . ibi ecclesia est." [The kingdom of Christ and the divine promise are not bound to Rome or to England or to France. Wherever the spirit of truth flourishes, where piety is true, where the institution of faith is infected by no errors . . . there the church exists (my translation).]

[31] Of course, none of these historians denies that Foxe's work contains evidence of England's growing national consciousness. Firth acknowledges that although Foxe never entertained the idea of an elect nation, this "does not diminish the fact that he did place his nation, with other European nations, in a historical context bounded by the prophecies of the Revelation" (*Apocalyptic Tradition in Reformation Britain,* 109). But such qualifications do not go far enough to account for the pervasive nationalism in *Acts and Monuments.*

mately accurate for Foxe, as I will argue. Bauckham rightly observes that Becon's characterization of Elizabeth as a conqueror of Antichrist is not "inflated millenarianism,"[32] but nonetheless such a characterization subtly redirects apocalyptic nationalism from history to the future, toward Christ's return. Apocalyptic imminence fuels as well as tempers nationalism in the Elizabethan period. Haller's elect-nation thesis misunderstands apocalyptic theology, but the anti-Haller position underplays nationalist enthusiasm.

The difficulty in determining the early Elizabethan attitude derives partly from a contradiction between historical circumstances (the hope for a national future resulting from the recent triumph of the English Church) and theological doctrine (the expectation of the imminent end of the world). I wish to describe this contradiction—of which most apocalyptic writers seem only vaguely aware—as *postmillennial foreclosure:* a phenomenon whereby England's success against Antichrist fuels the desire for a glorious English future, but the nonmillenarian expectation of an earth-destroying Apocalypse closes off the national future.[33] Christ arrives, as it were, too "post," the millennium having already occurred in history, unavailable for the future. I would also not ignore the economic resonance of the term: the Apocalypse forecloses on the debt sinful England owes to God, a debt that must be paid soon unless it is (as we shall see) deferred. From the nonmillenarian perspective there is no way to resolve logically the fundamental disparity between earthly and apocalyptic time. Indeed, when Elizabethan Reformers fixed their eyes on the New Jerusalem, the world became a rather sorry place in contrast—as Thomas Rogers suggested in his popular 1577 translation of Geveren's tract, when he asked rhetorically, "the gospel . . . casts his beams over all nations, and therefore what other thing shall we look for, but as Christ did foretell, a sudden downfall of this wretched world?"[34] Rogers's optimistic assessment of the conversion effort leads not to a happy earthly future but rather, vis-à-vis the Apocalypse, to worldly denigration.

We can see the effects of postmillennial foreclosure in the texts of

[32] The two quotations are from Bauckham, *Tudor Apocalypse,* 87, 128.

[33] Again, I use the term *postmillennial* to describe the *nonmillenarian* theology of the Tudors.

[34] Thomas Rogers, *Of the End of This World, and the Second Coming of Christ* (London, 1577), C4r. According to the *Short Title Catalogue,* this translation went through an impressive five editions between 1577 and 1589.

Aylmer and Bale, who qualify their nationalist hopes by contradict-
ing (*not* negating) their sense of the relation between England and the
Apocalypse. For example, in the paragraph in whose margin Aylmer
makes his "God is English" claim, he tells his countrymen that "you
fight not only in the quarrel of your country, but also and *chiefly* in
the defense of [God's] true religion, and of his dear son Christ" (my
emphasis). Alymer appears both to exaggerate and underplay the national equation simultaneously. Similarly, in a later passage strikingly glossed as "Christ's second birth in England," Aylmer has the
figure of "England" speak to her people:

> God hath brought forth in me the greatest and excellentest treasure
> that He hath for your comfort and all the worlds. He would that out of
> my womb should come that servant of Christ John Wyclif, who begat
> Huss, who begat Luther, who begat the truth. What greater honour
> could you or I have than that it pleased Christ as it were in a second
> birth to be born again of me among you?[35]

On the one hand Aylmer suggests that England might have a privileged role in the Second Coming by identifying the emergence of
"truth" with the English Wyclif and by referring to Christ's apocalyptic "second birth" in England. Yet Aylmer significantly qualifies his
conflation of England's national and religious identity. His brief genealogy of the true church's servants moves past Wyclif to the non-
English figures of Huss and Luther: the community of the true
church is finally *international*, not bound to a single nation. When
Aylmer hints at an "English" Second Coming—"it pleased Christ as
it were in a second birth to be born again of me among you"—the
phrase "as it were" distances him from a literal reference to the actual Apocalypse: he is willing to speak of Elizabeth or some future
English figure *as if* he or she marked the final triumph of the true
church, but he will not go further than that.

Thomas Betterage has written about the contradictory relation between praise for Elizabeth and apocalyptic expectation in martyrolo-
gies of the 1560s and 1570s, noting the "potential conflict between
the discourse of the world and that of the spirit."[36] This tension, as I

---

[35] The quotations are from Aylmer, *Harbor for faithful and true subjects*, P4v and
R1v.
[36] Thomas Betteridge, *Tudor Histories of the English Reformation, 1530–83*
(Aldershot, U.K.: Ashgate, 1999), 174.

have suggested, often takes the form of a narrative interplay between apocalyptic anticipation and deferral. Like Aylmer, Bale also revises his identification between Elizabeth and the apocalyptic future in *King John*, though in a different manner: he postpones the Second Coming rather than downplaying the national future. In the last speech of his play, a few lines after Nobility claims that Elizabeth is the apocalyptic angel, the character Civil Order expresses his wish for Elizabeth's long reign:

> Pray unto the lord that her grace may continue
> The days of Nestor to our souls' consolation;
> And that her offspring may live also to subdue
> The great Antichrist, with his whole generation,
> In Elias' spirit to the comfort of this nation;
> Also to preserve her most honorable counsel,
> To the praise of God and glory to the Gospel.[37]

Bale continues to speak of Elizabeth with apocalyptic language, but, surprisingly, removes the sense of apocalyptic imminence. Elizabeth, he suggests, will carry out a long, earthly reign, comparable to "the days of Nestor," and "her offspring" will hopefully continue to protect England far into the future. She is not an Emperor of the Last Days, but rather her presence seems to defer the Last Day. This national deferral makes an interesting contrast to the imminence of Christ's return in Bale's *Image of Both Churches*, in which he predicts that, because one of the four apocalyptic angels of Revelation 9:13 already "hath given his voice, I doubt it not but the other three *will shortly do the same.*"[38] Yet when he focuses on England, he feels the need to delay the end, making it possible for him to imagine an earthly future. Likewise, although Aylmer refers to the nearness of Christ's return ("now in the latter age of the world"), the conclusion to his tract defers this return when he speaks of Elizabeth both as an apocalyptic agent (to "cut off the head of that Hydra, the Antichrist of Rome") and as the begetter of an earthly, national future who "may many years carry the sword of our defense." This is the characteristic, if contradictory, rhetoric of postmillennial foreclosure: a gesture to merge the national and apocalyptic futures followed by an implicit acknowledgment that these futures remain incompatible.

---

[37] *John Bale's "King Johan,"* 147.

[38] John Bale, *The Image of both Churches after the most wonderful and heavenly Revelation of Saint John the Evangelist* (London, 1548), R3r (my emphasis).

Such an account of the relation between the discourses of nation-hood and eschatology—linked by historical circumstances but logi-cally opposed—allows us to give due attention to the national con-tent of much apocalyptic writing without reverting to the theological anachronism of Haller's elect-nation thesis. To do otherwise will cause us to misjudge the commitments of a post-Marian writer such as John Foxe. In 1556 he anticipated a Second Advent that would erase national identity in the process of delivering the elect from An-tichrist's persecution. In the 1560s, however, he perceives that the true church is aligned with the nation. He thus believes that En-gland's special contribution to the war against the false Church of Rome promises a glorious national future while simultaneously (if il-logically, from our perspective) still maintaining the conviction in an imminent and universal Apocalypse that would make temporal power and national identity irrelevant. We can see an apt example of the effect of postmillennial foreclosure by placing two sentences from *Acts and Monuments* side by side. Much as the 1563 preface ad-dressed to Queen Elizabeth had prayed that her rule continue "in long prosperity" (B2v), the 1570 preface likewise hopes Elizabeth will con-tinue "with long reign, perfect health, and joyful peace" (*1r)—in it-self a perfectly typical and unremarkable Elizabethan hope that the reign will flourish as long as possible. Yet it is difficult to reconcile this hope with the prayer Foxe offers in his 1570 preface addressed to the "congregation of Christ's universal Church," anticipating "the speedy Coming of Christ the Spouse, to make an end of all mortal misery" (1570, ☞2r). The cosmic "speedy Coming" logically cuts off "long reign" in the national future. To put it crudely: as a Christian, Foxe eagerly awaits the Promised End; as a nationalist, Foxe at times reveals an ambivalence about this end.

Apocalyptic expectation both encourages and cuts short nationalist enthusiasm in *Acts and Monuments*, sometimes in the same passage. Not only does Foxe often intermix deeply nationalist sentiments within his international conception of Protestantism, but, like Aylmer and Bale, he occasionally links this nationalism to the theme of the Apocalypse in *Acts and Monuments*. However—and this is why we cannot simply return to the elect-nation thesis—he never makes this link in an unqualified manner. Consider the following passage: "There hath been no region or country more fertile or fruit-ful for martyrs, than our own region of England" (1563, Ii6r). This is a suggestive statement of England's privileged role, for which Foxe goes on to offer two interpretations: "Whether it happeneth or cometh by the singular gift or privilege of God's divine grace, or else through the barbarous and foolish cruelty of such as at that time ruled and governed the church, is uncertain."[39] The first possibility Foxe offers ("privilege of God's divine grace") certainly has shades of Haller's elect-nation thesis. Yet Foxe refuses to ignore the second possibility of random, fallible, human agency—"foolish cruelty." England's relation to the apocalyptic true church is strikingly ambiguous in this passage: England teeters between having a genuinely privileged role and being a worse-than-usual example of worldly corruption. Much as we saw Aylmer and Bale do, Foxe gestures at conferring an elect status on England but then stops short of actually doing so. Given the simultaneous national and apocalyptic emphasis of his book, the question facing English Protestants in general confronted Foxe with a particular urgency: what kind of relation existed (or could exist) between the end just on the horizon and the new Elizabethan regime that seemed to promise a bright future for the emerging English nation?

Apocalyptic Anticipation and National Deferral

Foxe's subject matter is both national (martyrs in England) and universal (the apocalyptic true church), and he tells two parallel stories simultaneously in his twelve-volume book. The apocalyptic story of the true church begins with the Incarnation of Christ, continues with the early persecutions of Christians, the binding and releasing of Satan, the increase of persecution in modern times, the Reformation, and ends (or will end) with the final defeat of Satan by Christ and the rewarding of the faithful. Foxe also tells the story of the English nation. He begins with the history of the early English Church, goes on to discuss how medieval English kings tried to defend their nation against foreign powers, praises the contributions of John Wyclif to the reformed church, then focuses on the fate of English martyrs in the fifteenth and sixteenth centuries, and ends with the story of Elizabeth's life and accession. Thus, although the apocalyptic story has a prominent place in Foxe's narrative, it never simply absorbs the na-

---

[39] Warren Wooden, in *John Foxe* (Boston: Twayne Publishers, 1983), 34–36, uses this passage to demonstrate Foxe's commitment to the English nation. However, he does not comment on the ambivalent tone of the passage.

tional story. Rather, Foxe takes the conflict between nationalism and the Apocalypse, which in Elizabethan culture generally was an ideological difficulty, and reinscribes it in *Acts and Monuments* as a complicated relationship between story lines.

This shift to narrative structure as the venue of tension between England and the Apocalypse has an important consequence: it foregrounds the importance of the narrative ending. Because each story has its own beginning and middle, we might expect each to have its own conclusion. They almost do, but not quite. The story of the true church ends definitively with the Apocalypse. Yet the end of the English nation's story presents a problem. This story tells of persons and events in England's past that ideally help to make sense of the present. As such, Foxe often seems to offer the Elizabethan regime as *Acts and Monuments*'s narrative telos. The narrative begins and ends with enthusiastic addresses to Elizabeth, whose reign Foxe refers to as "these halcyon days" (1583, ¶2v). The account of Elizabeth's persecution under Mary and her eventual triumph is the last major episode of the book. And in a narrative that has charted time according to which English ruler was on the throne, Elizabeth and her regime clearly have a conclusive force. However, as we have already discussed, apocalyptic theology of the 1560s could not accommodate the idea of a temporal ruler bringing about the defeat of Satan or ushering in a golden age. The preaching of God's word, rather than the royal sword, would overcome Antichrist at the apocalyptic end of the world. Similarly, in *Acts and Monuments*, the Elizabethan regime is never fully imagined as a final ending to the narrative. Foxe always returns to the Apocalypse as his primary project: "to prosecute, by the merciful grace of Christ, the proceeding and course of times, till we come at length to the fall and ruin of the said Antichrist" (1570, T6r). In a description such as this, Foxe makes no mention of England because he imagines the apocalyptic end as universal, not national. Compelled by the conditions of Tudor apocalyptic theology, Foxe, in his formal descriptions of his work, has little choice but to depict the Apocalypse as the ending of both stories. And from an apocalyptic perspective, the Elizabethan regime is simply one more earthly stopping point in the journey to the Eternal Sabbath. When we focus on the function of the narrative ending in *Acts and Monuments*, the story of the true church does indeed *appear* to absorb the national story in that the narrative so often anticipates its apocalyptic conclusion.

Yet although Foxe cannot offer the Elizabethan regime as a narrative option equivalent to the Apocalypse, he nonetheless refuses to allow the apocalyptic story to swallow the story of the English nation. Indeed, he maintains the presence and importance of the national story through all the English editions of his book, even though the 1570 and later editions reveal a greater sense of eschatological pressure than does the 1563 edition. Recent scholars, seeking to avoid the anachronism of the elect-nation thesis, have sometimes underestimated the persistence of the national story in the narrative. For example, Richard Helgerson, one of the first scholars to see the ideological conflict in *Acts and Monuments* in terms of competing storylines, has argued that the book's narrative form does indeed function to collapse (for the most part) the national story into the apocalyptic story. Helgerson certainly does not ignore the strain of nationalism in *Acts and Monuments*, but he argues that the universal church to which the martyrs belong "is the community to which Foxe's sympathetic readers are instructed to pay their primary allegiance."[40] Helgerson goes on to demonstrate how the narrative design of the text itself works in favor of this universal community. Foxe encourages his readers to join with "an invisible and imaginary community whose reality is constituted by the deferral of sign to signified. Such a deferral takes the narrative form of a projection from persecution to an unseen triumph, a triumph that was figured but not exhausted by Elizabeth's assumption of the English throne" (266–67). For Helgerson, the narrative of *Acts and Monuments* promotes the story of the true church by constantly anticipating its apocalyptic ending, while it tends to dismiss or displace the present, national story.

Yet despite his shrewd insight about the link between eschatology and narrative progress, Helgerson underestimates the degree to which Foxe permits the national story to assert its presence by *resisting* the narrative ending. Foxe uses narrative form not only to promote the apocalyptic true church but also to represent the claims of the English nation. Helgerson thus at times inaccurately interprets national elements in *Acts and Monuments* as adumbrations of the apocalyptic end, suggesting, for example, that "like Constantine before her, Elizabeth could be seen as a type of the Emperor of the Last

---

[40] Richard Helgerson, *Forms of Nationhood: The Elizabethan Writing of England* (Chicago: University of Chicago Press, 1992), 247–94.

Days, the godly ruler who ends the persecution of the elect and institutes a period of Christian peace" (260). This sounds like the kind of
gesture Foxe would make if he in fact wished to subordinate the national story to the apocalyptic story, folding Elizabeth into an apocalyptic lineage. Yet Foxe never speaks of either Constantine or Elizabeth as an "Emperor of the Last Days."[41] In his most extended
discussion of this parallel (the 1563 dedication to Elizabeth), Foxe
emphasizes the advantage for England as a national, rather than apocalyptic, community:

> the Lord sent this mild Constantius, to cease blood, to stay persecution,
> to refresh his people. In much like manner what bitter blasts, what
> smarting storms have been felt in England during the space of certain
> years, till at last Gods pitiful grace sent us your Majesty to quench fire
> brands, to assuage rage, to relieve innocents. (B1v)

Foxe here specifies the national setting ("in England"), declining to
mention the presence of Antichrist or a sense of the imminent end of
time. Foxe's parallel in fact puts pressure on the standard convictions
of Tudor apocalyptic thought by suggesting an earthly permanence
for Elizabeth's regime, a regime very close to the end of the time: "so
we beseech [the Lord] to conserve you [Elizabeth] in *long prosperity,*
with the days not only of Constantius reign, but so with them whose
reign hath been *longest in any commonwealth*" (B2v; my emphasis).
There is very little sense of "the Last Days" here at all. On the contrary, Foxe's hope for a long national future, as with Aylmer and Bale,
forestalls the anticipated end of time. Indeed, Foxe himself almost
never refers to Elizabeth as figuring or serving any part in the coming

---

[41] Helgerson goes on in this paragraph to mention the apocalyptic content of the
portrait of Elizabeth contained in the initial letter C beginning the word "Constantine" in the 1563 edition of *Acts and Monuments,* which for Helgerson represents
the queen "triumphing over the papal Antichrist" (*Forms of Nationhood,* 260). Yet
Foxe believes Constantine begins the millennium, not that he ends it. John King,
whom Helgerson cites on this point, suggests that some apocalyptic conventions inform this portrait but does not see it as a representation of Elizabeth as an "Emperor
of the Last Days," concluding his discussion by affirming the *civic* resonance of the
image: "These associations coalesce in a powerful portrait in which Queen Elizabeth
carries the regal sword symbolic of the Tudor unification of ecclesiastical and secular
authority." See John N. King, *Tudor Royal Iconography: Literature and Art in an Age
of Religious Crisis* (Princeton: Princeton University Press, 1989), 154–56.

Apocalypse: he locates her in the national story.[42] Although her accession was a great triumph for Protestantism generally, as a feature of Foxe's narrative the national event subtly resists the conclusion of the apocalyptic story rather than anticipating it.

Rather than interpreting the Apocalypse as only the erasure of the national story, we need to attend to how this story "resists" the projected apocalyptic ending of the narrative. But what does this mean? We can usefully elaborate the pressure that the national story exerts on the narrative by using the terms set forth by Peter Brooks, who has argued that at the end of a narrative one gains a retrospective, totalized understanding of what has occurred. The ending sums up and even replaces the narrative events with a final meaning. He does not deny that there is a present experience of reading narrative events but points out that it is a present experience of reading events we understand already to be past:

> If the past is to be read as present, it is a curious kind of present that we know to be past in relation to a future we know to be already in place, already in wait for us to reach it. Perhaps we would do best to speak of the *anticipation of retrospection* as our chief tool in making sense of narrative, the master trope of its strange logic.[43]

"Anticipation of retrospection"—looking forward to a point at which one will gain a retrospective understanding of the present—is part of the double movement of narrative understanding. Yet Brooks also qualifies the anticipatory aspect of narrative in a striking way, observing that the ending, while being the moment of total meaning and confirmation, can also be seen as the moment of death—the point at which the narrative will cease to exist. Brooks arrives at this

---

[42] Helgerson does quote (*Forms of Nationhood*, 260) one of the rare instances in which Foxe explicitly links Elizabeth's accession to the defeat of Antichrist: "through whose true, natural, and imperial crown, the brightness of God's word was set up again to confound the dark and false-visored kingdom of Antichrist" (1570, OOOO4v). Yet it is significant that Foxe makes the monarch–Apocalypse connection in the context of the sacrifices of the Marian martyrs (Bishop Latimer's, in this case), and that in the next paragraph he goes on to speak of the Church of England's present peace as an achievement not of Elizabeth but of the martyrs, hoping that "we lose not that which *they* have obtained" (1570, OOOO4v; my emphasis).

[43] Thomas Brooks, *Reading for the Plot: Design and Intention in Narrative* (New York: Knopf, 1984; reprint, Cambridge: Harvard University Press, 1992), 23.

conclusion by relying on Freud's late understanding of death as the repetition sought after (and resisted) by Eros:

> We emerge from reading *Beyond the Pleasure Principle* with a dynamic model that structures ends (death, quiescence, nonnarratability) against beginnings (Eros, stimulation into tension, the desire of narrative) in a manner that necessitates the middle as detour, as struggle toward the end under the compulsion of imposed delay, as arabesque in the dilatory space of the text. (108)

Brooks imports this Freudian notion of the desired and resisted end into his own account of narrative movement. Narrative both anticipates the ending as its final meaning and resists it as its death; indeed, death and meaning become imbricated with one another as the goal of narrative. The end will always have this double charge, because it cannot confer meaning without also ending the existence of the narrative.[44]

It should be obvious that Brooks's notion of the narrative ending assumes an ideal case; in reality, most endings are not as conclusive as the theoretical ending that Brooks describes. Even he acknowledges that "we have no doubt foregone eternal narrative ends" (23). However, Brooks's theoretical conception of narrative and its ending becomes an almost literal description when applied to *Acts and Monuments* and the dilemma of postmillennial foreclosure. Foxe's apocalyptic story of the true church (indeed, any apocalyptic story) is an extreme example of a narrative anticipating its ending. The narrative of the true church strains at every moment to reach its conclusion, for, unlike any other narrative, its present moments are fully meaningful *only in terms of its end*. The death of the apocalyptic narrative is the same as its meaning—they are so entwined that the boundary between them almost disappears. Because one can never stand at a point in time that follows the Apocalypse, the apocalyptic

---

[44] Brooks's narrative version of psychoanalysis is well suited to describe many elements in Foxe's *Acts and Monuments*. Foxe often seems to allude to the relation between Eros and death in Christian thought, as when he reports Bishop Ridley's grim joke to his friends the day before his burning: "tomorrow I am to be married" (1570, YYYY4v). Also, the alignment of death and meaning is repeatedly and powerfully exemplified by the accounts of the martyrs, whose moment of death is almost always the moment at which they most fully communicate their meaning.

narrative is the only story of which one can never truly say "it has ended," only "it will end."

The story of the English nation, however, is a different matter. It has its beginning, its middle, and its end (ostensibly, the Elizabethan regime). If the national story truly concluded with Elizabeth—in the way a historical chronicle might—such an ending would of course finish off the narrative (be its death), but it would also confer meaning on the events of the narrative in obvious ways. However, the context of *Acts and Monuments* places Foxe's story of England in an unusual situation: its conclusion cannot be Elizabeth but rather must be the Apocalypse. A national story that concludes with the Apocalypse dies at its end without really receiving its expected meaning—precisely because such an ending is *indifferent* to the national story, functioning only to foreclose it. There is no way, within the orthodoxy of early Elizabethan theology, to see England's story as a necessary narrative building up to the apocalyptic end. In so far as is narratively possible, the apocalyptic end of the national story is all death and no meaning. Hence, the English story can only take on the function of *resisting* the end that Brooks describes as the counterpressure of narrative: "the compulsion of imposed delay . . . [the] arabesque in the dilatory space of the text" (108). Foxe never stages this resistance as anything but temporary (time itself works against it), but nonetheless he does stage it. The enthusiastic dedications and references to the queen, the celebration of the Englishness of the martyrs (as if their suffering were part of the story of England rather than the story of the true church alone), the occasional fuzziness of reference and topic ("the whole church of Christ, namely, of the church of England" [1576, TTTTt4v])—all these elements comprise the space and narrative mode in which Foxe gives vent to his patriotic sentiments, even while he acknowledges the coming of an end that will render such sentiments meaningless.

Although *Christus Triumphans* delayed the Apocalypse for the sake of repentance, urging its readers to prepare themselves for final judgment, the drama offered no expectations about a national future. *Acts and Monuments*, however, relies on narrative delay as the only means of imagining a national future that (temporarily) escapes eschatological foreclosure. This strategy is one that Foxe half chooses and half resigns himself to, a sought-after tactic as well as a forced position. His rhetoric of deferral often reveals a deep ambivalence, stemming from Foxe's profound uncertainty about what the near future will bring—English fruition or Christ's judgment? For example, ruminating on the current success of true religion in England, Foxe urges his readers that "[i]f god hath deferred his punishment, or forgiven us these our wicked deeds, as I trust he hath, let us not therefore be proud and high minded, but most humbly thank him for his tender mercies" (1570, e2r). Foxe's "trust" in divine forgiveness stands in tension with the uncertain status of delayed judgment: "*if* god hath deferred his punishment . . ." Just after this expression of hope, Foxe proceeds to reaffirm his conviction "that God yet once again is come on visitation to this church of England" and ponders what this good fortune will mean for the future: "And how grateful receivers we be, with what heart, study, and reverence we embrace what we have been given, that [question] I refer either to them that see our fruits, or to the sequel, which peradventure will declare." Once again, Foxe offers a deeply ambiguous sense of what England has achieved and what will become of it. Do the current "fruits" of English achievement suffice to convince outside observers of the nation's worthiness? Or must we wait to observe what the "sequel" will bring, a future outcome that "peradventure" tags as painfully uncertain.

Yet whatever the discomfort or illogic of apocalyptic postponement, it represents the only conceptual means Foxe possesses to imagine an English future vis-à-vis Christ's imminent return. Foxe sometimes gestures at deferral by insisting on a national element in his story or readership before elaborating eschatological implications. He attempts to create such a space for the English future at the end of the 1570 preface to "The True and Faithful Congregation of Christ's Universal Church . . . wheresoever congregated or dispersed through the Realm of England" (1570, ☞2r), a title that hints at a bifurcated sense of audience. Foxe interprets the last seventy years of persecution as analogous to the Babylonian Captivity, a period that "draweth now well to an end" (☞4v). He comments on this end with his characteristic ambivalence: "Now what the Lord will do with this wicked world, or what rest he will give to his Church after these long sorrows, he is our father in heaven, his will be done on earth." Worldly destruction or earthly continuance? Foxe goes on to elaborate these possibilities with a ship-at-sea metaphor:

> No man liveth in a commonwealth where nothing is amiss. But yet because God hath so placed us Englishmen here in one commonwealth,

also in one church, as in one ship together, let us not mangle or divide the ship, which, being divided, perisheth. . . . No storm so dangerous to a ship on the sea, as is discord and disorder in a weal public. What countries and nations, what kingdoms and empires, what cities, towns, and houses discord hath dissolved, in stories is manifest. (1570, ☞4v)

As Patrick Collinson has wryly noted of this passage, "now Foxe sounds like Hooker."[45] This ship of the commonwealth represents the English nation as both a political and religious community. Foxe emphasizes not the journey to a destination but rather the struggle for harmony in the present.

In Foxe's next paragraph, however, the ship of the nation turns into a different kind of vessel:

The Lord of peace who hath power both of land and sea, reach forth his merciful hand to help them that sink, to keep them up that stand, to still these winds and surging seas of discord and contention among us; that we may, professing one Christ, in one unity of doctrine gather ourselves into one ark of the true church together: where we continuing steadfast in faith may at the last luckily be conducted to the joyful port of our desired landing-place by his heavenly grace.

What starts out as a vision of England slips into a vision of the Apocalypse. Foxe abandons the national specification of the first ship, since the "one ark of the true church" must refer to an international entity. He also emphasizes the notion of a future end ("at the last") rather than focusing on the present, and thus the second ship, with its sure sense of destination, figures the impulse of narrative anticipation in *Acts and Monuments.*

Foxe does not conflate these two visions into a millenarian nationalism, yet he also does not disregard the ship of the nation in favor of the apocalyptic ark: why mention the first ship at all if the second is the only one that matters? Rather, Foxe offers the image of the ship of the nation, a ship with no overriding sense of destination (simply a "ship on the sea"), to insist on the importance of the present, national community, and only afterward acknowledges and celebrates

[45] Patrick Collinson, "John Foxe and National Consciousness," in *John Foxe and His World,* ed. Christopher Highley and John N. King (Aldershot, U.K.: Ashgate, 2002), 27.

the inevitability of "the joyful port of our desired landing-place." He paradoxically asks the reader to be a crew member of both the earthly ship of England and the heavenly ship bound for the Eternal Sabbath.

The national ship's lack of motion and progress calls attention to the limits of deferral in *Acts and Monuments:* Foxe delays the Apocalypse for the sake of national *existence,* not national achievement or development. The conditions of nonmillenarian theology prevent him from elaborating a specifically English apocalyptic future in any detail. I believe that Foxe's desire for a national future but inability to specify its relation to Christ's return partly accounts for the difficulty modern scholars have had in gauging the precise proportion of nationalism and apocalypticism in *Acts and Monuments.* It may also account for Foxe's curious ambivalence about the ending of his narrative. For example, both the 1576 and 1583 editions formally end with a brief section titled "Conclusion of the work," in which Foxe speaks one last time about the present reign of Elizabeth and the near future. In his comments he associates the progression of a narrative in a book with the progression of earthly time:

> During the time of her happy reign, which hath hitherto continued (through the gracious protection of the Lord) the space now of 18 [24 in the 1583 edition] years, as my wish is, so I would be glad the good will of the Lord were so, that no more matter of such lamentable stories may ever be offered hereafter to write upon. But so it is, I cannot tell how, the elder the world waxeth, the longer it continueth, the nearer it hasteneth to its end, the more Satan rageth; giving still new matter of writing books and volumes. (1576, TTTTt4v; 1583, FFFF4v)[46]

The confused combination of anticipation and deferral does not imply a settled relation between the nation and eschatology but rather signals Foxe's divided commitment to two irreconcilable temporalities. The passage makes it strikingly unclear what exactly is to be hoped for in the future. Of course, Foxe wants no more suffering and martyr stories, but what does he think will forestall them: the imminent Apocalypse or the continued reign of Elizabeth? That is, does the passage yearn for the end of time or seek to forestall this

---

[46] In an irony Foxe could not have predicted, this passage anticipates the many martyr stories, such as that of Bunyan, that editors added to Foxe's own stories in post-Elizabethan editions of *Acts and Monuments.*

end? Notice how the last sentence of the passage hurries time along to an anticipated conclusion ("it hasteneth to its end") but at the same time forestalls this conclusion by drawing time out ("waxeth," "longer," "more"). The sentence's syntax itself, with four short appositional clauses following one another, echoes the idea of time drawn out. The passage cannot decide whether it is going or staying.

Even the number of pages assigned to the various parts of the story in *Acts and Monuments* serves as part of the narrative resistance of the ending. More than the typical historical chronicle, *Acts and Monuments* offers a quite lopsided coverage of its material. The time period from the birth of Christ to the rise of Wyclif, 1,360 years, is covered in the first four books of the work. The time period from Wyclif to Elizabeth, about two hundred years, is covered in the last eight books. To put it another way, each of the first four apocalyptic ages delineated by Foxe receives a book's space of coverage; the fifth age receives eight books' space of coverage.[47] This is not such a surprising fact in itself; it simply suggests that Foxe has more to say about the time periods closest to his own. He himself notes the disparity in his coverage at the beginning of book 6: "in the compass of the said last three hundred years are contained great troubles and perturbations of the church . . . all of which things cannot be comprehended in one book: I have therefore disposed the said latter three hundred years into diverse books" (1570, Xx6v). Clearly, the arrangement of material has something to do with the amount of information Foxe has to communicate. Yet the disparity of his coverage is not only between the first four and last eight books: the eight-book coverage of the fifth age is itself lopsided. Books 5 and 6 cover 150 years, books 7 and 8 cover forty years, and book 9 covers six years (Edward's reign), whereas books 10 to 12 cover only five years (Mary's reign). The closer we get to the end, the longer the narrative is drawn out. Foxe allows the ever-slowing pace of *Acts and Monuments* to signify the increasing insistence of the English story on its presence, even as it

---

[47] In the 1570 edition of *Acts and Monuments*, the five apocalyptic ages—approximately three hundred years each—include the following: (1) the "suffering time" of the early church; (2) the "flourishing time" of the church, beginning with the accession of Constantine and the binding of Satan; (3) the "backsliding time" of the church; (4) the "time of Antichrist," beginning with the release of Satan from his thousand years of captivity; and (5) the "reformation and purging of the church . . . and how long it should continue more, the Lord and Governor of all times, he only knoweth" (e1r).

nears the end that has been anticipated throughout the narrative. The narrative's expectation of an apocalyptic conclusion strains toward the ending, but the number of details grows as the narrative continues, slowing its progress.

Foxe thus takes the tension between Apocalypse and nation implicitly present in a variety of discourses in Elizabethan culture and represents it in terms of opposing narrative pressures. Displacing the problem of postmillennial foreclosure onto narrative allows Foxe to negotiate the gap between nation and the Apocalypse without having to reach a philosophical or doctrinal resolution, a resolution that the conditions of early Elizabethan apocalyptic theology made impossible. He represents the conflict indirectly by use of the opposite pressures the two stories exert on the narrative. Millenarian nationalism is still decades ahead of *Acts and Monuments*; narrative form provides Foxe with a space to express hope for national existence in the future without denying the inevitability of the imminent end of time.

Spenser's Apocalyptic History

Spenser inherits Foxe's apocalyptic scheme and its major characteristics—historical application, Rome as the seat of Antichrist, the struggle between the two churches—and much of Spenser's poetry conforms to this scheme. His translations of the four apocalyptic sonnets in van der Noot's *A Theater for Worldlings* (1569) are not as explicitly antipapal as is his later poetry, but they do dramatize the cosmic struggle between Babylon and the true church. *The Faerie Queene* also echoes many of Foxe's tropes. Book I dramatizes the struggle of the two churches throughout apocalyptic history. Una, as the apocalyptic woman in white, represents the true church of Christ opposed to Duessa, the whore of Babylon. Arthur's intervention to assist Una in cantos vii and viii represents in part the protection of the true church by reformed nations, with a particular glance at the Tudor monarchy. Toward the end of the book, Redcross begins to figure the apocalyptic Christ defeating the dragon, Satan, at the end of time. Book V, as recent scholarship has revealed, relies on apocalyptic imagery to recount recent historical events, in ways similar to Foxe's treatment of English history, such as the rise of Wyclif. Like *Acts and Monuments*, *The Faerie Queene* offers a historical and nonmillenarian vision of the Apocalypse.

Nonetheless, England's apocalyptic landscape changed from 1570 to 1590, and Spenser registers these changes in his poem. As Richard Mallette has recently argued, the defeat of the Spanish Armada altered the manner in which some English thinkers wrote about the end of the world.[48] They begin to suggest that the final eschatological struggle will involve not only Christ's intervention but also an earthly, military battle between Protestants and the servants of Antichrist. I therefore adopt his term "post-Armada" to describe this phase of English apocalyptic writing, using it to delineate the apocalyptic optimism that the Armada victory stimulated from the 1590s through the early 1620s, when England's failure to enter the religious wars on the Continent quieted eschatological expectations for a while. Yet, although Mallette identifies book V of *The Faerie Queene* as the primary expression of this new rhetoric and sees book I advocating the earlier, Foxean view, book I represents one of the first post-Armada interpretations of Revelation, breaking substantially from earlier Elizabethan views. In placing the 1590 *Faerie Queene* within post-Armada apocalyptic writing, I draw some of my evidence from texts published after the poem. Yet I do so because the apocalypticism of book I more closely resembles that of later writers than it does early Elizabethan ones. In book I of his poem Spenser articulates two new ideas about his nation's future that become increasingly common in the 1590s and afterward: (1) England, though an earthly community, possesses a special character that may distinguish it from ordinary worldly corruption; and (2) the deferral of the end may signify not only a conceptual space for national existence but also a period of national achievement and development, suggesting that Christ's eventual return may confirm rather than only annihilate national identity. Book I does not envision a millenarian future, but it is future-oriented in its nationalism to a degree that earlier apocalyptic discourse is not, representing Spenser's most sustained attempt to imagine a relation between national and divine temporality.

Although much recent criticism has emphasized book I's moral and sacramental dimension over its historical application of Revelation, it has often overlooked the degree to which the narrative advances an idea of historical optimism by means of apocalyptic references.[49] Of course, Spenser has moral as well as historical points to

---

[48] See Mallette, "Post-Armada Apocalyptic Discourse."

[49] Some of the most influential interpretations of the moral over historical elements of book I's apocalypticism include Florence Sandler, "*The Faerie Queene*: An Elizabethan Apocalypse," in *The Apocalypse in English Renaissance Thought and Literature*, ed. C. A. Patrides and Joseph Wittreich (Ithaca: Cornell University Press,

make. In addition to his other significations, Redcross is a Christian Everyman, doomed to see through the glass darkly and in need of the intervening gift of grace. Yet the moral dimension of the story in no way mitigates the effort Spenser makes to imbue his characters with apocalyptic and national meaning, to communicate, in fact, a view of history on the same scale of ambition as *Acts and Monuments.* To say that the legend of Holiness expresses historical optimism is not to say that Spenser assumes every action in history will achieve moral success. Book I in fact is less forgiving than are the other books of the poem of its protagonist's repeated failure to achieve the virtue he supposedly represents. Rather, historical optimism means that Spenser, by explicitly linking his apocalyptic story with English identity, implies that human action within the general course of history can potentially contribute to the final cosmic victory.

The inclination to view the Apocalypse as the culmination rather than only judgment of history finds expression in many commentaries on Revelation after 1588. Mallette has noted the increased sense of militancy in these tracts, shrewdly linking it to the violence in book V of *The Faerie Queene.* Indeed, apocalyptic writers of the period regularly suggest that England's participation in European wars functions as a kind of confirmation of God's plan. Yet Mallette associates this militancy with a feeling of uncertainty about England's safety, "the unease about national self-preservation."[50] In fact, although post-Armada writers certainly acknowledge peril—Mallette quotes George Giffard's warning that England's enemies are "ready to overwhelm us"[51]—they are usually more confident than their prede-

---

1984), 148–74; and Michael O'Connell, *Mirror and Veil: The Historical Dimension of Spenser's "Faerie Queene"* (Chapel Hill: University of North Carolina Press, 1977), esp. 38–68. Joseph Wittreich describes the antihistorical interpretation succinctly when he claims that Spenser "joins the company of certain of his contemporaries who, within the context of the apocalypse, maintained a distinction between variable England and invariable Jerusalem, between the world of men and the angelic company, between an earthly paradise and the heavenly kingdom"; Wittreich, "Apocalypse," in *The Spenser Encyclopedia,* ed. A. C. Hamilton (Toronto: University of Toronto Press, 1990), 48. Yet the issue partly depends on who we think Spenser's "contemporaries" are. Do we mean Foxe, Fulke, Bullinger, and Jewel, who produced their apocalyptic texts in the 1560s and 1570s? Or do we mean Napier, Pont, Giffard, Prince James of Scotland, Dent, and Brightman, who, along with Spenser, wrote about Christ's return during the fifteen years after the Armada victory and before Elizabeth's death?

50 Mallette, "Post-Armada Apocalyptic Discourse," 150.

51 Ibid., 150; Giffard, *Sermons upon the Whole Book of Revelation,* A4r.

cessors about Antichrist's defeat *in history*. Whereas most early Elizabethan accounts of Revelation pointed to the raging strength of Rome as a sign of the approaching end, Giffard associates Antichrist's current decay with eschatological imminence: "the fifth angel, as we read chap. 16, hath poured forth his vial upon the throne of the beast, and that bloody kingdom of Antichrist waxeth dark, their brightness and glory is diminished, wherefore they be so vexed, that they gnaw their tongues for sorrow."[52] Commentators tied Antichrist's obvious death rattle to their confident prediction that the faithful would overcome God's enemies *before* Christ returned. Young Prince James of Scotland, writing about the apocalyptic meaning of the Armada battle in 1588, argued that Revelation prophesied earthly triumph over Britain's enemies: "God hath promised not only in the world to come, but also *in this world*, to give us victory over them."[53] Arthur Dent agreed, making the final defeat of Babylon distinct from God's final judgment: "the utter overthrow of the Pope, and all his adherents, shall be in this life a little before the coming of Christ unto judgement."[54] Post-Armada commentators' sense of a worldly victory over Antichrist, although still short of millenarian hope, encouraged many of them to think that God's apocalyptic victory might be a historical one, a drama in which human action could contribute positively to the saints' reversal of fortune.

Of course, the sense of the painful gap between human effort and apocalyptic judgment, what I am calling historical pessimism, did not disappear after 1588 but remained available as a perspective by which to interpret human effort in relation to end time. We can achieve a clearer sense of book I's vision of apocalyptic history by contrasting it to the view of history in book V, whose apocalyptic discourse confirms the sense of historical pessimism that reigns in the latter part of the poem. Kenneth Borris, who was one of the first critics to locate Spenser's poem between two phases of apocalyptic theology, intriguingly links Arthur's victories in the legend of Justice to the soon-to-emerge idea of the elect nation, suggesting that book V "may thus be a seminal text for that view, since the British cultural hero Arthur becomes its messianic vehicle, bringing deliverance for

---

[52] Giffard, *Sermons upon the Whole Book of Revelation,* A3v.
[53] James I, *Paraphrase of Revelation* (1588), in *The Works of the Most High and Mighty Prince James* (London, 1616), 80 (my emphasis).
[54] Dent, *Ruin of Rome,* Oo3v.

'all the people' to establish the reformed community (V.xi.34)."[55] However, most recent studies associate the apocalyptic features of the narrative with historical decline,[56] an interpretation that the proem to book V would seem to confirm. The inability of history to contribute positively to apocalyptic victory emerges in the first stanza:

> So oft as I with state of present time,
> The image of the antique world compare,
> When as mans age was in his freshest prime,
> And the first blossome of faire vertue bare,
> Such oddes I find twixt those, and these which are,
> As that, through long continuance of his course,
> Me seemes the world is runne quite out of square,
> From the first point of his appointed sourse,
> And being once amisse growes daily wourse and wourse.
>
>   (V.proem.1)

Spenser here, and in the stanzas that follow, locates paradise at the beginning of time and sees history as a process of decay. The references to the end of time, from this perspective, can only function as annihilation, as the world moves "toward his dissolution" (4.9) and human beings "arrive at their last ruinous decay" (6.9). To the degree that Spenser grants Elizabeth an apocalyptic agency in the present, she becomes a "Dread Soverayne Goddess" (11.1) who does not deliver her people from affliction but rather judges them for their sins:

---

[55] Kenneth Borris, *Spenser's Poetics of Prophecy in "The Faerie Queene"* (Victoria: University of Victoria Press, 1991), 79. Borris is careful to qualify book V's millenarian potential: "Spenser does not construct his allegory so as to evoke or preclude such anticipations" (80).

[56] Mallette, as we have mentioned, connects the aggressive militarism of the forces of Justice with the post-Armada impression that earthly warfare would help defeat Antichrist; yet he also emphasizes that the apocalyptic perspective of book V "comprehends human failure as deeply as tragedy does" ("Post-Armada Apocalyptic Discourse," 168). Mark Hazard reads Artegall's encounter with the Egalitarian Giant (V.ii) in terms of the apocryphal 2 Esdras, a link that potentially sanctions Talus's violence with divine prophecy. Yet Hazard sees the episode disavowing an apocalyptic "return to a golden age," suggesting that Spenser's "use of 2 Esdras points that discussion toward a sense of ultimate frustration about the incompatibility between human and divine justice, a frustration that implies the destruction of the merely human." See Hazard, "The Other Apocalypse: Spenser's Use of 2 Esdras in the Book of Justice," *Spenser Studies: A Renaissance Poetry Annual* 14 (2000): 177, 173.

"to thy people righteous doome aread" (11.4). The sentiment echoes Foxe's sense, during his exile, of the judgment awaiting his countrymen at the end of time: "I hope the vengeful anger of our father's rod will not wait long" (*CT* 225). Of course, the proem's pessimism about history does not necessarily extend to moral action in general. Artegall's struggles make clear that we are *morally* obliged to resist evil to the best of our ability, even if this resistance cannot contribute to the final *cosmic* triumph. To the degree that book V relies on an apocalyptic perspective, it implies a historical pessimism.

The effects of this pessimism become even clearer in the complex conclusion of the Mutability cantos, even though the tone here is not so obviously bleak as in the proem to book V. This pessimism lies again in history's inability to play a meaningful part in the cosmic conclusion to time. Indeed, the best interpretation of these cantos in recent years has demonstrated the degree to which temporality, in the form of the titaness Mutability's genealogical claims, represents precisely the force that threatens to overturn the Olympian metaphysics of political stability. Gordon Teskey elegantly explains that Dame Nature's decision against Mutability, rather than simply exposing the self-contradiction of rule by Change, betrays the repression of temporal origin required by any metaphysical order: "Authority can be defined as the power to compel the public forgetting of what is privately remembered: it is *hegemonic amnesia.*"[57] This moment of amnesia resonates with Prince Arthur's inability to find himself in history (in *Briton moniments* II.x.68), as well as with the need to account for the desperate state of Ireland ("Arlo-Hill," VII.vi.36–55) by means of a mythological fable that displaces the memory of national violence. In any case, the accuracy of Teskey's reading seems confirmed by the doubled aspect of Nature's decision against Mutability, namely, that change poses no threat because (1) it occurs according to Providential dictate (stanza 58), and (2) it will vanish at the end of time anyway (stanza 59). The strained logical relation between these two claims emerges forcefully in the following stanzas of canto 8, in which the narrator reveals that he is not comforted by Nature's first claim about Providential change: in the natural world, at least, Mutability "beares the greatest sway" (viii.1.5). What comforts him, finally, is not meaningful change in history but

---

[57] Gordon Teskey, "Mutability, Genealogy, and the Authority of Forms," *Representations* 41 (1993): 104–22; quotation at 108.

rather the annihilation of change at the Apocalypse, "that Sabaoths sight" (viii.2.9) that the narrator can only wistfully anticipate. As with the proem to book V, the gap between history and end time does not represent for Spenser moral nihilism, any more than the "curse" on Arlo-Hill relieves English colonists of their duty to exercise righteous violence in Ireland. Yet his sense of historical pessimism makes clear that this historical activity remains remote from Christ's victory over Antichrist at the end of time.

Yet if the later books of *The Faerie Queene* maintain a rather negative view of history in relation to the Apocalypse, why would Spenser represent a positive view of Revelation in book I? The answer lies in the special quality of salvational history that governs the first book of *The Faerie Queene.* Unlike book V, which posits an originary paradise followed by a history of decline and apocalyptic judgment, book I begins in the fallen world and traces a history of personal and cosmic salvation, leading to the renewal of paradise. David Quint has described the transition from book I to the later books as a "fall into history."[58] This phrase aptly describes the difference between book I and books II–VI, if we read "history"—as the Tudors sometimes did—as the wandering of earthy time isolated from, or at least imperfectly linked to, the Providence of God. In his later books, Spenser turns more fully to the historical pessimism of Foxe, who would like to believe that "God's divine grace" brought about England's historical capacity to produce godly martyrs for the apocalyptic true church but fears that the true cause may in fact be the "foolish cruelty" of England's rulers (1563, Ii6r). Foxe's rhetoric, simultaneously associating and alienating the nation from the divine future, responds to the strictures of postmillennial foreclosure, as I have discussed, and throughout much of his poem Spenser acknowledges the same strictures. In the legend of Holiness, by contrast, apocalyptic imminence does not simply annihilate history but potentially functions as history's culmination. We can see the entirety of book I as an experiment in historical optimism, an eschatology that suggests a unique (though not millenarian) relationship between the English future and Christ's return. In this sense of experiment I agree with Joseph Wittreich's claim that the poem "is finally not an historian's or a theolo-

[58] David Quint, *Origin and Originality in the Renaissance* (New Haven: Yale University Press, 1983), 154.

gian's but a poet's Revelation."[59] Not that poetry allows Spenser to rise above historical and theological concerns, and not that Spenser did not *really* care about the end of time, using it merely as a metaphor for the human condition. Rather, poetry encourages Spenser to try out heterogeneous approaches to the Apocalypse, allowing him to make it signify a variety of things in *The Faerie Queene*. In book I, Spenser explores what happens to national history when linked to a salvational narrative.

The Legend of Holiness: An English Apocalyptic Comedy

The first book of Spenser's poem, like Foxe's *Christus Triumphans*, constitutes a comedy in the sense that it emphasizes the final victory of God over the forces of earthly corruption. John King has appropriately drawn our attention to Spenser's reliance on the genre of Reformation drama "as a model for interpreting human history as a broad context for many particular 'tragedies' of elect saints, whose experience would undergo reversal at the millennium."[60] King's neutral description of history as a "context" for the final reversal is apt, I think. Foxe, who called his drama a "comeodia apocalyptica" (*CT* 200), optimistically anticipates the spiritual triumph of Ecclesia, the true church. However, he expresses pessimism about the role human history can play in this triumph, as Ecclesia makes clear: "Except by the coming of Christ, this beast cannot be destroyed. So we'll let him have this trophy untouched, because as far as I'm concerned I'm resolved to endure willingly whatever I endure since I endure it for the sake of Christ" (359). Foxe is eschatologically hopeful and historically skeptical—hence his disinclination to specify a national contribution to the defeat of Antichrist. It is significant that Spenser's contrasting sense of historical optimism in book I accompanies an equally contrasting national flavor in his apocalyptic comedy. We can easily identify at least three moments in the narrative that function as an apocalyptic "climax": Arthur's battle with Orgoglio and Duessa (canto viii), Redcross's vision of the New Jerusalem (canto x), and Redcross's victory over the dragon and betrothal to Una (cantos

---

59 Wittreich, "Apocalypse," in *Spenser Encyclopedia*, 48.
60 King, *Spenser's Poetry and the Reformation Tradition*, 222.

xi–xii). Each of these scenes participates in the comic structure of the narrative, presenting a reversal of fortune from affliction to victory for God's servants. The dispersal of one Apocalypse into several does not suggest apocalyptic reluctance or ahistorical application but rather that eschatology fuels the quest, a teleological counterbalance to romance digression. As Elizabethan commentators recognized, John's prophecy retells the end in several versions, with discrete accounts of the fall of the beast (Rev. 19), the binding of Satan (Rev. 20), and an account of the New Jerusalem (Rev. 21). Spenser makes his apocalyptic depictions distinct from earlier Elizabethan writers by including a national presence in each case, as if English participation constituted a necessary preliminary phase before eschatological disclosure can take place. Unlike *Christus Triumphans* or even *Acts and Monuments*, Spenser combines the figures of the true church and the apocalyptic Christ with the English figures of Elizabeth and Saint George. Spenser's identifications are almost unprecedented, as Florence Sandler cautiously notes: "the final appearance of Una in terms that suggest an identification with Elizabeth herself suggests some developments of the Tudor myth that go beyond Foxe's scheme."[61] Indeed, Spenser deliberately transforms Foxe's "comeodia apocalyptica" into an *English* apocalyptic comedy.

Spenser's legend of Holiness most closely parallels *Christus Triumphans* through the figure of Una. Claire McEachern's recent, exemplary reading of the representation of the English Church in book I suggests a double imperative in Una's identity: on the one hand, she must be self-identical to maintain her English uniqueness, yet on the other hand she must maintain an iterable relation to other churches (e.g., Duessa) in order to remain "legible" within the field of European nations.[62] Spenser may well have derived a model for this ambiguity of affiliation and distinction from Foxe's play. Ecclesia's double in this text is Pornapolis, the whore of Babylon, who falsely establishes herself as the true church, deceiving Ecclesia's sons Europus and Africus. Like Una, Ecclesia's disputed identity arises from the replicable nature of visual signs—"Would anyone who sees you think you're Ecclesia?" (*CT* 335) sneers Pseudamnus the Antichrist at the True Church. Also like Una, Ecclesia is on the one hand replicable,

---

[61] Sandler, "*Faerie Queene*," 162.

[62] Claire McEachern, *The Poetics of English Nationhood, 1590–1612* (Cambridge, Cambridge University Press, 1996), 35–82.

responding to Pornapolis's usurpation with the lament, "Oh, you make me not know who I am," but on the other hand she is divinely unique, asserting the unity of her nature and appearance: "The election of God remains fixed with this sign, that he knows who his people are" (333). The final comic reversal in both narratives relies on reestablishing the self-identity of the church, so that in Foxe the chorus can finally "see the bride herself" (361), whereas Spenser's Una, finally "well beseene, / Did seeme such, as she was" (I.xii.8.8–9). Yet, although McEachern is for the most part uninterested in the apocalyptic implication of this self-resemblance, we can discern the most important difference between Foxe's and Spenser's comedy in terms of their eschatology. Foxe, as we earlier discussed, imbues Ecclesia with an English resonance—she refers to herself as "an exile cut off from my country" (357)—but her transformation into the bride of Christ works to erase her national distinctiveness. In this last scene Foxe is careful to flank her with the international company of Europus and Africus: she ultimately represents the universal church of Christ. Indeed, as her son Africus sees the end approaching, he echoes Ecclesia's earlier doubt about identity, but this time in the ecstasy of apocalyptic triumph: "I'm so happy I don't know who or where I am" (365). Ecclesia's apocalyptic identity depends on the dissolution of national and topographical distinctions, reflecting Foxe's apocalyptic optimism but national pessimism in 1556.

The difference between the two texts depends partly on the disparate forms of reunion. Ecclesia's identity is clarified when she reunites with her earthly *sons*, whereas Una's identity emerges most explicitly when she prepares to take a *lover*, an Englishman who also signifies the apocalyptic Christ. By linking Una's self-revelation to the imminent consummation of her union with Redcross, Spenser reinflects Foxe's scheme to maintain rather than erase Una's national meaning. Thus, the point in canto xii at which Una's parallel to Queen Elizabeth culminates in the *Semper Una* reference to Spenser's monarch ("who in her selfe-resemblance well beseene, / Did seeme such, as she was, a goodly maiden Queene") appears to prepare for Una's self-unveiling as the wife of the Lamb described in Revelation 19:7–8, who clothes herself in radiant garments:

> For she had layd her mournfull stole aside,
> And widow-like sad wimple throwne away,
> Wherewith her heavenly beautie she did hide,

Whiles on her wearie iourney she did ride;
And on her now a garment she did weare,
All lilly white, withoutten spot, or pride,
That seemd like silke and silver woven neare,
But neither silke nor silver therein did appeare.

(I.xii.22.2–9)

The stanza of course literally describes an apocalypse, in the Greek
sense of uncovering: Una has "layd . . . aside" and "thrown away" her
covering. The contrast with *Christus Triumphans* helps us to appreciate Spenser's innovation in combining eschatological and national elements in Una, elements that earlier writers such as Foxe, Aylmer,
Bale, and Becon are unable to combine without complicated qualification. Although his allegory is circumspect, Spenser's narrative makes
it possible for us to suspect both that Elizabeth has been betrothed to
Christ and that the true church has married an Englishman.

Linking Redcross to the apocalyptic comedy of *Christus Triumphans* is more difficult because the only parallel could be Christ
the Groom. Spenser dramatizes the apocalyptic battle that Foxe can
only imply at the end of his play. As Frank Kermode notes, Spenser
turns Redcross from *miles Christi* (the traditional identity of Saint
George) into "Christ himself,"[63] suggesting his apocalyptic participation in the defeat of the Satanic dragon in canto xi. Recent critics
have disputed this claim, insisting that Redcross represents an Everyman Christian warrior—a "type" of Christ rather than Christ himself—and interpreting the many references to Revelation in this
episode as sacramental rather than eschatological.[64] Yet we need to
keep in mind that the Elizabethans did not see sacrament and eschatology as mutually exclusive. By the same token, the line between
Christ and his types was blurrier than we usually grant, as suggested
by the 1597 marginalia of John Dixon, which freely interprets the
dragon fight as a representation of Christ's redeeming sacrifice, of

[63] Frank Kermode, "Spenser and the Allegorists," in *Shakespeare, Spenser, Donne*
(New York: Viking Press, 1971), 43. Carol V. Kaske makes a similar claim about the
dragon episode, in "The Dragon's Spark and Sting and the Structure of Red Cross's
Dragon-Fight: *The Faerie Queene*, I.xi–xii," *Studies in Philology* 66, 4 (1969): 609–38.

[64] See Michael Leslie, *Spenser's "Fierce Warres and Faithfull Loves": Martial and
Chivalric Symbolism in "The Faerie Queene"* (Cambridge: D. S. Brewer, 1983),
104–18; and Kenneth Gross, *Spenserian Poetics: Idolatry, Iconoclasm, and Magic*
(Ithaca: Cornell University Press, 1985), esp. 130.

Queen Elizabeth's establishment of the true church in England, and of Christ's final victory over Satan.[65] True, Redcross is a "figure" for Christ Triumphant, but then so is the warrior "Faithful and true" in Revelation 19:11, whose precise designation is obscure enough that the Geneva glossers felt obliged to tell us that "[h]e meaneth Christ." Nor were these glossers blind to the ambiguity of Revelation's figural language, noting of the angel who chains Satan (20:1–3) that "[t]his Angel representeth the order of the Apostles, whose vocation and office was from heaven; or may signify Christ, who should tread down the serpent's head."[66] Sacramental office, end time, or both? In other words, the figural nature of Spenser's depiction would not have signaled to his readers a reluctance to equate Redcross and Christ. Rather, it is Spenser's persistent association between the knight's English identity and apocalyptic victory that would have struck his readers as innovative.

As with Una, Redcross takes on his eschatological function only after the disclosure of his English background as Saint George, suggesting that the knight requires both his apocalyptic and national identity before he can engage the dragon in canto xi. This coupling of identities appears quite deliberate if, as seems to be the case, Spenser himself initiated the "traditional" association between Saint George and the dragon-slaying Christ.[67] All the more striking, then, is the manner in which Spenser emphasizes rather than glosses over the difference between the national and heavenly roles, playing up Saint George's affiliation with the common people and with unsophisticated, folk conceptions of England. In the letter to Raleigh, Spenser refers to the knight as a "tall clownishe younge man" and "clownish person."[68] Contemplation reveals the knight's future identity as Saint

---

[65] John Dixon, *The First Commentary on "The Faerie Queene,"* ed. Graham Hough (Stansted, U.K.: privately published, 1964).

[66] *The Geneva Bible* (1560), HHh1r.

[67] It is often assumed that Spenser derives this apocalyptic identity for his knight from the Saint George tradition itself (after all, George had been a dragon-slayer since the twelfth century). Yet, as Harold Weatherby has observed, the actual evidence offers little indication that medieval or earlier Elizabethan writers saw the saint as an apocalyptic figure, despite the presence of the dragon. He concludes, "If we have come to think of Christ's defeat of Satan on Holy Saturday as a part of the Saint George myth . . . Spenser himself may be the mythmaker"; Weatherby, "The True Saint George," *English Literary Renaissance* 17, 2 (1987): 136.

[68] *The Faerie Queene*, 2d ed., ed. A. C. Hamilton (London: Longman, 2001), 717. Unless otherwise designated, all subsequent references are to this edition.

George in a description that implies a broadly-defined, popular community: "thou Saint *George* shalt called bee, / Saint George of mery England, the signe of victoree" (I.x.61.7–9). "Mery England," emerging explicitly into the poem for the first time, presents a folksy, archaic conception of the nation far from what we might expect of God's elect, though perhaps appropriate for a man brought up "in ploughmans state to byde" (x.66.5). Redcross's character, rather than raising England to apocalyptic heights, brings the Apocalypse down to earth. In Pocock's terms, Redcross's character functions to "secularize the sacred, by drawing the processes of salvation into that time which is known as *saeculum*."[69] Indeed, Spenser seems to insist on the necessary link between national humbleness and apocalyptic triumph. After Redcross slays the dragon, the crowd's reaction to him both revises and reaffirms his humble origins:

> And after, all the raskall many ran,
> Heaped together in rude rablement,
> To see the face of that victorious man:
> Whom all admired, as from heaven sent.
>
> (I.x.9.1–3)

As a figure of apocalyptic proportions ("as from heaven sent"), Redcross has surpassed the "raskell" and the "rude." Yet these terms also remind us of his humble, national origins: as Saint George, he is still one of them. Given this rhetoric of humility and triumph, and given the longstanding popular and national associations of Saint George in English culture,[70] Spenser seems to suggest an English connection different from that implied by Una's and Arthur's characters. That is, if Una as Elizabeth comes to represent the nation metaphorically, from above, Redcross as Saint George represents it metonymically from within. His character, unlike any figure in *Christus Triumphans*, encompasses both English provinciality and apocalyptic destiny, suggesting a distinct national element within a history struggling toward a cosmic and comic triumph.

This interpretation of Spenser's apocalyptic nationalism as historical optimism does not deny the self-reflexive quality of the narrative,

---

[69] Pocock, "England," 109.
[70] See Jonathan Bengtson, "Saint George and the Formation of English Nationalism," *Journal of Medieval and Early Modern Culture* 27, 2 (1997): 317–40.

which reveals itself as a representation rather than the actual consummation. As many critics rightly point out, Spenser circumscribes the apocalyptic betrothal of Redcross and Una with an admission of textuality: "Suffice it heare by signes to understand / The usual joyes at knitting of loves band" (I.xii.40.4–5). Yet Spenser's contemporaries would not have read this admission as a denial of apocalyptic imminence, and nor should we. In his prologue to *Christus Triumphans*, Foxe makes clear that his drama offers an Apocalypse with words, not things:

> we bring you Christ Triumphant. Perhaps it will not be long before stage representations will lie neglected; then indeed we will see all with our own eyes, when God sends in actual fact [re ipsa] what he now only promises. For now, do not be ashamed to view through a netting the images [simulachra] of things, which is all we play. (229)

Foxe's *simulachra* are Spenser's "signes": they both call attention to limits of representation while nonetheless anticipating the disclosure of *re ipsa*. Indeed, conspicuous figurality often characterizes apocalyptic narratives in the Reformation, because the expectation of the immediate Christ makes writers all the more aware of the need to describe this expectation with mediation. There is nothing new about book I's self-acknowledged representational status; rather, Spenser's innovation is his sustained transformation of Protestant apocalyptic comedy into an especially national story.

The New Jerusalem, Golden World, and England

Despite the optimistic inflection of apocalyptic nationalism in book I of his poem, Spenser must nonetheless confront the problem of post-millennial foreclosure that haunted Foxe's *Acts and Monuments* two decades earlier. After all, post-Armada apocalyptic thinking remained for the most part resolutely antimillenarian well after Spenser published the first installment of *The Faerie Queene*. Commentators refused to identify England literally with the New Jerusalem. As late as 1615 we find Thomas Draxe, in *An Alarm to the Last Judgment*, contemptuously dismissing millenarian expectations:

> They much mistake the matter, and are foully overseen, that expect a golden world, and expect an heaven and earth, and an exquisite refor-

mation of all things: whereas in so declining a world, they shall see the
Lord coming in the clouds sooner that this their dream come to pass.[71]

This passage seems to confirm Spenser's eschatological caution in
the Contemplation episode, in which he forestalls golden world
hopes by making clear the sinfulness of the world in relation to the
future New Jerusalem. Indeed, Contemplation's notoriously contradictory advice to Redcross raises the issue of the knight's national
identity in the most awkward manner, linking the disclosure of the
knight's Englishness to an Old Testament sense of original sin:

> And thou faire ymp, sprong out from English race,
> How ever now accompted Elfins sonne,
> Well worthy doest thy service for her grace,
> To aide a virgin desolate foredonne.
> But when thou famous victorie hast wonne,
> And high emongst all knights hast hong thy shield,
> Thenceforth the suit of earthly conquest shonne,
> And wash thy hands from guilt of bloudy field:
> For bloud can nought but sin, & wars but sorrowes yield.
>
> (I.x.60)

No golden world indeed. Why reveal Redcross's English identity in
the same stanza that exposes the vanity of earthly endeavor, especially in language that sounds disconcertingly close to Despair's earlier characterization of worldly effort (I.ix.43)? The condemnation of
"earthly conquest" rather infelicitously adumbrates the knight's designation as "Saint George" in the next stanza (x.61.8–9), inflecting
the name's etymology (*georgos*, earth-worker) toward worldly sin
rather than Adamic primordiality. Spenser even seems to cultivate
the awkward link between the two stanzas, as the last line of 61 suggests: "Saint George of mery England, the signe of victoree."
"Earthly" and "conquest" serve as an ominous analogue to "George"
and "victory." In "so declining a world," to use Draxe's phrase, only
Christ's arrival "in the clouds"—or, in Spenser's scene, the descent of
the New Jerusalem—will save England from its corrupt earthliness.
    Yet the antimillenarian caution about the golden world in post-

---

[71] Thomas Draxe, *An Alarm to the Last Judgement* (London, 1615), G6–G6v,
A5r–A5v.

Armada writers partly compensates for the futurist implications of their theology. As we have seen, these writers anticipate a military victory over Antichrist before the end of time, an attitude that Draxe himself echoes: "the ancient and mighty Roman Empire . . . is now so impaired, wasted and weakened that it hath lost all his former Majesty and Dominion, and retaineth only a bare and naked image, and picture, of that it formerly enjoyed."[72] A logical consequence of this pre-Advent victory, however, is a short period of earthly peace for the church before Christ's coming establishes the New Jerusalem. This future period of earthly life, though not the millennium, differs from the description of the Apocalypse in almost all early Elizabethan commentaries.[73] Patrick Forbes's 1613 exegesis, which confidently predicts that the reformed nations would bring down the whore of Babylon before the end of time, offers a good illustration of the revised historical scheme:

> Her destruction shall be by these self same Kingdoms and States, who before deceived with her, had been special props of Antichrist his power, but at last espying the abominations thereof, fall from him and become instruments of God his just indignation against the Whore.

Godly kingdoms will overthrow Rome, ending the tyranny of Antichrist on earth. But then what?

> there is a new face of a world, all enemies being so overthrown, as the Church hath a most graceful and quiet state, for that Satan . . . being now not only bound up for a thousand years as that first, but so as his destruction now begun holdeth on till that full point it shall have in the last judgment, and the Church her reign hereupon shall accordingly not be for a thousand years only, as at the first, but for evermore . . . she having no more to expect but the coming of her Lord for translating her to glory.[74]

Forbes takes care to establish his postmillennialist credentials and to identify Christ's coming as the inauguration of *heavenly* paradise, yet

---

[72] Ibid.

[73] As we have noted, Foxe's *Eicasmi*, published in 1587, postulates a penultimate period of calm between the fall of Antichrist and Christ's return.

[74] Patrick Forbes, *An Exquisite Commentary upon the Revelation of Saint John* (London, 1613), *5v, B11.

he acknowledges an interval between Satan's new binding and destruction at the Last Judgment, between the church's victory over Antichrist and its transfiguration by Christ's Second Coming. He thus looks forward to a penultimate earthly calm, a reward, as it were, for the earthly effort of "Kingdoms and States." Post-Armada apocalyptic writers discourage the hope for a millenarian golden world, but they anticipate a "new face of a world" that extends outside the historical struggle against Antichrist but that remains history nonetheless.

With this implication of a short future period of peace, a hiatus lodged between time and eternity, emerge new conceptions of the relation between the New Jerusalem and earthliness, especially English earthliness. For one thing, post-Armada commentators nearly all begin to insist, contra John Jewel and Thomas Rogers in the 1570s, that the earth will not suffer destruction at the Apocalypse but rather will physically endure in a purified form. The New Jerusalem will in fact descend from heaven to an earth that will persist through eternity.[75] Furthermore, many of them suggest a link between the promise of the New Jerusalem and the special role England will play in its achievement. They do not espouse a sense of England as an elect nation, for they continue to see the end of time as a universal affair, promising deliverance to the faithful in all nations.[76] Yet they begin to speak of England as leading an international consortium of godly nations against the forces of Antichrist. The international context of

[75] Giffard: "[John] calleth them new heavens and a new earth then, and saith that the old are passed away, not that the substance of the heavens and the earth that now are shall be abolished, but their estate shall be altered" (*Sermons upon the Whole Book of Revelation*, Dd7r). Dent: "By a new heaven and a new earth, is meant the renewed estate of heaven and earth, after this life in their quality, not in their substance. For we do believe according to scripture that his visible heaven, and this visible earth shall continue for ever, as touching their matter and substance" (*Ruin of Rome*, Oo4v).

[76] Giffard refers to the persecution of the saints in Revelation 20:9 to demonstrate the international effort against Antichrist: "The histories of these latter times do show that wheresoever in any country where popery had taken place, there were any that would not worship the beast. . . . For the tents of the Saints and the beloved city were in all lands where any did with pure and sincere faith worship the true God" (*Sermons upon the Whole Book of Revelation*, Cc8v). When describing the delights of the New Jerusalem, Dent brings up the question of membership: "But it may be demanded who shall dwell in this so glorious a City, and in this so great a light. Saint John answereth that *the people that are saved shall walk in it:* that is, all the Israel of God, all true believers" (*Ruin of Rome*, Qq2r).

England's leadership marks one of the primary differences between early Elizabethan and post-Armada apocalyptic discourse: Aylmer and Bale speak of their new queen's fight against Antichrist in England, but later commentators imagine a new, global prominence for their nation. For example, Giffard's account of his queen's efforts against the false church sets England on the international stage in an unprecedented manner:

> And by the singular blessing of God, our noble Queen hath been, and is the greatest defender and protector of the holy worship and true worshippers that is under heaven. The Churches in other countries have by her aid been much supported and relieved in their distresses. . . . The king of Spain, who hath given his power to the beast, sent his forces *anno 88* for to invade her land, and to throw down her excellent Highness, from that sacred authority and power in which almighty God hath placed her, and miraculously protected her, fighting from heaven against her enemies, even to the wonderment of the whole world.[77]

The new post-Armada esteem that England enjoys in the world's eyes derives in part from the almost reciprocal relation it has with God's Providence: Elizabeth acts to defend, protect, and aid the true church in the world, and God protects and fights for her from heaven.

Indeed, England's primary role in the apocalyptic end of the world guarantees the defeat of Antichrist on earth for many post-Armada writers. In a passage of *The Ruin of Rome* that considers the apparent improbability of such an earthly defeat, given the pope's considerable sway in Europe, Dent invokes England's commitment to the gospel:

> For they shall never set up Popery here in England, to stand and continue, do what they can. I must needs confess that our sins, being so horrible and outrageous as they are, and being grown to such an height and ripeness, do deserve some fearful vengeance. . . . But yet I hope, for his covenant's sake, for his great mercy's sake, for his name's sake, for his glory's sake, and for his Church's sake, he will be gracious and favorable unto us . . . yet this I say, and am persuaded of, that Popery shall never be established again in this kingdom; my reason is, because the everlasting Gospel carried abroad by the Angel that flieth in the mid-

---

[77] Giffard, *Sermons upon the Whole Book of Revelation*, A3r–A3v.

dest of heaven, shall spread still more and more throughout all the kingdoms of Europe.[78]

With the same reciprocal dynamic that Giffard employed, Dent shows how God's mercy on England's many sins allows the nation to make a significant contribution to the cosmic narrative. Surprisingly, God's glory and true church depend, at least in some sense, on English success, and the nation becomes a special space, immune to Antichrist's influence, where God's word first flourishes and germinates out to the rest of Europe. Not that Dent literally believes that Christ cannot get the job done without England; rather, his rhetoric attempts to carve out a future space in which England's contribution does not evaporate at Christ's Second Coming. Thus, post-Armada apocalyptic discourse, while denying a millenarian golden world, begins to cautiously postulate a future interval between history and eternity, as well as a sense of England as an exception to ordinary earthly corruption.

The peculiar rhetoric of Spenser's Contemplation episode represents an early attempt to formulate this revised relation between national time and apocalyptic time. As a nonmillenarian, Spenser refuses to specify an English New Jerusalem on earth. Yet he reserves for his nation a special relation to the heavenly city by associating earthly corruption with non-English space. The difficulty in revising the disparity between world and spirit, a division so important to the legend of Holiness, perhaps explains why Redcross's initial exchanges with Contemplation appear to bode so poorly for his nation's apocalyptic future. The knight's new preference for the New Jerusalem over the tower of Cleopolis—"this bright Angels towre quite dims that towre of glas" (I.x.58.9)—awkwardly recalls the early Elizabethan inference that the Apocalypse would erase rather than exalt national glory, because Cleopolis has functioned as an allegory for London, and for England generally. Contemplation's attempt to soften this awkwardness, an insistence that Gloriana (and thus, Elizabeth), is "heavenly borne, and heaven may justly vaunt" (x.59.9), feels a bit like a consolation for England's inferiority to the apocalyptic city. His claim that it behooves knights who "covet in th'immortall booke of fame / To be eternized, that same [Cleopolis] to haunt" (x.59.4–6) exacerbates this sense of consolation, since "covet" uncomfortably re-

[78] Dent, *Ruin of Rome*, A3r–A3v.

calls Redcross's earlier excessive enthusiasm for glory, and "eternized," respectable on its own, here rather unconvincingly echoes the "eternall peace and happinesse" (x.55.9) of the New Jerusalem. Indeed, the rhetoric of this stanza sounds a bit like the effects of post-millennial foreclosure in the prefaces to *Acts and Monuments*, in which Foxe's hope for Elizabeth's "long reign" (1570, *1r) comes into subtle conflict with his anticipation of "the speedy Coming of Christ the Spouse, to make an End of all Mortal Misery" (1570, ☞2r).

Precisely at this moment of contestation between Cleopolis and the New Jerusalem, Spenser introduces a third term into the discussion: the "English race" (x.60.1). We should pause here to consider the subtle oddness of this new term. Until this point, Cleopolis itself allegorically represented the English nation; Spenser in fact reinforces this correspondence only a stanza earlier by referring to the city's "Soveraigne Dame," reminding us of the parallel between Gloriana and Elizabeth.[79] But now, for the first time in book I, Spenser creates a distinct split between England and Faerieland. As readers, we must suddenly modify our earlier impression that the previous two stanzas presented a conflict between England and the New Jerusalem—the conflict was in fact between the Faerie city of Cleopolis (retrospectively uncoupled from England) and the New Jerusalem. Surprisingly, then, Redcross has *not* thus far been traveling through a type of English landscape, despite Gabriel Harvey's contrary view in "To the learned shepheard":

> So mought thy Redcrosse knight with happy hand
> victorious be in that faire Ilands right:
> Which thou doest vaile in Type of Faery land
> Elyzaes blessed field, that Albion hight.
> That shieldes her friends, and warres her mightie foes,
> Yet still with people, peace, and plentie flowes.[80]

Did Harvey simply get it wrong? McEachern appropriately notes that "Harvey's encomiuim seems to overlook the discrepancies between his vision of 'Eliza's blessed field' and the topography of the treacher-

---

[79] In the "Letter to Raleigh," Spenser writes that "[i]n that Faerie Queene I meane glory in my generall intention, but in my particular I conceive the most excellent and glorious person of our soveraine the Queene, and her kingdom in Faery land" (*Faerie Queene*, 716).

[80] "Commendatory Verses and Dedicatory Sonnets," in *Faerie Queene*, 722.

ous Faerieland."[81] Yet this is part of Spenser's point: the treacherous, sinful, earthly Faerieland does represent England and it doesn't, and it especially does not on Contemplation's mount in the presence of the New Jerusalem. Indeed, the introduction of England as a *third* term in the equation makes sense of the peculiar way in which Contemplation links his pronouncement of Redcross's national identity to earthly denigration in stanza 60. Contemplation associates his criticism of Redcross's earthliness with Redcross's identity as a Faerie knight; it is only when Contemplation speaks of Redcross's destiny as a saint in the apocalyptic city that he emphasizes the knight's Englishness:

> Then seek this path, that I to thee presage,
> Which after all to heaven shall thee send;
> Then peaceably thy painefull pilgrimage
> To yonder same *Hierusalem* do bend,
> Where is for thee ordained a blessed end:
> For thou emongst those Saints, whom thou doest see,
> Shalt be a Saint, and thine owne nations frend
> And Patrone: thou Saint George shalt called bee,
> Saint George of mery England, the signe of victoree.
>
> (x.61)

It seems, then, that Faerie and England here represent two distinct versions of earthly existence: the former, mired in sin, and disparate from the New Jerusalem; and the latter, characterized by its saintly patronage and possibly commensurate with the apocalyptic future. Spenser is unable or unwilling to deny the disparity between earth and heaven, but he makes Faerieland, rather than England, bear the brunt of this disparity. The *georgos* implication of "Saint George of mery England" avoids the corruption of "earthly conquest" and "guilt of bloudy field" from the previous stanza (x.60.7, 8) because it is an English *georgos*. Faerieland may continue to suffer incursions from the papist threat of Archimagos and Duessas, but, as Dent promises, "they shall never set up Popery here in England, to stand and continue, do what they can." By making Faerieland signify non-English space, Spenser can emphasize England's heavenly rather than worldly quality, focusing on his nation's connection to the Apoca-

---

[81] McEachern, *Poetics of English Nationhood*, 35.

lypse through the mediation of a specifically English saint: "For thou . . . / Shalt be a Saint, and thine owne nations frend / And Patron" (61.6–8). The English future escapes postmillennial foreclosure.

Yet what is the relationship between England and the apocalyptic city, exactly? Will Saint George be one national saint among many, England's specific representative in the city along with the representatives of other nations? This is the kind of question that post-Armada commentators discourage, despite their conviction that the New Jerusalem will be on earth, as Giffard testily illustrates: "I will not enter here to dispute with what creatures the Lord will furnish the earth withal."[82] Nor will Spenser, who appears deliberately ambiguous about this issue. His vision is not millenarian, and his New Jerusalem represents heavenly reward in general as much as it does a specifically apocalyptic future. The unspecified relation between England and the apocalyptic city leads to Redcross's confusion about how to value world and spirit, as he attempts both to delay (stanza 62) and hasten (stanza 63) his entry to the New Jerusalem. Jeffrey Knapp, in a subtle explanation of Redcross's failure to return to England at this point, argues that Spenser cultivates this ambiguity: "the English must reject a premature, pastoral identification of their island with Paradise, in favor of a sense of England as completed only when God's work is, when that part of the world not-English, and so estranged from God, has been apocalyptically returned to the fold."[83] Indeed, as Knapp's comment implies, in order to avoid Draxe's "golden world" error, the episode defers not only the Apocalypse but also Englishness, projecting both into a future that will yield a "Saint George." Yet, more confusing still, Spenser also projects Englishness back into the past, producing an atavistic vision of "mery England" derived from folk tradition. Redcross fails to return to his nation not only to avoid a premature millenarianism but also because Contemplation offers the knight an England that no longer exists. For Spenser, the cost of resisting national erasure at the Apocalypse, the cost of asserting historical optimism in the face of eschatology, the cost of

---

[82] Giffard, *Sermons upon the Whole Book of Revelation*, Dd7r. Hugh Broughton, in his *Revelation of the Holy Apocalypse* (London, 1610), speaks of "the heavenly Jerusalem *in this world*," but like Giffard feels that inquiry into the details is unwarrented: "to search out of what sort it shall be, the Law . . . forbiddeth us to search curiously" (Nn1v).

[83] Jeffrey Knapp, *An Empire Nowhere: England, America, and Literature from "Utopia" to "The Tempest"* (Berkeley: University of California Press, 1992), 131.

imagining "a new face of a world" (Forbes in 1613) instead of "a sudden downfall of this wretched world" (Rogers in 1577), resides in the emptying of the national present into both an apocalyptic future and an archaic past. Purifying England by means of abjecting sinful Faerieland allows Spenser to maintain an ambiguous relation between the nation and the end of history, but this strategy exorcises the complicated present (associated with Faerie) into an idealized English past and future. Whereas Foxe's apocalyptic nationalism loses England in the future, Spenser's loses it in the now. The cost of Spenser's gesture should remind us that he denigrates Faerie here as a local expedience, an experiment with history, as it were. Elsewhere in *The Faerie Queene,* such as II.x, the Faerie lineage of Sir Guyon is much freer of sinfulness than is the British lineage of Arthur. Spenser privileges English worldliness here because he is trying to unite salvational history with national history in book I, attempting to find an association between English time and the divine future that earlier writers found so elusive.

Spenser and English Achievement

Spenser is a poet who dislikes closure, often qualifying the victories of his heroes at the last moment or deferring expected conclusions or consummations. Some of these deferrals occur in the midst of apocalyptic imminence, leading many critics to agree with Kenneth Gross's assessment that Spenser is an "antiapocalyptic" writer.[84] As our discussion suggests, however, eschatological delay is built into the Book of Revelation itself and into the Renaissance genre of apoc-

---

[84] Gross, *Spenserian Poetics,* 127. Interestingly, Gross actually invokes this term only when qualifying it. Yet his account of the postponed wedding foregrounds the trope of deferral: "Book I's Eden of the end becomes, if not the original Eden of loss, then, strangely, an Eden of deferral, even while the interrupted marriage foreshadows all later deferrals in the poem" (130). Mallette similarly calls book V "an Apocalypse postponed" ("Post-Armada Apocalyptic Discourse," 168). John Watkins refers to Spenser's "retreat from apocalypse"; Watkins, " 'And yet the end was not': Apocalyptic Deferral and Spenser's Literary Afterlife," in *Worldmaking Spenser: Explorations in the Early Modern Age,* ed. Patrick Cheney and Lauren Silberman (Lexington: University of Kentucky Press, 2000), 173 n. 3. Mark Hazard represents a rare holdout, observing that "It is thus not correct to say, as some critics do, that Spenser is against apocalyptic thought because he is against millennial hope" ("Other Apocalypse," 177).

alyptic writing, cropping up in Foxe, Bale, and Aylmer. There is no
denying Spenser's especially marked tendency toward eschatological
deferrals. Some of them respond to the problem of a national future
within apocalyptic time, what I have called postmillennial foreclosure, in the way *Acts and Monuments* does. Take, for example, the
conclusion of Merlin's prophecy, which we examined in chapter 2:

> But yet the end is not. There *Merlin* stayd,
> As overcomen of the spirites powre,
> Or other ghastly spectacle dismayd,
> That secretly he saw, yet note discoure.
>
> (III.iii.50.1–4)

I previously argued of this episode that the prophetic vision of the national past results in an eschatological displacement of history. We
can also describe this episode in terms of Tudor apocalyptic theology:
with no millenarian future on the horizon, national history runs cat-
astrophically into the end of time. John Watkins has recently suggested that Merlin's final phrase functions as a deferral of the Apocalypse, implying that "history has not yet reached its culmination"
and thus signifies a "retreat from millenarian confidence."[85] Scripture of course offered plenty of examples of apocalyptic postponement,[86] and bracketing Watkins' anachronistic use of "millenarian,"
I agree that the conclusion of the prophecy creates eschatological
delay. Yet it also creates eschatological imminence. Merlin's echo of
Christ in Matthew 24:6—"but yet the end is not"—was sometimes
called the "little Apocalypse" by commentators and read as a sign of
the approaching end.[87] The catastrophe of the "ghastly spectacle" de-

---

[85] John Watkins suggests that the penultimate vision of Elizabeth—"Then shall a
royall virgin raine, which shall / Stretch her white rod over the Belgicke shore"
(iii.49.6–7)—"depicts Elizabeth in unmistakably millenarian terms" and represents a
"millenarian culmination" ("Apocalyptic Deferral and Spenser's Literary Afterlife,"
160). Yet, as I hope our discussion thus far has made clear, no sixteenth-century com-
mentator would think of such a vision as that of a "millenary" or "chiliast," per se.

[86] E.g., 2 Thessalonians 2:2–3.

[87] In Matthew 24, Christ's statement initiates his prophecy of the end of the world
(24:7–51), in which he makes promises that Tudor commentators commonly took to
signify apocalyptic imminence. For example, Christ assures his listeners that "for
the elect's sake those days shall be shortened" (24:22) and that the end will come
within "this generation" (24:34). John Napier, in *Plain Discovery of the Whole Revelation of Saint John*, refers to Matthew 24 to show that, although Revelation technically predicts a date of 1789 as the end of the world, it will probably happen sooner:

rives not from the idea that history may continue but rather that it
may end too soon, cutting off the national future. Spenser's use of
"the end is not" functions as a miniature of Foxe's own representational strategy, because the phrase both invokes and postpones the
ending of the historical narrative. On the one hand, the statement
does literally end the narrative, ideally promising to confer meaning
on and closure for the story just related. On the other hand, its apocalyptic content nullifies the national specificity of that story, and so
"the end is not" takes on an almost hortatory force: let the end not
come yet; let the ghastly spectacle be postponed. As in the proem to
the legend of Justice, the apocalyptic ending of Merlin's prophecy
judges history and consumes it.

The deferral at the end of book I does something else. Although
Spenser certainly registers the sadness of all believers who must wait
longer for Christ's return—Redcross leaves Una "to mourne"
(I.xii.41.9)—this delay does not yield a "ghastly spectacle" (as in Merlin's prophecy), nor does it lead to the "righteous doome" of the
world's "dissolution" (as in the proem to book V). Spenser critics have
perhaps underappreciated the difference between the apocalyptic
ending in book I and the later books. After four stanzas that liken the
betrothal of Una and Redcross to the union of Christ and the true
church in Revelation 19 and 20, Spenser has the knight depart
abruptly:

> Her joyous presence and sweet company
> In full content he there did long enjoy,
> Ne wicked envie, ne vile gealosy
> His deare delights were able to annoy:
> Yet swimming in that sea of blisfull joy,
> He nought forgot, how he whilome had sworne,
> In case he could that monstrous beast destroy,
> Unto his Faerie Queene backe to returne:
> The which he shortly did, and Una left to mourne.
>   (I.xii.41)

Stanza 41's concluding "mourne" is certainly shocking after the account of Redcross's pleasure: joyous, sweet, delights, joy. Indeed, his

---

"Not that I mean that . . . the world shall continue so long, because it is said that for
the Elects' sake the time shall be shortened" (12). On the label "little Apocalypse,"
see Borris, *Spenser's Poetics of Prophecy*, 11.

departure gives the lie to the suspiciously conclusive "full content." Even though Spenser has prepared us for this parting (xii.18), we are still surprised to learn that Una remains the church militant rather than the church triumphant. Yet unlike Spenser's other apocalyptic interruptions, which appear to promise only disaster or decay, the following stanza is remarkably noncatastrophic:

> Now strike your sailes ye jolly Mariners,
> For we be come unto a quiet rode,
> Where we must land some of our passengers,
> And light this wearie vessell of her lode.
> Here she a while may make her safe abode,
> Till she repaired have her tackles spent,
> And wants supplide. And then againe abroad
> On the long voyage whereto she is bent:
> Well may she speede and fairely finish her intent.
>
> (I.xii.42)

The stanza releases us back into history, metaphorized as a ship, peopled now not with mourners but with "jolly Mariners"—indeed, the shift from "mourne" to "jolly" is as dramatic as the tonal shift in the previous stanza. This return to history no doubt prepares us for the continuation of the poem, but also gives us a history with a sense of purpose: "fairely finish her intent." Spenser's eschatological deferral does happen for the sake of a continuing history (as with Merlin's prophecy), but not just any old history—it also demands a history of teleological action.

Many post-Armada apocalyptic writers issue a similar call to cosmic action. We can see this partly in their new sense of militancy, which they sometimes regard not only as a pre-Advent possibility but as a necessity, a required postponement of Christ's return. Dent explains that

when the seventh Angel bloweth the seventh trumpet, then cometh the end of the world: But the sixth Angel hath sounded the sixth trumpet long ago, as appeareth by the effects: Therefore it cannot be long ere the seventh Angel blow. But Rome must fall down finally, *before the seventh Angel blow*, as hath been shown before.[88]

---

[88] Dent, *Ruin of Rome*, Mm2r (my emphasis).

The passage both anticipates and delays the end, somewhat reminiscent of Foxe's sense of apocalyptic imminence at the end of *Acts and Monuments:* "But so it is, I cannot tell how, the elder the world waxeth, the longer it continueth, the nearer it hasteneth to its end, the more Satan rageth; giving still new matter of writing books and volumes" (1576, TTTTt4v). As we have discussed, Foxe's sentence appears to both wish for and postpone the Apocalypse, an event that will end England's future as well as Foxe's book. Yet whereas Foxe can imagine the continuation of history only as the scene of Satan's rage, Dent has a plan of action in mind: kill Antichrist. Dent defers not only for the sake of continued earthly existence but also earthly *achievement.* Such a conception of pre-Advent history makes possible specifically national action. John Napier, praising Prince James's spiritual steadfastness in 1593, urges his monarch not only

> to abide constant and courageous against that day of the destruction of the Apostatic seat and city, in case (God willing) it fall in your time: *but also in the mean time,* until the reformation of that Idolatrous seat, to be preparing and purging you Majesty's own seat and kingdom from all enemies of that cause. . . . For shall any Prince be able to be one of the destroyers of that great seat, and a purger of the world from Antichristianism, who purgeth not his own country?[89]

Napier hopes the Apocalypse will happen soon ("God willing"), yet he defers the end by imagining a "mean time," an interval of earthly history in which the human enemies of Antichrist participate in his destruction. Such participation links the nation (in this case Scotland) to Christ's final victory, because James may become "one of the destroyers of that great seat." Like Dent, then, Napier defers the Apocalypse not to avoid the annihilation of national history but rather to give it eschatological meaning.

In this context it is important to remember *why* Redcross leaves Una: "Backe to returne to that great Faerie Queene, / And her to serve six years in warlike wize, / Gainst that proud Paynim king, that workes her teene" (I.xii.18.6–8). He leaves to take military action in the world, to assault the "Paynim king"—a figure for evil in general, of course, but also for Antichrist, the final foe in the eschatological

---

[89] Napier, *Plain Discovery of the Whole Revelation of Saint John,* A3v–A4r (my emphasis).

battle. Indeed, Spenser suggests that the knight will achieve apocalyptic victory in history, having the king confidently predict an eventual consummation of the marriage between Redcross and Una: "Ye
then shall hither back returne againe, / The marriage to accomplish
vowd betwixt you twain" (xii.19.8–9). Redcross can return to the
Apocalypse only after defeating Antichrist in history. The deferral is
lamentable ("hard necessity" [19.1], the king calls it) but also necessary if history is to contribute to (rather than merely wind down to)
the Apocalypse. Spenser in book I, like his contemporaries in the
1590s, revises the early Elizabethan idea of merely holding on until
Christ arrives into an optimistic notion of active participation, imbuing the end of time with a national meaning, to some degree. The crucial difference here consists of the cosmic participation, not martial
action in itself. After all, the conclusion of the Mutability cantos invokes eschatological armies ("that Sabaoths sight" [VII.viii.2.9]), but
in such a way that makes national effort irrelevant, consigning the
English to languish as "in-dwellers" (VII.vii.55.9) within the cursed
realm of Ireland. Book I's contrasting sense of historical preparation
for Christ's return does not deny the spiritual, moral meaning the effort holds for Redcross as Everyman. As an individual Christian, the
knight undergoes experiences revealing that we must patiently fortify
our faith as well as fight as soldiers against Antichrist in history:
Spenser insists on both the external history and internal conscience.

Post-Armada commentators insist on the same thing, despite their
historicism. Giffard writes to his fellow Englishmen that their salvation may depend on England's victory: "none shall inherit that glory,
but conquerors. We are in a battle, if we fight valiantly, and overcome
our enemies, we shall be crowned: but if we be overcome and led away
captive, as prisoners taken in the wars, how can we be saved?"[90] Giffard here surprisingly sets the stakes at almost millenarian heights,
suggesting that an English triumph over Antichrist, rather than faith
alone, will determine the fate of his readers' souls. Here we have
apocalyptic nationalism at its most alarming, where fighting the
good fight is not enough: your nation has to win. In the next sentence, however, he recasts the locus of this battle: "We have a corrupt
nature, full of sin and sinful lusts, and the devil worketh in it very
strongly: and if we do not subdue it, and vanquish Satan, we are taken
as prisoners and held captive." Antichrist in Rome shifts into the

---

[90] Giffard, *Sermons upon the Whole Book of Revelation*, Ee1v.

devil in our souls, from history to mind, from England to Everyman—
perhaps a symptom of the nonmillenarian limit of post-Armada discourse. Yet Giffard also believes in the eschatological battle in history, a struggle requiring both Christian faith and the English sword.

Deferral does indeed seem to inhere generally in apocalyptic narratives, but its specific manifestations produce quite divergent effects.
Christus Triumphans defers the end for the sake of spiritual repentance in the present, an impulse that continues to inform deferrals in
subsequent apocalyptic texts as well. Yet *Acts and Monuments* addi-
tionally employs deferral as a conceptual space for national existence,
a means of resisting national erasure at the end of time. Book I of *The
Faerie Queene* develops this conceptual space into an imperative for
national achievement, in which England can potentially make a positive contribution to the final cosmic victory. The possibility of cosmic participation does not negate the moral and spiritual meaning of
Spenser's narrative; it simply makes that meaning matter in an additional way. *Acts and Monuments* and book I of *The Faerie Queene,*
while avoiding a millenarian vision, anticipate the more explicit
sense of national participation that English writers begin to imagine
in the 1640s and 1650s. Was this arc of apocalyptic development that
I describe inevitable? Surely not. Yet it seems to respond to the increasing need to locate national time within a conception of God's eschatological plan, to make the English and divine futures commensurate even as the disparity between them manifested itself with
unprecedented obviousness.

4 POETICAL HISTORY
Spenser and Milton Ornament the Nation

British Union and the Problem of Historical Fiction

The obvious advantage of apocalyptic history for Renaissance English writers was that it was true. However tricky Foxe and Spenser found its application to national time, John's prophecy brought with it a biblical certainty. Revelation might express its truths in allegories, but it did not use "fiction." The same could not be said about Arthurian history. Despite some isolated attempts to imbue Arthur with a messianic character, the charge of fictionality began to undo the historical authenticity of the Brutus and Arthur narrative as the sixteenth century drew to a close. William Paruus's complaint that Geoffrey of Monmouth rehearsed "fabulous dreams" represents a common objection to the narrative: it lacked the substance and solidity of true history, making it unworthy of the nation's heritage.[1] Indeed, the emptiness of fiction posed a threat to the Arthur story in ways precisely the inverse of the threat posed by the problem of the monument we discussed in chapter 2. Whereas the antiquarian defenders of Geoffrey feared that the remains of the British past were

[1] John Leland reports Paruus's opinion, in *Assertio Inclytissimi Arturii Regis Britanniae* (London, 1544); trans. Richard Robinson in *A Learned and True Assertion of the Original, Life, Actes, and Death of the Most Noble, Valiant, And Renowned Prince Arthur, King of Great Britain* (London, 1582), fol. 36v.

too *physical,* dangerously susceptible to material transience, Geoffrey's critics found his story too *phantasmal,* devoid of real content, comprising nothing but fables. Fiction's emptiness marred the truth of history.

Many early Tudor defenders of Geoffrey in fact agreed with his critics' assessment of fiction's effect on history, leading them to vigorously deny the presence of fable in the Arthur narrative. John Bale lamented that so many English chronicles were unreliable—"we find for true histories, most frivolous fables and lies"—yet suggested that the *Historia Regum Britanniae* was in fact a vital piece of true history that demonstrated England's past greatness under the reigns of "king Brennus . . . great Constantine . . . and Arthur."[2] John Dee insisted in his *Brytanici Imperii Limites* that the falsehood of many British chronicles threatened to obscure the true account of national history expressed in the *Historia:* these false histories had "both confounded the truth, with untruths: and also, have made the truth it self to be doubted of, or the less regarded, for the abundance of their fables, glozings, untruths, and Impossibilities, inserted in the true history, of King Arthur."[3] Neither Bale nor Dee deny that a great deal of their nation's historiography contains—and suffers from—the emptiness of fiction; they simply wish to preserve Geoffrey's narrative from such an accusation. As scholars have long observed, when prominent historical writers such as William Camden expressed their doubts about the *Historia*'s accuracy later in the century, support for the narrative as pure history began to erode.[4] By the early seventeenth century, the majority of England's increasingly skeptical historiographers agreed with George Hakewill's assertion that "the whole narrative of Brute" is "rather poetical than historical."[5]

As the *Historia*'s historical authenticity began to slip away, however, some English writers began to exploit its new identity as fiction. They took their cue no doubt from earlier Geoffrey-defenders who, less absolute than Leland, Bale, or Dee, tried to finesse the problem of

---

[2] John Bale, *The New Year's Gift* (London, 1546); reprinted in John Chandler, *John Leland's Itinerary* (Dover, N.H.: Alan Sutton, 1993), 9, 10.

[3] John Dee, *Brytanici Imperii Limites* (BL Add. MS 59681), fol. 27r.

[4] For some classic accounts of this development, see T. D. Kendrick, *British Antiquity* (London: Methuen, 1950), esp. 108–9; and F. J. Levy, "The Making of Camden's *Britannia*," *Bibliothèque d'Humanisme et Renaissance* 26 (1964): 70–97.

[5] George Hakewill, *An Apology or Declaration of the Power and Providence of God in the Government of the World,* 2d ed. (London, 1630), 9.

fiction by deemphasizing the issue of historical accuracy, stressing instead the need for historical continuity itself. Attempting to salvage Arthur from Polydore Vergil's assault, William Lambard suggested that historical accuracy was secondary to the need for an origin:

> if he shall seek to discredit the whole work, for that in some parts it containeth matter, not only unlikely, but incredible also: then shall he both deprive this Nation of all manner of knowledge of their first beginning, and open the way for us also to call into question the origin and antiquities of Spain, France, Germany, yea, and of Italy his own country: in which, that which Livy reporteth of Romulus and Remus, Numa and Aegeria, is as far removed from all suspicion of truth, as any thing whatsoever Galfride writeth, either of Brute, Merlin, or King Arthur himself.[6]

Lambard does not defend the *Historia* in terms of its truthfulness but rather as an enabling condition of knowledge. To dismiss the entire work will "deprive this Nation of all manner of knowledge of their first beginning," a deprivation as contagious as it is calamitous—once it happens to one nation, it can happen to all nations. The need for an origin implicitly forces the *Historia* into a threshold space between truth and fiction.

Some "post-Camden" writers extended this idea by dropping the pretense of historical accuracy almost entirely, suggesting that a fictional continuity was as good as a historical one. After all, poetry had a long tradition of preserving ancient deeds for posterity. James I and his representers (such as Ben Jonson and Inigo Jones) do not seem to have cared much about the historical accuracy of Geoffrey's *Historia* when employing Brutus and Arthur as figures of legitimacy for the new king. In the various proclamations, parades, and masques that liken James to monarchs of the past, Brutus and Arthur stand somewhere between the "historical" figures of Solomon, David, Julius Caesar, and Augustus, and the fictional figures of Jove and Aeneas.[7] Justifying his use of Brutus in *Part of the Coronation Entertainment* (1604), Ben Jonson not only accepted but promoted the idea of fictional continuity: "Rather than the City should want a Founder, we

---

[6] William Lambard, *The Perambulation of Kent* (London, 1576), 69.
[7] See Jonathan Goldberg, *James I and the Politics of Literature* (Baltimore: Johns Hopkins University Press, 1983; reprint, Stanford University Press, 1989), 33–54.

choose to follow the received story of *Brute*, whether fabulous or true, and not altogether unwarranted in Poetry: since it is a favor of Antiquity to few Cities to let them know their first Authors."[8] Jonson sets aside the issue of historical accuracy—"whether fabulous or true"—to suggest that the fiction of poetic writing is necessary to protect against the threat of historical loss (to "want a founder"). Even the ambiguity of "Authors" here—historical founder or poet?—plays on the permeability between history and fiction. Writers seeking the ancient British past were obliged to confront the dilemma of poetical ornamentation described by Sir Walter Ralegh: "Historians do borrow of Poets, not only much of their ornament, but somewhat of their substance. Informations are often false, records not always true, and notorious actions commonly insufficient to discover the passions, which did send them first on foot."[9]

The willingness to treat ancient British history as a useful fable emerged in part out of the increasing inclination of many English historians to turn to the more recent, Saxon past as a source of national heritage. In contrast to the mythical Britain of Geoffrey, Saxon England was historically knowable and provable.[10] Richard Rowland, who wrote under the name Vestegan, mounted in 1605 one of the earliest arguments that the English ought to search for their true origins in "our ancient English Saxon Kings," lamenting the inclination of earlier English writers to treat "the antiquities of the Britains as if they properly appertained unto Englishmen, which in no wise they do or can do, for that their offsprings and descents are wholly different."[11] Throughout much of his work, Vestegan took pains to showcase his methodological precision and historical skepticism. Although he cautiously accepted the historical existence of Brutus, he mocked the naïve trust in his Trojan identity ("these things hardly will be believed"), arguing that available evidence pointed to a more

---

[8] Jonson, *Ben Jonson*, 11 vols., ed. C. H. Herford, Percy Simpson, and Evelyn Simpson (Oxford: Clarendon Press, 1925–54), 7:92.

[9] Walter Ralegh, *The History of the World* (London, 1614), II.21.6; reprinted in Sir Walter Ralegh, *Selected Writings*, ed. Gerald Hammond (New York: Penguin, 1986), 170.

[10] On the early Stuart interest in the Saxons, see Richard T. Vann, "The Free Anglo-Saxons: A Historical Myth," *Journal of the History of Ideas* 19 (1958): 259–72; and R. Schoeck, "Early Anglo-Saxon Studies and Legal Scholarship in the Renaissance," *Studies in the Renaissance* 5 (1958): 102–10.

[11] Richard Vestegan, *Restitution of Decayed Intelligence in Antiquities concerning the most Noble and Renowned English Nation* (Antwerp, 1605), †2r, †3v.

modest, Gallic background for this ancient personage (M2r, M3v–N4r). Brutus, Vestegan thus implied, provided neither a link to classical glory nor a line that persisted up to the present: "By all this we may see to what great uncertainty this ancient name of Britain is now brought." The Saxons, by contrast, offered a historical story of continuity and endurance, remaining "the corps and body of the realm" even through the Danish and Norman invasions (M1v, V2r). Although Vestegan's sneering correction of John Foxe, who anachronistically calls the fourth-century Helen "English" rather than British, probably derives in part from his Catholicism, it also stems from his persistent desire to maintain a separate English tradition and identity (†4v). The shift from the Britons to the Saxons thus offered at least two advantages: it permitted a national history more firmly based on empirical records, less tainted by fiction, and it distinguished an *English* national community from the more heterogeneous and overtly problematic notion of "Britain."

"Britain" had of course emerged as quite problematic in the early years of James's reign, when the new king attempted a union—both political and cultural, both state and nation—between the kingdoms of England and Scotland.[12] Vestegan's own dislike of or at least indifference to the proposed Union may be signaled by the way his dedication to James curiously ascribes Anglo-Saxon rather than British origins to the Scottish king. Many other writers who resisted this union, often out of deeply anti-Scottish sentiment,[13] vigorously articulated a sense of English nationhood distinct in territory, of course, but also distinct in time. In some of these tracts, England emerges as a latter-day community, superior to the barbarous antiquity—and historical obscurity—of the Britons. According to Sir Henry Spelman, one of the leading antiquaries of his day,

> if the honorable name of England be buried in the resurrection of Albion or Britannia, we shall change the golden beams of the sun for a

[12] For a useful background on the Union issue, see Brian Levack, *The Formation of the British State: England, Scotland, and the Union, 1603–1707* (Oxford: Clarendon Press, 1987).

[13] Anti-Union writers expressed xenophobic feelings intensely and repeatedly in this period. Francis Osborne characterized the Scots as mere thieves in his "Traditional Memoirs": "They beg our lands, our goods, our lives / They switch our nobles, and lie with our wives; / They pinch our gentry, and send for our benchers, / They stab our sargeants and pistol our fencers." Quoted from Levack, *Formation of the British State*, 195; see also 193–97.

cloudy day, and drown the glory of a nation triumphant through all the world to restore the memory of an obscure and barbarous people, of whom no mention almost is made in any notable history author but is either to their own disgrace or at least to grace the trophies and victories of their conquerors the Romans, Picts and Saxons.[14]

Spelman strikingly implies here a willingness to conceive of England as product of modernity, a community whose origins do not go back to the beginning of history but rather constitute merely one event of many within history. He does not deny that the Britons rather than the English derive from an ancient lineage but conceives of their antiquity as an obscurity. Articulating the English community in the present requires that one *not* remember ("resurrection," "memory") the British past. Pure, historically specific, and historically valid Englishness comes at the cost of an ancient heritage.

Many historical writers were unwilling to pay this cost, and this is why fiction emerges as so crucial to the issue of Union and nationhood. Arthur B. Ferguson has recently observed that, despite the historiographical skepticism during and after the late-Tudor period, "the English still needed a beginning . . . without finding a vanishing point for their historical perspective, they felt a sense of intellectual insecurity."[15] It is this sense of insecurity that made the prospect of a British Union attractive to some English historical writers. "British" history reached back to the early events of civilization, linked the nation to a classical past via the Trojans, and provided a King Arthur who maintained a thriving native Christian kingdom independent (it was claimed) of the Church of Rome. Philip Schwyzer describes the situation lucidly:

Whether or not they took any interest in Wales per se, [pro-Union writers] saw in Britain the potential for greatness to which mere Englishness—lacking the crucial advantages of antiquity and insularity—could never attain. To exchange England for Britain was to change some thou-

---

[14] Henry Spelman, "Of the Union" (date of composition, ca. 1604); printed in *The Jacobean Union: Six Tracts of 1604*, ed. Bruce R. Galloway and Brian P. Levack (Edinburgh: Scottish History Society, 1985), 170.

[15] Arthur B. Ferguson, *Utter Antiquity: Perceptions of Prehistory in Renaissance England* (Durham, N.C.: Duke University Press, 1993), 101.

sand years of chaos, strife, and a foreign yoke for two and a half millennia of history guided by divine providence and prophesy.[16]

Schwyzer, like several other recent critics,[17] goes on to characterize the Union debate's national question in terms of topography—the various indeterminate borders between England, Scotland, and Wales. These exemplary interpretations reveal that English identity was constituted not from within but rather on its periphery, in terms of the heterogeneity of a multinational context that the idea of Englishness both relied on and sought to repress.

Yet these discussions tend to overlook the manner in which the Union debate also produced a crisis of *historical* identity, forcing a choice between two versions of the national past that earlier Tudor writers had pretended were nearly identical. Arthur Kelton, celebrating the historical continuity that Geoffrey offered the nation—"How many kings successively, / One after other, here did remain / Of one dissent, line, and progeny"—could in 1547 blur the distinction between British and English in the extended title to his work: "... *Britons and Welshmen are Lineally Descended from Brute.*"[18] If "Welshmen" represent the modern-day inhabitants of Wales, then "Britons" must in some vague manner represent everyone else in England. The Union debates made such convenient blurring quite difficult, demanding a somewhat awkward choice between England or Britain. William Harbert, the Welsh author of the pro-Union *Prophecy of Cadwallader* (1604), in which he calls James I "our second Brute," wrote a less confident plea for Union two years later. *England's Sorrow, or, A Farewell to Essex* (1606) offers a national lament

---

[16] Philip Schwyzer, "Purity and Danger on the West Bank of the Severn: The Cultural Geography of *A Masque Presented at Ludlow Castle, 1634,*" *Representations* 60 (1997): 28.

[17] See, e.g., David Baker, "Imagining Britain: William Shakespeare's 'Henry V,'" *Shakespeare, Spenser, Marvell, and the Question of Britain* (Stanford: Stanford University Press, 1997), 17–65; and Claire McEachern, "Putting the 'Poly' Back into *Poly-Olbion*: British Union and the Borders of the English Nation," in *The Poetics of English Nationhood, 1590–1612* (Cambridge: Cambridge University Press, 1996), 138–91.

[18] Arthur Kelton, *Chronicle with a Genealogy* (London, 1547), sig. e4r, t.p. On Kelton's confusion, see Andrew King, *"The Faerie Queene" and Middle English Romance: The Matter of Just Memory* (Oxford: Clarendon Press, 2000), 176–78.

that we might see as the historical counterargument to Spelman's anti-Union demand for modern, knowable origins:

> Oh where is Britain? Where is she?
> What? Smothered in forgetful sepulcher?
> Exiled from man's reviving memory?
> Oh no, let England like a child prefer
> That well known title of her ancestor:
> I know the neighbor sisters of this Isle
> Will greatly glory in so good a style.[19]

Significantly, the initial question of location—*where* is the nation?—transforms into a question of *when* in the language of "forgetful sepulcher," "reviving memory," and "ancestor." In Harbert's view, "England" cannot simply merge into an ancient heritage but rather remains incomplete in itself. It is a child that will come into its true identity, and avoid a bastardizing modernity, by acknowledging its derivation from its parent, "Britain." Philemon Holland, the translator of Camden's *Britannia* in 1610, similarly links the issue of spatial and cultural unity to the recognition of British antiquity. Translating Camden's observation that the term "Britain" neared extinction during the Saxon period, Holland adds his own commentary to Camden's text:

> now after 800 years or thereabout come and gone, even while we are perusing this work, King James invested in the Monarchy of the whole Isle, by the propitious favor and grace of God. . . . to the end that this said Isle, which is one entire thing in itself, encircled within one compass of the Ocean . . . should also bear one name . . . Great Britain.[20]

The union of England and Scotland under James offers, in Holland's view, a powerful continuity in both time and space. The idea of Britain thus differed importantly from the Englishness of the Anglo-Saxonists: rather than national singularity, it promised a sense of

---

[19] William Harbert, *England's Sorrow, or A Farewell to Essex* (London, 1606), sig. B1r. Schwyzer ("Purity and Danger on the West Bank of the Severn," 27) quotes this passage to offer an example of the link between the river Severn and the Union debates in the seventeenth century.

[20] William Camden, *Britain*, trans. Philemon Holland (London, 1610), 141.

unity over cultural diversity, and rather than a distinct historical modernity, it offered the continuity of tradition.[21]

Unfortunately for Union advocates, fewer and fewer Englishmen believed that ancient British history was true. The minor irony of Holland's celebration of the British name is that he offers it in a translation of a text that convinced many readers after 1586 that early British history was in fact myth. One of the effects of a fabulous British past was to expose the proposed Union as a latter-day fiction. The unification of Britain represented for some English writers both a *restoration* of an ancient heritage and a fictive *novelty*, the artificial yoking together of the disparate traditional cultures of England, Scotland, and Wales. "Britain" thus emerges in some Union debate writing as simultaneously hoary and recent. Ben Jonson's *Masque of Blackness*, performed during the heat of the Union question in 1605, represents another example of the alienation of national space emerging from the alterity of national time. The masque shrewdly registers the nation's dependence on a peripheral otherness for its identity in that "Britannia" reacquires its ancient name only upon the arrival of Niger and his black Ethiopian daughters to the island:

> Britannia, which the triple world admires,
> This isle hath now recovered for her name;
> . . . .
> With that great name, Britannia, this blest isle
> Hath won her ancient dignity and style,
> *A world divided from the world*, and tried
> The abstract of it in his general pride.[22]

---

[21] This is not to say that all pro-Union writers insisted on Brutus as the island's historical founder. John Clapham, in his *History of England* (London, 1602), retitled *History of Great Britain* in 1606 to emphasize the pro-Union point, expressed doubt about Brutus and called the pre-Roman Britons barbarous. Edward Ayscu's *A History Containing the Wars, Treaties, Marriages, and Other Occurents between England and Scotland from King William the Conqueror, until the Happy Union of them Both in Our Gracious King James* (London, 1607) came to similar skeptical conclusions about his nation's early period. Nonetheless, most pro-Union writers accepted Brutus at least in order to highlight the Union's value as a form of antiquity.

[22] Ben Jonson, *Masque of Blackness* (1605); reprinted in *The Norton Anthology of English Literature*, 7th ed., 2 vols. (New York: Norton, 2000), 1:1295–1303, ll. 127–28, 132–35.

Here Jonson trumpets the twin advantages of union, insularity and antiquity. The passage presents Britannia as a restoration of tradition: the nation has "recovered" its name and thus its "ancient dignity." Immediately after this claim, however, Jonson notes the novelty of Britannia:

> For were the world, with all his wealth, a ring,
> Britannia (whose *new* name makes all tongues sing)
> Might be a diamond worthy to enchase it,
> Ruled by a sun, that to this height doth grace it.
>   (Ll. 136–39; my emphasis)

Although "new name" might carry the sense of "newly reinstated," it also calls attention to the identity of Britannia as a latter-day conceptualization, a conspicuously *invented* identity. In *Masque of Blackness*, the temporal ambiguity (ancient or new) of the British nation in the present functions as an analogue to the historical ambiguity (fact or fiction) of that nation's origin in the past—"whether fabulous or true," as Jonson puts it in the *Coronation Entertainment*. The threat of fiction makes Britain awkwardly older and newer than England, simultaneously.

This is not to say that defenses of the ancient British past and the *Historia Regum Britanniae* as authentic history ended altogether after Camden. Far from it. Yet such defenses had to finesse the question of historical authenticity even more delicately than earlier Tudor defenses did. Edmund Bolton, a friend of Sir Robert Cotton, who for a short time assisted John Speed with his *History of Great Britain*, argued for the validity of the *Historia* in a theoretical treatise about historiography that clearly reflected the demands of national origin. Bolton never published *Hypercritica*, and probably wrote most of it in 1621, after the hopes for a British Union were mostly dead.[23] Yet the treatise is very sensitive to effects of the Union debate on national historiography. Metaphorizing the telling of history as navigation, Bolton explains that

there is a Necessity to sail through the National Quarrels of Britain, which the Union wisheth should be forgotten, but that the Adamantine

---

[23] On the date of the text's composition, see D. R. Woolf, *The Idea of History in Early Stuart England* (Toronto: University of Toronto Press, 1990), 192 n. 67.

Laws and Nature of the Task permits it not, and may be called the Quarrel of Nations. And these Winds and Tempests are the Reason why the mutual Victories and Overthrows between England and Scots, and between English and Welsh, and between English and Irish, etc., are never related with sufficient Freedom or Sincerity by newest Historians.[24]

Like Jonson, Bolton recognizes that contemporary "Britain" itself is a kind of fiction, a convenient construct for promoting unity in the present, erasing or revising the truth of history. The truth of history resists the effects of this "imagined community," to borrow Anderson's well-known phrase. Indeed, Bolton's treatment of the Union question reveals a limit of Anderson's thesis for nationhood: some communities, Bolton implies, are more imagined than others, and their members will not always accept their pasts as overtly *imaginary*. Bolton's treatise is in fact characteristic of early-Stuart historiography in its demand for objectivity and accuracy in historical method, repeatedly asserting sentiments such as "truth is the sovereign praise of an History" and "indifference and even dealing are the Glory of Historians" (85, 91). Bolton seems ready to subordinate both Union and temporal continuity for the sake of historical truth, in which the national past comprises a series of changes and conflicts.

Yet the treatise is also characteristic of much early-Stuart historiography in its quiet acknowledgment that a history of discontinuity may not be sufficient. When coming to Geoffrey's *Historia*, Bolton begins to sound like his more lenient Tudor predecessors:

> There is a great complaint among some of the most Learned, against *Galfridus Arthurius*, or *Galfridus Monumenthensis*, for want of Truth and Modesty, as creating a Brute unto us for the Founder of our *Britain*. But who is he that, proving it to be a Fiction, can prove it withal to be his? If that Work be quite abolished, there is a vast Blank upon the Times of our Country, from the Creation of the World till the coming of *Julius Caesar*, not *terra incognita* it self being less to be known then ours. . . . Nevertheless out of that very Story (let it be what it will) have Titles been framed in open Parliament, both in *England* and *Ireland*, for the Rights of the Crown of *England*, even to entire Kingdoms. And

---

[24] Edmund Bolton, *Hypercritica*; reprinted in *Critical Essays of the Seventeenth Century, 1605–1650*, 3 vols., ed. J. E. Springarn (Oxford: Clarendon Press, 1908), 1:105–6.

though no Parliament can make that to be a Truth which is not such in the proper Nature thereof . . . yet are we somewhat the more, and rather tied to look with favour on the Case. Therefore it pleased me well, what once I did read in a great Divine, that *in Apocryphis non omnia esse Apocrypha*. And that very much of *Monmouths* book, or pretended Translation *de Origine & gestis Britannorum* be granted to be fabulous, yet many Truths are mixed. (86)

Bolton rehearses the standard Tudor line that a few falsehoods do not invalidate a work of history as a whole. Yet the contradiction here is much starker than in Lambard, because the Tudor writer made no programmatic claims about the necessary objectivity of the historian. Lambard in 1576 privileges national continuity over historical accuracy; Bolton in 1621 tries to privilege both. Bolton relents on his demand for historical truth only in the case of English history, treating that history as a special exception because it stands in such desperate need of a narrative, threatened by a "Vast Blank." Yet the exceptionality of the English past forces him into methodological inconsistency, leading him to assert truth's invulnerability to human bias and will (the votes of "Parliament") and yet also acknowledge truth's susceptibility to interpretation, the imperative "to look with favour on the Case." National history, he implies, may require a certain tolerance of fiction. Yet it is a requirement that he cannot fully accept. After defending Geoffrey at some length (86–91), and after acknowledging the nation's need for historical continuity—"I incline very strongly to have so much of every Historical Monument or Historical Tradition maintained, as may well be holden without open absurdity"—Bolton reveals the limited value of a quasi-fictional heritage: "My Histories notwithstanding begin at *Julius Caesar*" (91). Bolton will abstractly concede the need for an ancient British past to fill in the "vast Blank," but cannot bring himself to describe what such a history would be like. Indeed, in his following brief summary of the necessary "parts" of a national history, he begins with "The Roman Period" (100). National history ought to begin with the ancient Britons, but one can only tell it from the Roman Conquest; historians should strive for historical accuracy above all but ought also to regard national tradition; history exposes discord, but it creates unity. The inconsistencies of *Hypercritica* are more intense than other historical writing of the period in quantity rather than in quality. English writers like Bolton, unwilling simply to settle on a late-Saxon beginning, struggled between two irreconcilable imperatives: the need for historical continuity and the fact of historical loss.

This problem forces me to clarify my earlier assertion that the British history served as a "useful fable" for post-Camden writers. In fact, the English could not so simply replace a historical origin with a purely fictional or even purely exemplary one, tempting as it might be. Regarding exemplarity, we might have expected historians simply to place the *Historia Regum Britanniae* in the same category as certain classical histories such as the *Cyropaedia*, the historical accuracy of which humanists usually subordinated to moral value. Thomas Blundeville's important theoretical treatise, *The True Order and Method of Writing and Reading Histories* (1574), despite its insistence that historians faithfully describe what happened in the past, expresses contempt for scholars without a moral understanding of the past, who "having consumed all their life time in histories, do know nothing in the end, but the descents, genealogies, and pedigrees of noble men, and when such a king or Emperor reigned, and such like stuff."[25] Why not treat the *Historia* as an exemplary story without worrying too much about its accuracy? Yet although Renaissance writers found it easy to do this with Greek and Latin histories, they came to Geoffrey with a special need: they wanted an origin. National history had to tell them not only how to behave virtuously but also from where they came, making dates, names, and "such like stuff" indispensable.

The *Historia*'s etiological function similarly resisted its transformation into pure fictionality, despite the manner in which the category of historical fiction—what Renaissance writers often called "poesie historical"—sometimes encompassed fully invented narratives. George Puttenham could approvingly say of historical poets in general that they "used not the matter so precisely to wish that all they wrote should be accounted true" and that some of their narratives were "wholly false."[26] Yet the requirements of national history demanded that *some* of what Geoffrey wrote should be accounted true. Even Ben Jonson's cavalier acceptance of a fictionalized past— "we choose to follow the received story of *Brute*, whether fabulous or

---

[25] Thomas Blundeville, *The True Order and Method of Writing and Reading Histories* (London, 1574); reprinted in *Huntington Library Quarterly* 2 (1940): 149–70.
[26] George Puttenham, *The Arte of English Poesie* (London, 1589), reprinted in *The Arte of English Poesie: A Facsimile Reproduction* (Kent, Ohio: Kent State University Press, 1970), 55.

true"—has not absolutely given up on the hope for historical credibility: the story might, after all, be true. The *Historia* could not, as pure fiction, satisfy England's etiological need; it had to function in the threshold space between fact and fable, as historical fiction.

Arthur Ferguson's recent discussion of "poesie historical" properly characterizes the genre as a "hybrid concept" and suggests that in the sixteenth century it "could lay credible claim to the as yet ill-defined region between fact and fiction."[27] His learned study clarifies the status of poetry in relation to Renaissance debates about history and myth, but may slightly underestimate the degree to which a hybrid "poesie historical" emerged as a *forced* position for some national historians. They could see the dichotomous effects of historical fiction only as a mixed blessing, the answer to their problem and the sign of their problem's inevitability. On the one hand, fiction filled in the gap between past and present opened by a lack of records or a failure of memory; on the other hand, fiction threatened the hard-gained (albeit limited) knowledge of the ancient past with its contaminating emptiness, causing "the truth it self to be doubted of," as Dee complained. Fiction thus emerged as a compromise measure, better than nothing but not as good as a fully credible origin. After all, the strict rule of historical accuracy might encourage Bolton to drop the entire British pretense, but his nation is, as he notes, "*tied* to look with favour on the Case" (my emphasis). Indeed, for all its promise of continuity, fiction to some degree replicated the etiological paradox of national historiography, in which the effort to find an origin called attention to its absence. To avail ourselves again of Certeau's notion of the uncanny effect of modern historiography: "it is an odd procedure that posits death, a breakage everywhere reiterated in discourse, and that yet denies loss by appropriating to the present the privilege of recapitulating the past as a form of knowledge."[28] Jonson's "want" of a founder, Harbart's "forgetful sepulcher," Bolton's "vast blank"—national historiography takes these figures as its motivating starting point and uncannily returns to them as its conclusion. Fiction bridged the empty gap between past and present and yet emerged as empty itself, to some degree, replacing one absence with another. English writers needed fiction to fill out the historical narrative, embel-

---

[27] Ferguson, *Utter Antiquity*, 120, 122.
[28] Michel de Certeau, *The Writing of History*, trans. Tom Conley (New York: Columbia University Press, 1988), 5.

lishing it on the outside, so to speak, making it easier to see. This outside decoration, however, threatened to turn history into *mere* ornament, an external form with no inner substance.

Of course, the Renaissance treated poetry as an "ornament" in both senses. The ornamental quality of verse, its use of sound and rhetorical figures, added the trimmings of beauty and delight to poetry and yet also constituted poetry's very being. George Puttenham, in a chapter of his treatise titled "Of Ornament Poetical," employs a common body and clothes metaphor to describe the relationship between poetry and poetic figure:

> And as we see in these great Madams of honor, be they for personage or otherwise never so comely and beautiful, yet if they want their courtly habiliments or at leastwise such other apparel as custom and civility have ordained to cover their naked bodies, would be half ashamed or greatly out of countenance to be seen in that sort and perchance do then think themselves more amiable in every man's eye when they be in their richest attire, suppose of silks or tissues and costly embroideries, than when they go in cloth or in any other plain and simple apparel. Even so cannot our vulgar Poesy show itself either gallant or gorgeous, if any limb be left naked and bare and not clad in his kindly clothes and colors, such as may convey them somewhat out of sight, that is, from the common course of ordinary speech and capacity of the vulgar judgment.[29]

Like women's bodies, poetry possesses neither dignity nor maximum beauty without ornament. Poetic figure serves as the clothing to poetry's otherwise naked body. The question remains, of course, as to whether such clothing might also artificially conceal poetry's inherent loveliness. Puttenham teasingly glances at this possibility by encouraging his readers to imagine the naked, desirable woman under the fine clothes. He appears to compromise finally on the inner/outer beauty issue by characterizing poetic ornament as a natural part of poetry ("kindly clothes") rather than as only an artificial addition. Ornament may cover poetry on the outside, but poetry is not really poetry without it.

Poetic theory regularly reveals this ambiguity about whether ornament resides on the outside or inside of poetry. Some versions of the

[29] Puttenham, *Arte of English Poesie*, 149.

relationship treat ornament as an external and nonessential, even distracting, element of poetry. Sidney insisted that prose counted as poetry, "verse being but an ornament and no cause to poetry."[30] In his *Timber*, Jonson similarly conceives of ornament as merely extra, noting approvingly the opinion of a poet he once knew: "For he denied figures to be invented for ornament, but for aid; and still thought it an extreme madness to bend, or wrest that which ought to be right." Ornament represents that aspect of poetic figure that distorts rather than assists poetry's natural effects. Like Puttenham, Jonson employs the body and clothes metaphor but emphasizes the effect of deceitful concealment: "For whilst they think to justify their ignorance by impudence, and their persons by clothes, and outward ornaments, they use but a commission to deceive themselves."[31] The ambiguity of ornament's location, outside on the body or inherently inside, persists when writers try to define the proper relation between fiction and history. To return to Ralegh's observation about historians in his *History of the World:*

> For it was well noted by that worthy Gentleman Sir Philip Sidney, that Historians do borrow of Poets, not only much of their ornament, but somewhat of their substance. Informations are often false, records not always true, and notorious actions commonly insufficient to discover the passions, which did sent them first on foot.[32]

As often happens in Renaissance descriptions of historical poetry, ornament slides into substance, the exterior becomes interior. Ralegh suggests that fiction does provide a substance for historians, filling in the gaps when data are missing but not filling them in with truth. *The substance of fiction makes history itself ornamental.*

The "ornament" goes a long way in explaining the Renaissance link between history and poetry. It captures fiction's identity as a *supplement* to history, an addition that both repairs and calls attention to an original lack, in the manner Derrida has so influentially de-

---

[30] Philip Sidney, *An Apology for Poetry*, ed. Forrest G. Robinson (New York: Macmillan, 1985), 21.

[31] Ben Jonson, *Timber, or Discoveries*, ed. Ralph S. Walker (Syracuse, N.Y.: Syracuse University Press, 1953), 40, 32.

[32] Ralegh, *Selected Writings*, 170.

scribed.[33] Yet it also articulates the Renaissance conception of poetry as both grand and inconsequential, the memorial of kings and Sidney's "ink-wasting toy." We should keep in mind that church furnishings, the decorative objects that Reformation debates labeled as either useful props or empty idols, were called "ornaments."[34] The ornament oscillates between the real and unreal, the useful trimming and the empty distraction. Both Spenser and Milton rely on the figure of the ornament to articulate their sense of the relationship between history and poetry. For both writers, ornamental fiction serves as a compromise between their nation's need for historical continuity and the fact of historical loss. In *The Faerie Queene* Spenser uses fiction as a threshold figure that engages the uncanny gap between past and present, an ornament that puts living flesh on the bones of history. In his *History of Britain* Milton similarly tries to use fiction as an ornament of history, clothing the naked body of truth with the trappings of poetic invention. For both writers, ornamental fiction revives the national past and yet threatens to turn that past into an empty shell, void of the substance of truth.

Before we turn to Spenser and Milton, however, I examine briefly one more example of the link between the Union debate and the problem of historical fiction. It perhaps seems peculiar to contextualize a study of Spenser and Milton with this debate, because Spenser writes over a decade before the crisis begins and Milton writes two decades after Union hopes were dead. Yet *The Faerie Queene* anticipates, and the *History of Britain* reflects, the painful sense of historical heterogeneity that the Union debates thematized in the early seventeenth century. Like Jonson and Bolton, Spenser and Milton see

[33] Jacques Derrida, "Structure, Sign, Play in the Discourse of the Human Sciences," in *Writing and Difference* (Chicago: Chicago University Press, 1978), 278–93, esp. 289.

[34] *OED*, s.v. "ornament,"definition 1b, quotes two examples: "such ornaments of the Church, and of the ministers, shall be retained" (*Act of Uniformity* [1559]); and "the inventory of all the popish ornaments that remained at the Church of Calsterworth" (*English Church Furnishings* [1565]). Spenser, in two contexts involving ambiguous church spaces, chooses to use the term in *The Faerie Queene*. The first is Kirkrapine's notoriously problematic church spoliations, in which he robs temples "of their ornaments" (I.i.17.2)—are these ornaments sacred or idolatrous? The second follows the masque of Cupid, when Britomart, trapped in Busyrane's second room, spends her time "gazing on that Chambers ornament" (III.xii.29.2)—are these ornaments appropriate or inappropriate objects of Britomart's attention?

that to abandon fables is also to risk losing ancient and pure origins, to consign the nation to Spelman's belated modernity. Both authors explore the idea that fiction, as an ornament to history, might mitigate this historical heterogeneity, producing a greater sense of unity in the national past. In this regard, *The Faerie Queene* and the *History of Britain*, despite their historical and generic disparities, both bear an important affinity with Michael Drayton's *Poly-Olbion*.

Several critics have appropriately described *Poly-Olbion* (1612, 1622) as a Union debate poem, because it engages the British and Saxon past as a means to interpret the relation between the various localities of the nation. Songs IV–IX in particular feature a debate between the Welsh and English rivers, appealing respectively to British and Saxon traditions. As chorography, *Poly-Olbion*'s spatial effects are diverse: critics have characterized the poem as a subordination of monarchy to national space, as a mournful epitaph for the failed Union, and as a celebration of regional, local identity within the nation.[35] Yet critics tend to agree about its historical duality, the division between Drayton's credulous assertions about Britain's ancient past and John Selden's skeptical annotations urging readers not to mistake poetry for history. D. R. Woolf has said of *Poly-Olbion* that "poetry and history were never split further apart than in this work where they alternate."[36] Ferguson suggests that Drayton had no real historical intentions but rather asked Selden to do the historical annotations "so that he might leave himself free to serve more freely in his chosen capacity as poet."[37] Yet although the division between the verse and the annotations is undeniable, each "side" of the text is itself internally divided between history and fiction. Within his fable of talking rivers, Drayton does in fact have serious historical purposes. He complains in his preface that many readers would "rather read the fantasies of forraine inventions, than to see the Rarities and Historie of their owne Country delivered by a true native Muse."[38]

---

[35] Subordination of monarchy: Richard Helgerson, *Forms of Nationhood: The Elizabethan Writing of England* (Chicago: University of Chicago Press, 1992), 107–47 (esp. 117–20), 139–46; mournful epitaph: Schwyzer, "Purity and Danger on the West Bank of the Severn," 28–31; celebration of the local: McEachern, "Putting the 'Poly' Back into *Poly-Olbion*," 138–91.

[36] Woolf, *Idea of History*, 212.

[37] Ferguson, *Utter Antiquity*, 128.

[38] *The Works of Michael Drayton*, ed. J. William Hebel, 4 vols. (Oxford: Shakespeare Head Press, 1933), 4:v*. Subsequent parenthetical references to prose passages

He offers instead (albeit through his topographical characters) the story of "Britain-founding Brute" (1:310) and "Arthur's ancient seat, / Which made the Britaines name through all the world so great" (3:395–96), expressing dismay that his countrymen now doubt the literal truth of the Lord of Camelot: "Ignorance has brought the world to such a pass / As now, which scarce believes that Arthur ever was" (6:273–74). His repeated invocation of "ancient Bards" does not represent only a poetic gesture but rather, as John E. Curran, Jr., has shown, harkens back to Tudor antiquarian debates about the likelihood that pre-Roman British poets may have preserved their history in popular songs, making Geoffrey's *Historia* a written record of an authentic oral tradition.[39] Rather than abandoning historical accuracy, Drayton implies that ancient British history is stable enough to endure poetic ornamentation without damage. In his preface he urges his readers not "to remaine in the thick fogs and mists of ignorance" but rather to "see the ancient people of this Ile delivered thee in their lively images" (v*). "Lively images" represents his conception of fiction as ornament—helpful elaboration of historical truths, bringing life and vigor to ancient events.

Selden's annotations likewise mix history and fiction, despite the scholar's hostility toward stories of the ancient British past. He makes clear in his introduction that the presence of fiction in putatively historical accounts of the nation activates his critical faculties:

And indeed my jealousy hath oft vexed me with particular inquisition of whatsoever occurs, bearing not a mark of most apparent Truth, ever since I found so intolerable Antichronisms, incredible reports, and Bardish impostures, as well from Ignorance as assumed liberty of Invention in some of our Ancients; and read also such palpable Fauxeties, of our Nation, thrust into the World by Later Time. (viii*)

Fiction attacks the truth on both ends of history, initiated by the ancients and extended by latter-day national partisans. To the degree that he condemns fabled origins, his comments resemble Sir Henry Spelman's demand that the nation give up unverifiable tradition and

---

are by page numbers in this edition, whereas references to verse are by book and line number.

[39] John E. Curran, Jr., "The History Never Written: Bards, Druids, and the Problem of Antiquarianism in *Poly-Olbion*," *Renaissance Quarterly* 51, 2 (1998): 498–525.

accept a more recent starting point. Like Bolton, Selden implies that the English have an unusually difficult time coming to terms with their past, lamenting in the "illustrations" to book 1 that England seems to be the only modern nation still trying to maintain a fictional heritage:

> and indeed, this critique age scarce any longer endures any nation, their first supposed Authors name, not Italus to the Italians, not Hispalus to the Spaniard, Bato to the Hollander, Brabo to the Brabantine, Francio to the French, Celtes to the Celt, Galathes to the Gaul, Scota to the Scot; no, nor scarce Romulus to his Rome, because of their unlikely and fictitious mixtures. (21)

Other nations have thrown off their invented eponymous founders; why can't England? Yet Selden's invocation of "this critique age" is not without ambivalence. He recognizes that the denial of a founder produces anxiety as well as clear-sighted truth. Indeed, shortly after the previously quoted passage, Selden relents on his characterization of historical credulity as an especially English failing, describing the Briton/Welsh story symptomatic of a larger, European pathology: "These things are the more enforced by Cambro-Britons, through that universal desire, bewitching our Europe, to derive their blood from Trojans" (22). Selden then makes a halfhearted concession about early national history and the Brutus story: "Briefly, seeing no National story, except such as Thucydides, Xenophon, Polybius, Caesar, Tacitus, Procopius, Cantacuzen, the late Guicciardin, Commines, Macchiavel, and their like, which were employed in the state of their times, can justify themselves but by tradition . . . you shall enough please Saturn and Mercury, presidents of antiquity and learning, if with the Author you foster this belief" (22–23). In a sense, the brilliance of Selden's sentence resides in its successful effort to say nothing definitely. We can only "justify" the national story by means of tradition, not history alone, which suggests that the English past will remain incomplete without recourse to fiction. Yet fiction here continues to be alien to history, because belief in Brutus will please not history's patron, Clio, but only the poetic figures of Saturn and Mercury. Indeed, Selden undercuts his assertion that no nation can justify its past without tradition by inserting, as a subordinate clause, a list of ten writers who justify their nations with history. Selden grants the English need for tradition but continues to see it as a disruption of historical truth. As Anne Lake Prescott suggests of Selden, "his notes are . . . a study in urbane ambivalence."[40]

Drayton's ambivalence emerges from the other side of the problem. That is, he grants the need for historical truth but continues to regard such truth as the annihilation of the national past. Ornamental poetry, ostensibly decorating the facts of history, ends up constituting the soil out of which those facts can grow in this first place. Defending the historical existence of Arthur, Drayton explains how a few fictions in past accounts of the British king have created unwarranted skepticism in modern readers. Initially, his comments resemble John Dee's complaint that past fictions have caused "the truth it self to be doubted of":

> Some credulous Ages layd
> Slight fictions with the truth, whilst truth on rumor stayd;
> And that one forward Time (perceiving the neglect
> A former of her had) to purchase her respect,
> With toyes then trimd her up, the drowsie world t'allure,
> And lent her what it thought might appetite procure
> To man, whose mind doth still varietie pursue;
> And therefore to those things whose grounds were verie true,
> Though naked yet and bare (not having to content
> The weyward curious eare) gave fictive ornament.
>
> (6:277–86)

Fiction continues here as the ornament of solid truth, but its effects are more negative than in Drayton's earlier recommendation of "lively images." Historical truths are the "grounds" of the Arthur story, but they no longer compel respect on their own, "naked yet and bare" like Puttenham's embarrassed ladies. Past generations applied "fictive ornament" to these grounds, using fables as the "toyes" that "trimd" historical truth with pleasing extras, gaining the attention of a bored audience, a bit like Sidney's poet who entices the recalcitrant reader to virtue by hiding moral lessons in fictions "as have a pleasant taste."[41] Yet the exemplary function of poetry will not serve Drayton's etiological need, because the presence of fiction has produced calamitous skepticism among the English readership. Dray-

---

[40] Anne Lake Prescott, "Drayton's Muse and Selden's 'Story': The Interfacing of Poetry and History in *Poly-Olbion*," *Studies in Philology* 87, 1 (1990): 128–35.

[41] Sidney, *Apology for Poetry*, 38.

ton's double bind is that while fiction makes the past interesting, it also makes the past incredible. This dilemma grows worse as Drayton shifts his argument to defend fiction as the necessary medium of history:

> And surelie I suppose, that which this forward time
> Doth scandalize her with to be her heinous crime,
> That hath her most preserv'd: for, still where wit hath found
> A thing most cleerlie true, it made that, fictions ground:
> Which shee suppos'd might give sure colour to them both:
> From which, as from a roote, this wondred error grow'th
> At which our Cricticks gird, whose judgements are so strict,
> And he the bravest man who can contradict
> That which decrepit Age (which forced is to leane
> Upon Tradition) tells; esteeming it so meane,
> As they it quite reject, and for some trifling thing
> (Which Time hath pind to Truth) they all away will fling.
>
> (6:289–300)

Fiction oscillates between the ornament of the past and its substance in these verses. Human wit, Drayton suggests, makes historical truth the "ground" of fiction, as earlier, but after line 292 we cannot be sure which is ground and which is trimming. The fiction–history relationship gives "colour"—figural elaboration—to "both" history and fiction (fiction no longer simply ornaments history), and this relationship turns into the "roote" from which emerges a false, unbelievable history. Fiction provides the needed medium—indeed, the ground—for history's survival, but fiction contaminates and ruins history in the process. Small wonder, then, that when Drayton restates Selden's concession that national history needs "Tradition," he redescribes fable as "some trifling thing / (Which Time hath pind to Truth)." This recategorization of fiction as decoration and history as content compensates for the painful observation Drayton has already made: fiction is a trifling ornament that allows ancient history to reach the present at all.

Drayton and Selden are thus not simply opposed as antiquarian and poet, but rather the obscure origin of their nation divides each of them between these two roles. They both acknowledge, in fact, that early history "forced is to leane / Upon tradition," much as Bolton concedes that his nation is "tied to look with favour on the Case." This is the sense in which a hybrid "poesie historical" emerges as a forced position for these early Stuart writers, torn between a need for origin and an increasing historiographical skepticism, compelled by the Union question to choose between a truncated though verifiable Saxon history or an ancient but fabulous British one. It is of course tempting to read this early-modern perception of the necessary presence of fiction in history as a postmodern insight about the invented quality of all historical facts and all origins. Yet to do so with too much abandon obscures the dilemma that Bolton, Selden, and Drayton faced in their historical moment. They indirectly concede the fictiveness of origins and yet also insist that such an origin could never be etiologically valid. They struggle with the suspicion, voiced obliquely by Spelman, that the English nation may be a relative novelty, a product of latter-day history whose beginnings do not extend to antiquity, and at the same time they find this suspicion intolerable, continuing to search for their lost past. It is this ghostly sense of a past, one there and not there, that Spenser engages in his own "poesie historical," *The Faerie Queene*.

Spenser and the Fiction of Life and Death

Ruines of Rome, a poem very much concerned with the physical remains of the past, speaks directly to Spenser's anxiety about the antiquarian understanding of history:

> O mervelous great change:
> Rome living, was the worlds sole ornament,
> And dead, is now the worlds sole moniment.[42]

As we saw in chapter 2, the material monument, ostensibly a means to recover the past, threatens to lose that past in its self-consuming transience. Arthur's *Briton moniments* (*FQ* II.x) ends prematurely with a "there" on the last page, the mark of history's physical presence and its material interruption. Similarly, in the passage just quoted, Rome as the world's "moniment" represents the physical

---

[42] Edmund Spenser, *Ruines of Rome*, 11. 404–6, in *The Yale Edition of the Shorter Poems of Edmund Spenser*, ed. William A. Oram, Einar Bjorvand, Roland Bond, Thomas H. Cain, Alexander Dunlop, and Richard Schell (New Haven: Yale University Press, 1989).

tomb of history, the death of the past. Yet Rome as "ornament" expresses a living history, as if ornamental expression could redeem or
resurrect the monument as a vital posterity. Of course, in Spenser's
pessimistic translation of Du Bellay's pessimistic poem, the process
only works in one direction, from ornament to monument, from life
to death. Yet in other parts of his oeuvre, Spenser explores the possibility that fiction, as the ornament of history, could reverse the process and raise his nation's past from the dead. He is sensitive to the
risk of fictional ornament, its tendency to shift from trimming to entire substance, and his use of the word in general ranges from the
sense of "just elaboration" to "dangerous distraction."[43] Yet Spenser,
like most of his peers, unwilling to accept an entirely fabulous national origin, takes seriously the notion of a hybrid "poesie historical" wherein fiction supplements historical facts. To the degree that
he imagines this hybrid as successful, fiction's ornamentation of history works like Drayton's "lively images," putting flesh on the bones
of the past. If the monument and prophecy constitute one axis of
Spenser's engagement of his nation's past, the other axis involves the
interplay of fiction and history.

Spenser does not ignore the double-edged quality of fable but acknowledges it and even exploits it. Much as *Briton moniments* (*FQ*
II.x) and Merlin's prophecy (III.iii) explore both the capacities and
limitations of monumental and prophetic history, *The Faerie Queene*
dramatizes fiction's ability to both enliven and empty out the historical content of his national narratives. Spenser values ornamental fiction as a form of temporal continuity but also values the potential
emptiness of fiction as a means to acknowledge the tentative link the
nation in fact has with its origins. In as far as his historical poetry is
partially fictional, Spenser can creatively imagine a strong continuity
in British history, even if not entirely supported by the "hard facts" of
his documentary sources. Yet, in making this fictionality conspicuous, Spenser to some degree accepts the uncanny gap that reasserts itself in the English historical narrative. This relation, ideally, allows
Spenser to avoid simply fictionalizing the narrative of English history
(which would empty out all historical content from the continuity he

---

[43] The opposite senses sometimes appear in close proximity in *The Faerie Queene*.
The holy cross on Redcross Knight's shield "is set for ornament" (II.i.27.7), whereas
Arthur strips Duessa of her "proud ornaments" (II.i.22.6).

seeks), while acknowledging that without the fiction of poetry, this history is divided and incomplete. Spenser thus places poetry within the gap between England's past and present. Over twenty years ago, Michael O'Connell suggested a similar function for Spenser's poetry when he observed that in *The Faerie Queene*, "we find it is poetry which stands between history and the present."[44] Yet O'Connell did not sufficiently recognize the elusiveness of this "between," because in fiction the threshold between past and present is liminal—both a link and a gap, both presence and absence. Poetry's position between history and the present results not only from the fullness of poetry but also from the lack that marks history. Spenser's historical fiction represents, in Certeau's words, "a labor of death and a labor against death."[45]

Of course, my claim that Spenser takes early national history seriously *as history* goes against the grain of recent criticism, much of which contends either that Spenser disbelieved Geoffrey's narrative entirely or that the question of historical accuracy is irrelevant to Spenser's true purposes.[46] To do so, however, makes the unlikely assumption that Spenser was somehow ignorant of, indifferent to, or immune to the historiographical controversy surrounding the figure of Arthur and the *Historia*, and that he believed he could employ Arthur without invoking that controversy for his readership. As I hope the preceding section of this chapter shows, Camden's *Britannia* did not end this controversy in 1586. If any thing, his comments and ambiguous conclusions fueled the fire of the debate about the historical status of figures like Brutus and Arthur. Hence the archival rigor of the two national histories in *The Faerie Queene* (II.x and III.iii), in which Spenser consults, follows, and revises his sources with what appears to be great historiographical care. Even scholars who take seriously the issue of historical controversy surrounding

[44] Michael O'Connell, "History and the Poet's Golden World: The Epic Catalogue in *The Faerie Queene*," *English Literary Renaissance* 4, 2 (1974): 242.

[45] Certeau, *Writing of History*, 5.

[46] T. D. Kendrick saw Spenser's treatment of the Brutus story as one of incredulous amusement (*British Antiquity*, 126–29). Ferguson similarly claims that Spenser imagines *Briton moniments* as fanciful as *Antiquitie of Faerie lond* (*Utter Antiquity*, 124). Andrew King offers a subtler sense of Spenser's historical problem but also asserts that "Arthur's historicity" is not at stake in *The Faerie Queene* ("*Faerie Queene*" and Middle English Romance, 180).

Arthur often emphasize the exemplary rather than etiological force of the poem's historical dimension.[47] Yet although Spenser certainly believes, like everyone else in the sixteenth century, that history ought to teach virtue to the present, he does not accept an exemplary fable over a true etiology without a qualm. Spenser does perceive that, after Camden, some fiction may be unavoidable, but he still hopes to identify a starting point not entirely fictional, a historical lineage from which his monarch and nation "derived arre" (II.x.4.2). The letter to Ralegh confirms this balance between the exemplary and etiological value of history, offering comments that strongly imply, contra Puttenham,[48] that the "poet historical" must preserve at least some historical accuracy in his narratives. Despite what some critics suggest, Spenser here distinguishes between the poet historical and the historiographer *not* in terms of fact and fiction—which would simply free the poet historical from the constraints of fact—but rather in terms of the order of their narratives.[49] Furthermore, Spenser appears confident that even a "fact-based" poet historical will be able to offer moral lessons, suggesting in his letter (contra Sidney) that history can

[47] For example, John E. Curran, Jr., offers an excellent account of how Camden's skepticism about the *Historia Regum Britanniae* influenced Spenser's account of British history in *Briton moniments;* Curran, "Spenser and the Historical Revolution: *Briton Moniments* and the Problem of Roman Britain," *Clio* 25, 3 (1996): 273–92. Curran discusses Spenser's historical crisis in terms of "the Galfridian form of patriotism" (276) and history's relation to "glory" (292). Yet Camden did not think he was being unpatriotic when he expressed modest doubts about Geoffrey, and Spenser's *View of the State of Ireland*, as we will see, expresses a strong patriotism while condemning fictionalized origins. The Tudor Geoffrey-defenders were not more patriotic than the skeptics, but they did feel the need for an ancient past more urgently. *Briton moniments*'s conflict is not only between glory and historical truth but also between etiology and historical loss.

[48] Puttenham, *Arte of English Poesie*, 55.

[49] S. K. Heninger argues for the fact–fiction distinction: " 'An historicall fiction,' then, is a story which has been made by an author as opposed to the accurate account of an actual occurrence. . . . Later in the Letter, Spenser will differentiate between the method of 'a Poet historical' and that of 'an Historiographer' in exactly these terms"; Heninger, *Sidney and Spenser: The Poet as Maker* (University Park: Pennsylvania State University Press, 1989), 379. Yet Spenser makes his distinction between chronology and *récit*, not between fictiveness and accuracy: "an Historiographer discourseth of affairs orderly as they were done, accounting as well the times as the actions, but a Poet thrusteth into the middest, even where it most concerneth him"; Spenser, "Letter of Authors," in *The Faerie Queene*, ed. A. C. Hamilton (New York: Longman, 2001), 716.

teach virtue as well as can fiction.[50] The historical poet therefore need not abandon fact for fable in order to fulfill his moral purposes. The letter even registers a concern about the potential misuse of poetic narratives, voicing an annoyed condescension toward those readers who read fiction for the sake of its "variety of matter" rather than for "profite of the ensample."

Spenser's serious though conflicted attitude toward national origins and their relation to fiction also appears in *A View of the State of Ireland*. Scholars have long called attention to the skeptical comments about Brutus in a cancelled passage of the treatise, in which Irenius, mocking the Irish pretension of a Spanish origin, concedes that "the Irish do herein no otherwise than our vain Englishmen do in the Tale of Brutus, whom they devise to have first conquered and inhabited this land, it being impossible to prove that there was ever any such Brutus of Albion or England, as it is that there was any such Gathelus of Spain."[51] If we assume that Irenius speaks directly for Spenser, and that Spenser's historical ambivalence played no part in the cancellation of this passage in all but one manuscript of the *View*, then these comments represent disbelief indeed. Slightly later, however, arguing for the historical subjection of Ireland to England, Irenius insists that "it appeareth by good record yet extant, that King Arthur, and before him Gurgunt [i.e., Geoffrey's "Gurguit"], had all that island in his allegiance and subjection" (52). Here Irenius, and perhaps Spenser, seems to accept the historical existence of two ancient English kings—Arthur and Gurguit—mentioned in the *Historia*. Andrew Hadfield has persuasively argued that Spenser's credulity

---

[50] For example, Sidney praises Xenophon for using fiction to beautify some of the events surrounding Cyrus's reign, a gesture that proves, according to Sidney, that fable teaches virtue more ably than does history (Sidney, *Apology for Poetry*, 33–34). Spenser, by contrast, distinguishes Xenophon not from the historian but rather from the philosopher (Plato), offering no hint that the historical content of the narrative impedes its exemplary function. If anything, Xenophon's poetic modifications come under Spenser's censure that nowadays "nothing [is] esteemed of, that is not delightful and pleasing to common sense"; "Letter of the Authors," 716. On Spenser's admiration of history in the letter, see also Wayne Erickson, *Mapping "The Faerie Queene": Quest Structures and the World of the Poem* (New York: Garland, 1996), 22–24.

[51] *View of the State of Ireland*, 44. For an account of this passage's absence in the manuscripts, see *Spenser's Prose Works*, ed. Rudolf Gottfried, Variorum Spenser (Baltimore: Johns Hopkins Press, 1949), 86, 506–16.

about Arthur derives in part from the willingness of some Renaissance historiographers to validate parts of ancient British history for the sake of their imperialist hopes in Ireland.[52] The likelihood that Hadfield is right should also put us in mind of E.K.'s skepticism about Arthur in the "April" section of *The Shepherd's Calender*—although these comments seem to refer to the Arthur of Chrétien de Troyes rather than Geoffrey of Monmouth.[53] In any case, while the *View*'s colonialist goals no doubt exert an influence on Spenser's claims about his nation's history, some English colonialists found it perfectly possible to disbelieve Geoffrey and at the same time affirm Ireland's historical subjection to England. Andrew Hadfield himself has recently written about such a colonialist, John Milton, who vitriolically denies Arthur's historical existence (in the *History of Britain*, as we shall see) but who nonetheless insists in his *Observations* (1649) that the English are the historical masters of the Irish.[54] Colonialism encouraged but did not require certain forms of historical credulity. Spenser appears skeptical of Brutus and credulous of Arthur, and the evidence about his general belief in early British history remains ambiguous in the *View*.

Spenser's colonialist treatise does reveal, however, the dangers of too much skepticism about national origin. In chapter 2 we noted the historiographic sophistication of the *View*, its willingness to compare different versions of the same story, to consider the effects of linguistic traditions, and to emphasize the value of physical evidence about the past. Part of its mission, then, is to share "many sweet remembrances of antiquity" (43), but in such a way as to cleanse antiquity from the contaminating effects of fiction, the "most fabulous and forged" assertions of Irish chroniclers (46). Yet Spenser's historiographic rigor threatens to dismantle antiquity altogether. His attempt

[52] Andrew Hadfield, "Briton and Scythian: Tudor Representations of Irish Origins," *Irish Historical Studies* 28, 112 (1993): 390–408.

[53] E. K. glosses April's reference to the Ladies of the Lake as follows: "For it was an old opinion amongst the Ancient Heathen, that of every spring and fountain was a goddess the Sovereign. Which opinion stuck in the minds of men not many years since, by means of certain fine fablers and loud liars, such as were the Authors of King Arthur the great and such like, who tell many an unlawful leasing of the Ladies of the Lake, that is, the Nymphs"; *Yale Edition of the Shorter Poems of Edmund Spenser* (New Haven: Yale University Press, 1989), 82. There is no Lady of the Lake in the *Historia Regum Britanniae*.

[54] See Andrew Hadfield, "The English and Other Peoples," in *A Companion to Milton*, ed. Thomas N. Corns (Oxford: Blackwell, 2001), 174–90, esp. 186–89.

to deny the Irish a Spanish origin, depriving them of a historical basis to resist English rule, forces him to question the origins of all nations. Indeed, although Ireneus initially says that the Irish make their Spanish claim "without any good ground" (44), he goes on to suggest that even if the derivation is true, the many centuries of cultural mingling in Spain make it impossible to say what really counts as Spanish as distinct from other nations. These putative colonizers "had left no pure drop of Spanish blood, no more than of Roman or Scythian" (50). The denial of "pure" blood signals Irenius's rhetorical strategy: both the Irish and Spanish have such heterogeneous origins that no single derivation can constitute a legal claim for autonomy. Yet the revelation about heterogeneity, inspired by Ireneus's historiographical zeal, does not stop with two nations. Although Ireneus at first derogates Spain's hybridity, suggesting that such an origin would not be "greatly glorious" to the Irish (49), he soon revises his evaluation of the Spaniard:

> So surely is he a very brave man, neither is that any thing which I speak to his derogation; for in that I said he is a mingled people, it is no dispraise, for I think there is no nation now in Christendom, nor much further, but is mingled, and compounded with others: for it was a singular providence of God, and a most admirable purpose of his wisdom, to draw those Northern Heathen Nations down into those Christian parts, where they might receive Christianity, and to mingle nations so remote miraculously, to make as it were one blood and kindred of all people, and each to have knowledge of him. (51)

Mingling is God's plan, and modern nations should feel no shame about it. The full import of this "ripping of ancestors," as Eudoxus terms it, emerges in Spenser's view of Providential heterogeneity. To understand history properly and truthfully is to "rip up" the past, to see that no nation has a clear or pure origin, not even England. Hence the necessity of the various claims about English unoriginality in the *View:* that "the English were, at first, as stout and warlike a people as the Irish," that the Saxons learned literacy from the Irish rather than the other way around, that "it is even the other day that England grew civil" (21, 47, 70). Ireneus's criticism of England's "vain" belief in Brutus takes on an additional resonance in this context, because the wish for a pure origin is itself a form of vanity—selfish, delusory, even irreligious. The Irish belief in a pure Spanish origin is similarly "most vain," and their "vanity" encourages their continued production of "forged histories" (49). Nations must give up fiction and accept the historical truth about themselves, the truth that Sir Henry Spelman implies a few years later in his argument against uniting nations: they are products of modernity.

Yet is Spenser really so content to abandon fabled antiquity for the truth of historical belatedness? Let us keep in mind Judith Anderson's observation that the tract's multifaceted rhetoric about history and fable is "indicative not of a totally assured view but of one aware of unsettling complexities in questions of truth and still very much in process."[55] Indeed, Spenser's condemnation of fiction leaves his nation rather high and dry without an origin, and to a certain degree without a stable identity. Significantly, the discussion about national mixing leads almost immediately to comments about the Old English, who now resemble the Irish, and the language changes from "mingling" to "degeneration."[56] Eudoxus cannot believe that these former English citizens would forget their proper derivation: "Could they ever conceive any such dislike of their own natural countries, as that they would be ashamed of their name, and bite at the dug from which they sucked life?" (69). The indeterminate effect of mother's milk on the child metaphorizes the lack of an origin that could determine national identity in the present. Indeed, Irenius's answering use of the metaphor makes clear that mother's milk now displaces rather than confirms proper origin and identity, in the forms of interracial marriage and language acquisition: "I suppose that the chief cause of bringing in the Irish language amongst them was specially their fostering and marrying with the Irish, the which are two most dangerous infections; for first the child that sucketh the milk of the nurse, must of necessity learn his first speech of her, the which being the first inured to his tongue, is ever after most pleasing unto him" (71). Sucking "life" shifts to "infection," and we are put in mind of Thomas Scanlan's suggestion that the *View*'s ambiguities stem in part from "the difficulties of constructing a colonial identity in the absence of a coherent national identity."[57] The modernity of nations emerges as historical truth and prevents Irish etiological claims from impeding En-

[55] Judith Anderson, "The Antiquities of Fairyland and Ireland," *Journal of English and German Philology* 86:2 (1987): 199–214, at 205.

[56] E.g., *View of the State of Ireland*, 54, 67, and 68.

[57] Thomas Scanlan, *Colonial Writing and the New World, 1583–1671* (Cambridge: Cambridge University Press, 1999), 71.

glish imperialism, but Spenser's historiographic skepticism, denying the nation a pure and ancient origin, implicitly leads to English degeneration in the present.

The *View* finds this distressing lack of origins both indisputable and unacceptable. As a historical writer, Spenser does not accept Jonson's willing transformation of the national past into pure myth. Yet he feels even more conflicted than Selden about the deleterious effects of "this critique age," perceiving more intensely than he the need for a tradition to justify the nation, however dubious the historical content of such a tradition. The *View* keenly registers the etiological paradox of English historiography: the "ripping" (adducing) of ancestors also rips up ancestors, dispels the pious, crucial fictions that gave them existence. *The Faerie Queene* responds to this dilemma, especially books II and III, by using fiction to articulate an "eternall union . . . /Between nations different afore" (III.iii.49.1–2). Spenser names this national union "Tudor," a present identity that resolves past national difference. Yet this sense of unity extends beyond the present back into the past, reconceiving Saxon and British history as *Tudor* history, uniting disparate storylines into a single etiology. Spenser realizes he cannot do this without the aid of fiction, the very element that ruins true antiquity in the *View*. The poem thus employs fable to imagine a link to the past but not so much as to empty out this link's historical content. Of course, Spenser knows that such ornamentation risks precisely this emptying, the threat that national vanity will turn the past into fable. Yet *The Faerie Queene* is not simply a poet's fictionalization of the *View*'s historiographical problems. Spenser's hybrid historical poetry employs fiction as an ambiguous countermeasure to historical loss but also as an acknowledgment of this loss, of the incapacity of bare, unornamented history to find its way to the present. Fiction's ornamentation of the past both fulfills history and signals history's incompleteness.

Spenser thus exploits and magnifies a quality of fiction that Elizabethan literary theory had obliquely noted for some time: the link between poetry and nothingness. S. K. Heninger's magisterial study of the poet figure shows that the late Elizabethans came to see poetry as a world-creating discourse rather than an imitation of reality. For all its advantages, however, this conception risks turning poetry into a dangerous unreality: "The poem tends to etherealize into speculation, tends to evaporate into idle thoughts of what should be or might be, tends to metamorphose into fantasies and misconceptions and delusions."[58] Indeed, despite Aristotle's claim that poetry expresses universal truths, and therefore possesses its own authenticity beyond history, some Renaissance accounts acknowledged that fiction created meaning out of nothing. In the *Apology*, Sidney praises poetry for its ability to teach virtue, but his suggestion that the poet "nothing affirms, and therefore never lieth,"[59] while freeing poetry from the charge of falsehood, also implicitly deprives it of truth. Poetry teaches morality but has "nothing" to say. Puttenham likewise praised the poet's ability to invent things from nothing but imaginative power, asserting the divine nature of such power: "It is therefore of Poets thus to be conceived, that if they be able to devise and make all these things of them selves, without any subject of verity, that they be (by manner of speech) as creating gods."[60] An impressive claim, but perhaps dubious praise in the end, since divine creativity in humans comes at the cost of "verity" and requires a parenthetical caution against blasphemous literalism: "by manner of speech."

The peculiar nothingness of poetry emerges even more explicitly when commentators compare it to history. Thomas Blundeville distinguishes between history and poetry precisely in terms of the calculus between something and nothing. Of the historian: "some do make *of so much as much*, as true Philosophers and Historiographers, whose office is to tell things as they were done without either augmenting or diminishing them, or swerving one iota from the truth." Of the poet: "some do make *much of nothing*, as God did in creating the World of naught, and as Poets in some respect also do, whilest they feign fables and make thereof their poesies and Poetical Histories."[61] Historians create an equivalent discourse out of a commensurate material, whereas poets create an imaginary discourse out of nothing. Blundeville's assessment of poets, like Puttenham's, is at least slightly ambivalent—they possess a godlike talent yet "feign fables" rather than tell truths. God does not feign, but poets have to do so. If history is something and fiction is nothing, then historical fiction is something in between, a threshold figure. Spenser uses this ambiguous figure as a compromise between the need for a national

---

[58] Heninger, *Sidney and Spenser*, 249.

[59] Sidney, *Apology for Poetry*, 57.

[60] Puttenham, *Arte of English Poesie*, 20.

[61] Blundeville, *True Order and Method of Writing and Reading Histories*, 164 (my emphasis in both quotations). Blundeville is loosely translating Francesco Patrizi, *Della historia diece dialoghi* (Venice, 1560), at this point in *The True Order*.

origin and the fact of historical loss. In this context, the liminality of historical fiction—both there and not there, godlike creativity and empty fancy—emerges to some degree as the appropriate response to the uncanny gap between past and present. Spenser takes the forced position of "poesie historical" and tries to occupy it as an advantage.

Between the living ornament and the dead monument, between the flesh-and-blood past and the historical corpse, Spenser imagines what we might call a ghostly history. His link to the past animates his nation's posterity but also conceives of that posterity as spectral and intangible, possibly lost in fable. My account of this "ghostly" dimension of *The Faerie Queene*'s national representation derives partly from Isabel E. Rathborne's suggestive "conception of Faeryland as a mythical land of fame inhabited largely by dead heroes."[62] The poem records the fame of the past but implicitly alienates it from a living present. Rathborne, of course, offered a mostly optimistic view of the exemplary force of dead heroes, yet Spenser often calls attention to the elusiveness of a memory between life and death and between past and present. Think, for example, of the turret of the House of Alma, where we encounter the middle sage who "could of things present best advise" (II.ix.49.2). On the one hand, this sage is the figure of balance for and connection between the unstable temporal extremes that surround him, flighty Phantastes (the future) and decrepit Eumnestes (the past). On the other hand, he is the only figure in the turret without a name, a sign of the curious absence that accompanies his liminal status. He holds future and past together effectively, yet Spenser imagines his threshold condition as a ghostly one, both there and not there.

Spenser suggests a similar status for his fiction in the proem to book II, where he famously counterposes the "painted forgery" of fiction and the "just memory" of history (II.proem.1.4, 5). He employs the opposition to set up a defense of the value of his poetic world but also to acknowledge the limitations of fiction in relation to national history. Spenser mocks literalist interpretations of Faerieland by pretending to offer real-life analogues such as Peru, the Amazon, Virginia, and even the moon (II.proem.2–3), showing that we cannot judge poetry according to the terms of reality. Nor, however, can we treat poetry as entirely separate from the facts of reality, especially

[62] Isabel E. Rathborne, *The Meaning of Spenser's Fairyland* (New York: Columbia University Press, 1937; reprint, New York: Russel and Russel, 1965), 151.

the historical reality of the nation's origin. Significantly, the proem's focus shifts from place to time, as Spenser asks Elizabeth to see "in this antique ymage thy great auncestry" (4.9). Is he still joking? Yes and no. The fabulous events of book II's narrative do not literally represent the queen's heritage, but they may carry and animate—may ornament—historical elements of that heritage, such as the existence of King Arthur and the line of monarchs in *Briton moniments* (II.x). Fiction does not offer the unreality of "painted forgery," but neither does it idealize reality to the point at which historical truth no longer matters. It offers something between an empty nothing and an idealized something: an "antique ymage" that resurrects history by means of the visualizing, spectralizing power of poetry. Indeed, we can distinguish Spenser's "antique ymage" from Drayton's "lively images" in that Drayton hopes to make history live whereas Spenser seeks to make it undead.

This ghostly view of the past permits Spenser a degree of latitude with his characters, who at least suggest national origin even if their activities fall outside the historical chronicles. Arthur, Arthegall, and Britomart derive from historiography or lead to it, and Spenser ornaments their basic historical identity with fiction. As such, they work to consolidate time and produce what Wayne Erickson calls "a pattern of temporal mediations."[63] Their movement in and out of Faerieland links the disparate historical worlds of fifth-century Britain and sixteenth-century Tudor England that crowd around its peripheries. I claimed in chapter 2 that Spenser's Arthur is almost historical but not quite. Fiction responds to this limitation, as Andrew King has noted, by replacing the moribund and childless Arthur of the chronicles with the romance figures of Arthegall and Britomart, whose fictional union will give birth to a line of kings.[64] Furthermore, although all three characters are Britons, their fictional flexibility allows them to imply a sense of national unity in the past. Saxon Redcross can amiably tell British Britomart that "you and your country both I wish welfare, / And honour both" (III.ii.10.8–9), even though in history their countries are at war. Likewise, the vaguely historical figure of Angela—the name appears in the chronicles but with none of the details that Spenser invents (III.iii.55–56)[65]—can

[63] Erickson, *Mapping "The Faerie Queene,"* 6.

[64] King, *"Faerie Queene" and Middle English Romance,* 183.

[65] Carrie Anne Harper, *The Sources of "The British Chronicle History" in Spenser's "Faerie Queene"* (Philadelphia: John C. Winston, 1910), 168.

supply Britomart with her armor that hangs in King Ryence's church with the other Saxon "ornaments" (59.1). This sharing of the vaguely historical Angela with the fictional Britomart echoes the scenario described by the motto on Arthegall's armor, "Achilles armes, which Arthogall did win" (III.ii.25.6)—in which the fictional son of Peleus yields weapons to the vaguely historical Arthegall. The fiction–history hybrid created by Britomart and Angela's intersection contributes to the national union of the Saxon and British pasts, yielding a British heroine wearing Saxon arms.[66] By moving these characters in and out of history and fiction, Spenser suggests that the distance between *Briton moniments* and Merlin's chronicle is not unbridgeable: a character such as Britomart can span the temporal gulf between King Uther's reign (II.x.68.1 and III.iii.52.5–9) and that of King Conan (III.iii.29).

Yet the ghostly historicity of both Spenser's characters and landscape also acknowledges the unsubstantial quality of the historical links they create. For one thing, Spenser's refusal to specify the borders between the fictional and historical worlds, his unwillingness even to coordinate these borders around a manifested center such as Cleopolis—unlike earlier Italian epics that usually provide such a center—creates a temporal blurring. John Steadman has described this effect as a "fragmentation of time": "[Spenser] does not merely disintegrate it; he dissolves it, reducing time and space alike to indefinite extension, an indeterminate continuum."[67] Indeed, Spenser's fiction both mediates and shatters history. The indeterminacy between full and partial time marks Spenser's characters as well. Arthur, Britomart, and Arthegall can play on the margins of Spenser's two historical narratives but cannot fully enter. Even though *Briton moniments* depicts the historical stage on which Arthur is born and on which he will one day act, a violent interruption—"There abruptly did it end" (II.10.68.2)—divides history from the fictional Arthur. Spenser represents Britomart's shift from fictional romance (III.ii) to historical fate (III.iii) as a radical change in identity. And when Arthegall enters English history (III.iii.27), he does not join Arthur as his half brother—a union that might suggest a strong homogeneity between history and fiction—but rather, as Harper notes,

---

[66] Noted by Michael O'Connell, *Mirror and Veil: The Historical Dimension of Spenser's "Faerie Queene"* (Chapel Hill: University of North Carolina Press, 1977), 84–85.

[67] John M. Steadman, *Moral Fiction in Milton and Spenser* (Columbia: University of Missouri Press, 1995), 85.

replaces Arthur in the historical chronicle.[68] In as far as Arthegall and Arthur come together at all before book V, they do so not by gradual approximation but by displacement. Thus, Spenser emphasizes the duality rather than the unity of his characters' hybrid nature, and he imagines their travels between fiction and history as quantum jumps rather than smooth transitions.

Perhaps the example that most reveals the delicate gain and cost of the ghostly link between past and present is the figure of Conan, Britomart and Arthegall's son. At first glance, this figure would seem to promise a firm link between Spenser's two historical narratives as well as a strong homogeneity between history and fiction. Conan stands precisely between past and future in that he rules England after the last king mentioned in *Briton moniments* (Uther) and before the first ruling king named in Merlin's prophecy (Vortipore).[69] And he stands exactly between history and fiction in that he is the son of the (originally) fictional Britomart and Arthegall and is the father of the fully historical Vortipore. In other words, the figure of Conan offered Spenser an excellent occasion to emphasize the unity within his hybrid narrative, should he have chosen to do so. Yet even to call this figure "Conan" assumes more than Spenser actually tells us, for Spenser never names him. After Arthegall is "[t]oo rathe cut off by practice criminall / Of secret foes" (III.3.28.8–9), Merlin informs Britomart:

> With thee yet shall he leave for memory
> Of his late puissance, his Image dead,
> That living him in all activity
> To thee shall represent. He from the head
> Of his coosin *Constantius* without dread
> Shall take the crowne, that was his fathers right,
> And therewith crowne himselfe in th'others stead.
>
> (iii.29.1–7)

Although Spenser speaks of him as a figure who recovers the past ("for memory") and who rectifies an interruption in royal lineage, Conan ends up confirming the fact of historical loss as much as he re-

---

[68] Harper, *Sources of "The British Chronicle History,"* 144.

[69] Although technically Constantius ruled before Conan (III.iii.29. 5), Spenser only mentions Constantius as he loses his crown; Spenser also, contrary to his sources, cast suspicion on the legitimacy of Constantius's reign: "[Conan] shall take the crowne, that was his father's right" (iii.29.6).

pairs it. His own rule is curiously tenuous, almost emptied out by its dependence on an absent authority ("the crowne, that was his fathers right") and its status as a replacement ("he . . . shall . . . crowne him-selfe in th'others stead"). As a "memory" of his departed father, Conan in fact foregrounds the paradox of his representational status: he is an "Image dead" that signifies the past by "living."

The liminal status of memory here once again recalls Michel de Certeau's description of historiography's attempt to recover historical loss: "[historical] discourse is incessantly articulated over the death that it presupposes, but that the very practice of history contradicts. For to speak of the dead means to deny death and almost to defy it. Therefore speech is said to 'resuscitate' them. Here the word is liter-ally a lure: history does not resuscitate anything."[70] I suggest that the figure of Conan parallels Certeau's notion of the historiographical "lure": Conan points to the death that Merlin's prophecy both relies on for motivation and seeks to deny. Merlin speaks of Conan as a res-urrection of the dead past (Arthegall) for the living present (Brito-mart), but the figure remains, to a considerable degree, a precarious threshold between the past and present, an "image dead . . . living."

King Conan emerges as the ghost of history, a resurrection of the national past that does not fully live but maintains a phantom pres-ence. Fiction makes this resurrection possible in the first place, and, significantly, Conan's war against the Mercians in the next stanza represents one of the few events in Merlin's prophecy that Spenser en-tirely fabricates. Spenser declines to name Conan because his identity and status are so indeterminate: does he belong in the past or present? Is he fiction or history? This indeterminacy perhaps explains why Spenser, after Conan's fictional battles, curiously shifts to the conditional voice: "And *if* he then with victorie can lin, / He shall his dayes with peace bring to his earthly In" (iii.30.8–9; my emphasis). The pure past or future is always indicative: events did happen or will happen. However, fiction's intervention here pushes the future into the potential. The tentative and conditional voice in these verses nicely reveals the cost of relying on fiction for historical continuity: Spenser can represent a celebratory link between England's past and present, but a troubling insubstantiality haunts such a link. The con-nection is there, but Spenser creates it, so to speak, out of thin air.

This conception of Spenser's fictional ornamentation of history as

[70] Certeau, *Writing of History*, 47.

a spectral image of the past illuminates the status of the Elfin *Antiq-uitie of Faerie lond* (II.x.70–77) and its relation to *Briton moniments*. Critics have disagreed about the Elfin chronicle's meaning, labeling it variously as pure fiction, idealized history, political flattery, and his-torical allegory. Many interpretations agree in general with Harry Berger's view that the two chronicles are dichotomous, representing "two utterly irreconcilable points of view," the real and the ideal.[71] David Lee Miller has suggestively described the Elfin chronicle as an idealized "ahistorical 'history.'"[72] Richard A. McCabe, Erickson, and others, however, have pointed to the historical references in the Elfin chronicle, arguing that the two narratives cannot be so neatly distin-guished.[73] The difficulty in specifying real or ideal resides in part from what we might call the uneven historicity of *Antiquitie of Faerie lond*. Until stanza 75, historical identification with the Faerie monarchs is speculative at best. Yet then, because Spenser has told us elsewhere that Tanaquill (stanza 76) represents Queen Elizabeth, it seems hard to deny that in stanza 75, Elficleos, Elferon, and Oberon represent Henry VII and his sons, Prince Arthur and Henry VIII. Spenser makes this Tudor lineage smoother by conveniently omitting the reigns of Edward and Mary, thus emphasizing national unity, al-beit a rather forced unity. Given that Spenser makes historical identi-fication so easy in the later stanzas, he seems to discourage us from ascribing a strong historicity to the earlier ones by making them opaque. Rather, the cleaned up history of the end of the chronicle emerges as the happy consequence of the unbroken *fictional* continu-ity of the earlier parts. An origin ("Elfe" [71.1]) that so absolutely gov-erns its narrative extension, an origin from which "all Faryes spring, and fetch their lignage right" (71.9), and that manifests itself in every subsequent king by means of the repeated root name, "Elf," can occur only in a history heavily ornamented by fable. Such a history need not foreground antiquarian concerns such as belief and skepticism, as with *Briton moniments*'s treatment of the origin of giants (x.8). It also can afford to skip over the details of history, as with the Elfin

[71] Harry Berger, Jr., *The Allegorical Temper: Vision and Reality in Book II of Spenser's "Faerie Queene"* (New Haven: Yale University Press, 1957), 104.

[72] David Lee Miller, *The Poem's Two Bodies: The Poetics of the 1590 "Faerie Queene"* (Princeton: Princeton University Press, 1988), 206.

[73] Richard A. McCabe, *The Pillars of Eternity: Time and Providence in "The Faerie Queene"* (Dublin: Irish Academic Press, 1989), 95–103; Erickson, *Mapping "The Faerie Queene,"* 93. See also Hamilton's annotations on II.x.70–76 in the 2001 edi-tion.

chronicle's cheerful acknowledgment that the reigns of seven hundred kings "were too long their infinite contents / Here to record, ne much material" (x.74.5–6). Indeed, the Elfin chronicle's "infinite contents" reveal its ghostly status: its fictions are both infinite and empty, too vast to describe and too phantasmal to see distinctly.

This enhanced vision of history potentially produces two rhetorical effects. The clearly invented orderliness of the Elfin chronicle confirms by contrast the historical authenticity of *Briton monuments* and its imperfect, heterogeneous story. Conversely, the structural parallel of the two narratives—each offering genealogies that link past and present—may compromise the historical status of British chronicle, exposing the manner in which anyone can gather together a group of names and call it antiquity. That is, the Elfin chronicle's etiological excessiveness indirectly reminds us that the story of Brutus may emerge from national "vanity" rather than true history, as Spenser warns us in the *View*. Much as *Briton moniments* relies on Merlin's prophecy for its status as a material monument (as we discussed in chap. 2), it relies on the Elfin story's fiction to confirm the historical content of its narrative as well as that content's susceptibility to fable. *Antiquitie of Faerie lond*'s missing details are indeed not "much material" to its goals as a fictionalized history; they are, however, the very thing that gives history its content.

Yet whatever risks *Antiquitie of Faerie lond* poses to history, its difference from *Briton moniments* signals Spenser's serious historiographical intentions, as I have suggested. He refuses simply to collapse history into fiction, maintaining fable as the ambiguous ornament of the national past. His attempt to maintain this compromise between historical loss and historical continuity throughout book II and most of III emerges more sharply when we reach Paridell and Britomart's conversation about history (III.ix). Here, for the first time, Spenser represents Geoffrey of Monmouth's narrative as a pure fable, an etiology with no historical content. Fiction's decoration of history becomes history's substance, all icing and no cake.

As Heather Dubrow has noted, this episode represents the third telling of England's national history, and this fact encourages us to compare the episode with the two earlier installments of English history, *Briton moniments* and Merlin's prophecy.[74] The episode does not only retell the earlier stories: Spenser carefully gives to Paridell the beginning

---

[74] Heather Dubrow, "The Arraignment of Paridell: Tudor Historiography in *The Faerie Queene*, III.ix," *Studies in Philology* 87, 3 (1990): 312–27.

of Geoffrey of Monmouth's narrative. Spenser also links this narrative to the earlier ones by having Paridell mention "aged *Mnemon*" (III.ix.47.4), which recalls the figure of Eumnestes in the House of Alma. Just as Arthur and Britomart respond to the historical narratives they read or hear, Spenser has Hellenore respond to the historical narrative she hears (ix.52). Yet although Dubrow sees the episode's historiographic engagement as one that "destabilizes the earlier ones" and that exacerbates "the anti-closural uncertainties of the two earlier episodes,"[75] I argue that it also does just the opposite. This third installment of the nation's story smoothes away the *historiographic* controversy surrounding Geoffrey's chronicle by turning history into epic fiction.

Throughout much of Paridell's account of Troy and Rome, Spenser highlights the problem of historical loss. Although the theme of *translatio imperii* would seem to offer an ideal vehicle for historical continuity, Spenser initially emphasizes its discontinuous elements: "For noble *Britons* sprong from *Troians* bold, / And *Troynovant* was built of old *Troyes* ashes cold" (ix.38.8–9). Underlying the transmission of glory from Troy to London is the discontinuity of the new— "*Troynovant*" cannot help but advertise its distance from "*old* Troyes ashes cold." Both Paridell and Britomart initially comment on the inevitable effects of mutability in the story of Troy, what Paridell calls "direfull destinie" (ix.33.5) and what Britomart calls "mans wretched state" (ix.39.8).[76] Indeed, Paridell's inclination to forget England in his narrative is not only a function of his dubious character but also speaks to the anxiety Tudor historians felt about their nation's isolation from the classical past. Paridell's "heedlesse oversight" (ix.46.2), initially leaving out the British story, reminds the reader of the historical discontinuity that threatens throughout this episode.

The episode is not entirely bleak, however. Spenser once again relies on the historical–fictional hybridity of his characters in order to suggest a link between past and present. He has Britomart interpret as her own etiology Paridell's account of Troy, "from whose race of old / She heard, that she was lineally extract" (ix.38.6–7). That Brito-

---

[75] Ibid., 316, 317.

[76] Mihoko Suzuki argues that Paridell's and Britomart's comments on Troy (III.ix.33 and 39) are diametrically opposed, revealing Paridell's self-centeredness and Britomart's devotion to the public good. See Suzuki, "'Unfitly yokt together in one teeme': Vergil and Ovid in *Faerie Queene*, III.ix," *English Literary Renaissance* 17, 2 (1987): 172–85, esp. 179–83. However, their comments are also quite similar in that they both emphasize the idea of decay in time.

mart is a British woman "lineally extract" from the Trojan people confers the continuity of epic history to English history. This continuity is most strongly expressed when Britomart supplies England's connection to the classical past with what seems to be a prophetic inspiration of her own:

> There there (said *Britomart*) a fresh appeard
> The glory of the later world to spring,
> And *Troy* againe out of her dust was reard,
> To sit in second seat of soveraigne king,
> Of all the world under her governing.
> But a third kingdome yet is to arise,
> Out of the *Troians* scattered of-spring,
> That in all glory and great enterprise,
> Both first and second *Troy* shall dare to equalise.
>
> (ix.44)

Britomart here articulates the link between Troy, Rome, and Britain in one of the most succinct and complete expressions of historical continuity in *The Faerie Queene*. Unlike Britomart's earlier comments about historical loss (9.39), this stanza downplays the gaps between Troy's three manifestations. She mention's Troy's "dust" only in the context of Troy's reincarnation: "And *Troy* againe out of her dust was reard." She entirely skips over Rome's fall, moving quickly to the third Troy, England, that stands as the competitive equivalent of the earlier Troys: "That in all glory and great enterprise, / Both first and second *Troy* shall dare to equalise." Although Mihoko Suzuki rightly observes that England will eventually have to fall in order to "equalize" Troy and Rome, rhetorically speaking the stanza emphasizes duration and continuance, occluding the threat of decay.[77] In as far as is possible, Britomart imagines history here as a smooth transition rather than as a series of breaks. Indeed, Britomart's inspired cry of "There there" recalls and corrects the self-consuming "There" of *Briton moniments* (II.x.68.2) and the apocalyptic "There" of Merlin's prophecy (III.iii.50.1). Although these earlier instances of the word functioned as interruptions of history, Britomart's exclamation seeks to repair the link between past and present.

This historical consolidation relies, ironically enough, on the

---

[77] Ibid., 184.

episode's willingness to jettison historical content. Britomart can translate epic continuity to the British past only in as far as she identifies herself with the fictional story of Troy's fall. However, the context has become so deeply fictional—going back to Paris's abduction of Helen—that Britomart's proclamation empties out historical content even as it resists historical discontinuity. Notice, for example, how the status of Brutus alters in this episode from *Briton moniments*. However unbelievable Spenser's readers found the story of Brutus in the British chronicle, they encounter it in a historical narrative that also includes indisputably true events, such as the arrival of the Romans and later the Saxons. At most, Brutus ornaments but does not dissolve the historical consistency of *Briton moniments*. Paridell's account, conversely, turns early British history into epic fiction, explicitly paralleling Brutus's arrival to the accounts of the *Iliad* (ix.33–35) and the *Aeneid* (ix.41–43). Britomart thus gains an ancestor in Brutus, but an ancestor who, like herself, derives from the poetic imagination rather than from antiquarian investigation.

This is not to say that replacing a historical with a fictional rendition automatically glorifies the national past in an unproblematic manner. Fictional origins are not necessarily free of moral ambiguity, as Paridell's account of Aeneas reveals:

> Anchyses sonne begot of Venus faire,
> (Said he,) out of the flames for safegard fled,
> And with a remnant did to sea repaire,
> Where he through fatall errour long was led
> Full many yeares, and weetlesse wandered
> From shore to shore, emongst the Lybicke sands,
> Ere rest he found. Much there he suffered,
> And many perils past in forreine lands,
> To save his people sad from victours vengefull hands.
>
> At last in Latium he did arrive,
> Where he with cruell warre was entertaind
> Of th'inland folke, which sought him backe to drive,
> Till he with old Latinus was constraind,
> To contract wedlock: (so the fates ordaind.)
> Wedlock contract in bloud, and eke in blood
> Accomplished, that many deare complain:
> The rivall slaine, the victour through the flood
> Escaped hardly, hardly praisd his wedlock good.
>
> (ix.41–42)

Although Spenser perhaps intends the depressing tone to reflect Paridell's unheroic character, he also sees keenly into the bleaker aspects of the *Aeneid* itself. Aeneas forges an origin for Rome, but "many deare complaind"—much as Arthur notes "how dearly dear" (II.x.69.3) the memory of the national past is to the present—revealing the suffering behind the victorious history. Spenser offers W. R. Johnson's interpretation of Virgil's poem *avant la lettre*. Similarly, Brutus's arrival in Albion is marked by conflict:

> For that same Brute, whom much he did advaunce
> In all his speach, was Sylvius his sonne,
> Whom having slaine, through luckles arrowes glaunce
> He fled for feare of that he had misdonne,
> Or else for shame, so fowle reproch to shonne,
> And with him led to sea an youthly trayne,
> Where wearie wandring they long time did wonne,
> And many fortunes prov'd in th'Ocean mayne,
> And great adventures found, that now were long to sayne.
>
> At last by fatall course they driven were
> Into an Island spatious and brode
> The furthest North, that did to them appeare:
> Which after rest they seeking far abrode,
> Found it the fittest soyle for their abode,
> Fruitfull of all things fit for living foode,
> But wholy wast, and void of peoples trode,
> Save an huge nation of the Geaunts broode,
> That fed on living flesh, & druncke mens vitall blood.
>
> (ix.48–49.1–2)

The parallels are numerous and obvious. Both Aeneas and Brutus "fled" from their original homes. "Fatall errore" (41.4) compels Aeneas's movements, whereas Brutus endures "wandering . . . by fatall course" (48.7, 49.1). Their arrival at their new homes in each case involves overcoming hostile natives. Ambiguities about the value of nation-founding abound in this episode.

Yet the historiographical point is clear: both of these narratives offer fictional origins for their nations. History per se is not at stake in the link between Troy, Rome, and Britain. By going back so far in the past, Spenser does what he refused to do in his earlier historical narratives: he fully fictionalizes history and stops worrying about the accuracy of his narrative. In doing so, he can suggest a continuity between past and present that he cannot suggest in his earlier narratives, in which he keeps history and fiction apart. The price of this fictional continuity, however, is that fiction now replaces rather than ornaments history. For example, fiction here does not mediate between the present and the historical cities of London and Lincoln but rather *supplants* these cities:

> [Brutus's] worke great *Troynovant*, his worke is eke
> Faire *Lincolne*, both renowmed far away,
> That who from East to West will endlong seeke,
> Cannot two fairer Cities find this day,
> Except *Cleopolis*. . . .
>
> (ix.51.1–5)

Cleopolis has earlier been the Faerie ornament for English London, the former belonging to *Antiquitie of Faerie lond* and the latter belonging to *Briton moniments*, maintaining the fiction–history hybridity of Spenser's poetry. Here, however, the disparity between Troynovant and Cleopolis is not a tension between history and fiction. Rather, both cities seem to compete on the same plane: it is hard to tell if "from East to West" (l. 3) designates a space in the world or in Faerieland. In fact, it hardly matters, because at this point in the episode Spenser has collapsed his earlier distinction between fiction and history. Brutus's deeds give England a past, not because the deeds are true but because his narrative resembles great epic narratives of nation-founding. In his attempt to negotiate the uncanny gap between England's past and present, Spenser quietly drops his earlier ambitions of historical rigor and exclusively adopts (we might even say, resigns himself to) the creative role of the poet. Jonson, as we have seen, would decide a few years later "to follow the received story of *Brute*, whether fabulous or true, and not altogether unwarranted in Poetry." Spenser's formula in III.ix is more extreme: he follows the story of Brutus *insisting* that it is fabulous and suggests that it is *only* warranted in poetry.

Yet even here Spenser registers a sense that a continuity achieved so purely by fiction is marked by a peculiar emptiness. When Paridell boasts that "my linage I derive aright" (III.ix.36.1) from the invented sequence of Paris, Parius, and Paridas, he reminds us of the fictional "Elfe" derivation of *Antiquitie of Faerie lond*. Yet Paridell's claim even more obviously stems from the "vanity" that the *View* condemns as the cause of fictionalized origins. Britomart, deriving herself "from Trojans bold" (III.ix.38.8), risks precisely the same charge of vanity. The power of fiction in this episode both creates dearly needed etiologies and exposes these origins as narcissistic projections from the present into the past. Perhaps this is why Spenser sets Hellenore's response to the narrative in such striking contrast to the earlier responses of Arthur and Britomart. At first, it seems that the urgency of the national past has made an impact on Hellenore, for Spenser tells us that she listens "with vigilant regard, and dew attent" (ix.52.3). However, the next verse suddenly undercuts this suggestion: "Fashioning worlds of fancies evermore / In her fraile wit" (52.4–5). What, then, do the words "vigilant" and "dew" mean exactly in the previous line? This moment of attentive inattention, beyond simply representing Hellenore's moral deficiencies, reminds us of both the promise of poetry—its ability to create golden worlds— and its danger, its seductiveness, its meretricious polysemeity. Indeed, "fashioning worlds of fancies" is precisely what poets do; it is a description of the grandeur of poetic creation and the emptiness that underlies it. Spenser does finally give us a "famous history to be enrold / In everlasting moniments of brasse" (ix.50.7–8), allowing the ornament of fiction to resurrect the dead monument of history. Yet he also reveals that in the process, fiction is likely to take over history completely, leaving the nation only with the "fabulous and forged" origins that the *View* warned against.

Milton's *History of Britain* and the Naked Truth

The most famous fact about Milton's Arthurian epic is that he did not write it. We know of his intentions to compose such an epic from several documents he wrote during the 1630s. The Trinity manuscript reveals his interest in a number of figures from pre-Norman history. The letter to John Baptista Manso and the "Epitaphium Damonis," both composed around 1639, mention explicitly Milton's desire to write an Arthurian epic. In the letter to Manso, Milton hopes some day to "recall in my poetry the kings of my native land, and Arthur, who caused wars even beneath the earth."[78] In the "Epi-

---

[78] Quoted from *The Riverside Milton*, ed. Roy Flannagan (New York: Houghton Mifflin, 1998), 234. All subsequent references to Milton's poetry are made parenthetically from this edition.

taphium," Milton proposes to write about English history all the way
from Brutus to Arthur:

> I myself will sing the ships of Troy through the Rutupian Sea, the old
> kingdom of Inogene, daughter of Pandrasus, the chieftains Brennus and
> Arviragus, and old Belinus, and finally the Amorican settlers, under the
> law of the Britons, next Igraine pregnant with Arthur by fatal fraud—
> Gorlois's counterfeit face and false arms, the fakery of Merlin. (*River-
> side Milton*, 242)

Like Eudoxus in the *View of the State of Ireland*, Milton in these
texts seems partly driven by the "sweet remembrances of antiquity,"
wishing to resurrect a national heritage and "recall [revocabo] . . . the
kings of my native land." Early in his career, then, Milton seems
ready to heed the call of many Elizabethan and early Stuart poets and
recount the story of his nation in an epic-romance setting. His comments about this proposed historical poem two years later in *Reason
in Church Government* (1641) similarly emphasize the goal of recalling a past that earlier generations have failed to preserve. After Italian
acquaintances praised several of his youthful poems and urged him to
persist in his poetic endeavors, Milton tells us that

> I began this farre to assent both to them and divers of my friends here
> at home, and not lesse to an inward prompting which now grew daily
> upon me, that by labour and intent study (which I take to be my por-
> tion in this life) joyn'd with the strong propensity of nature, I might
> perhaps leave something so written to aftertimes, as they should not
> willingly let it die. These thoughts at once possest me, and these
> other. That if I were certain to write as men buy Leases, for three lives
> and downward, there ought no regard be sooner had, then to Gods
> glory by the honour and instruction of my country. For which cause,
> and not only for that I knew it would be hard to arrive at the second
> rank among the Latines, I apply'd my selfe to that resolution which
> Ariosto follow'd against the perswasions of Bembo, to fix all the indus-
> try and art I could unite to the adorning of my native tongue; not to
> make verbal curiosities the end, that were a toylsom vanity, but to be
> an interpreter & relater of the best and sagest things among mine own
> Citizens throughout this Iland in the mother dialect. That what the
> greatest and choycest wits of Athens, Rome, or modern Italy, and
> those Hebrews of old did for their country, I in my proportion with this

over and above of being a Christian, might doe for mine: not caring to be once nam'd abroad, though perhaps I could attaine to that, but content with these British Ilands as my world, whose fortune hath hitherto bin, that if the Athenians, as some say, made their small deeds great and renowned by their eloquent writers, England hath had her noble atchievments made small by the unskilfull handling of monks and mechanicks.[79]

Several goals of historical writing come together in this passage. The memorializing function of historical poetry—"leave something so written to aftertimes"—works to reverse the deleterious effects of the "unskilfull handling" of earlier, monkish writers. Such memorializing combines with the didactic function of poetry, "the honour and instruction of my country." Despite his injunction against "verbal curiosities," neither here nor in his earlier Latin texts does Milton emphasize the distinction between history and fiction, as his invocation of Ariosto suggests. In fact, the paragraph in *Church Government* that follows the one just quoted goes on to muse on a number of different poetic models, some partly historical and some purely fable. Milton's only concern at this point about truth versus falsity takes the form of a quiet dig at those readers of poetic history "who will not so much as look upon Truth herselfe, unlesse they see her elegantly drest" (*CPW* 1:818). Rhetorical or fictional clothes may have to ornament the body of truth, but Milton gives little sense here that serious harm results from this necessity.

Despite these signs of enthusiasm, Milton never wrote a national epic. In fact, he expresses disdain for such national topics in the epic he did end up writing over thirty years later. In *Paradise Lost*, we first encounter Arthur and his peers in Hell with the fallen angels, when Milton relates that the demonic army was even more spectacular than "what resounds / In fable or romance of Uther's son / Begirt with British and Armoric knights" (1:580–81). Here, Arthur's reign is merely a "fable." In fact, of the nine literary armies that Milton compares to the demonic army at this point in the narrative, the Arthurian army is the only one Milton singles out as fictional. Milton indirectly pursues this criticism of national epic at the beginning

---

[79] *The Complete Prose Works of John Milton*, 8 vols., ed. Don M. Wolfe (New Haven: Yale University Press, 1953–82), 1:811–12. Subsequent references to Milton's English prose are made parenthetically to this edition, abbreviated as *CPW*.

of book 9, complaining that the "chief mastery" of earlier epic poems has been "to dissect / With long and tedious havoc *fabled* knights / In battles *feigned*" (9:29–31; my emphasis). It seems that Milton can now only imagine a national, Arthurian epic as a distasteful fiction. Why the change in attitude?

There may be many reasons why Milton changed his mind about writing his proposed national epic, but in this chapter I focus on the problem that Milton seems to emphasize in these passages—that the Arthur stories are "feigned." The national history Milton actually did write, his *History of Britain*, represents a conflicted response to the problem of fiction and the conditions of national historiography in seventeenth-century England. In this history he comes to see fiction to some degree as Spenser did, as the ornament of history. Yet unlike Spenser's ornament, which seeks to resurrect the dead monument and puts flesh on the bones of history, Milton more commonly thinks of fable as the garment of history, the clothing that covers the naked body of truth. For Spenser, history is dead or alive, whereas for Milton history is naked or clothed. And although Spenser tries to find a compromise between the fiction–history dilemma with the notion of a ghostly history, Milton finally cannot bring himself to conceive of such a middle ground in the *History of Britain*. He finds himself caught between two intolerable situations: the body of true history clothed in fables that make it presentable but false, or the naked truth, the authentic but unpresentable story of his nation. This double bind is part of the reason Milton finds it so difficult to speak of "the beginning of Nations," as he puts it in his *History*, so difficult that he eventually finds biblical etiology the only fit topic for his epic.

After Milton returned to England from Italy in 1639, he plunged into an exhaustive study of English history, presumably to prepare himself for the composition of his national epic, as his comments in *Church Government* suggest. The notes of his *Commonplace Book* for the next five years reveal his readings in Bede, William of Malmesbury, Stow, Holinshed, Speed, Sir Thomas Smith, Lambarde, Camden, Hayward, Hardyng, Buchanan, Spenser, Ralegh, Bacon, Selden, and Gildas, in addition to many classical and European historians. This research led not to a national epic but instead to a national history, the first four books of which Milton began writing sometime in the late 1640s; Nicholas von Maltzahn has argued persuasively for

1649, a date Milton himself suggests in the *Second Defense*.[80] Milton concluded, or rather abandoned, his *History of Britain* probably by the mid-1650s, having produced a six-book work that started with the founding of Britain and ended with the Norman invasion in 1066. He did not attempt to publish it until 1670, after he had written *Paradise Lost*. Each book of the work defines an age. Book 1 covers the pre-Roman period of English history, starting with the story of Brutus. Book 2 gives an account of the Roman occupation, whereas book 3 relates the reigns of the British kings after the Romans leave, including that of King Arthur. Book 4 treats the Saxon domination, and books 5 and 6 cover the incursions of the Danes, up to the Norman invasion. Milton stopped here without continuing the narrative up to his own time.

It is tempting to see the *History of Britain* as the fulfillment of Milton's early plans to write a national epic. Milton certainly imagines the *History* filling the same gap in English history that he expected his epic poem would fill. He begins book 2 of his narrative by comparing the historian of a nation to a wise man who,

> knowing that when he conquers all things else, he cannot conquer Time or Detraction, wisely conscious of this his want as well as of his worth not to be forgott'n or conceal'd, honours and hath recourse to the aid of Eloquence, his friendliest and best supply; by whose immortal record his noble deeds, *which else were transitory*, becoming fixt and durable against the force of yeares and generations, he fails not to continue through all posterity, over Envy, Death, and Time, also victorious. (*CPW* 5:40; my emphasis)

Milton sees himself as preserving England's story for posterity, much as he hoped ten years earlier that, by writing his Arthurian epic, he might "leave something so written to aftertimes." We must not underestimate the memorializing and etiological thrust of *History of*

---

[80] Nicholas von Maltzahn, *Milton's "History of Britain": Republican Historiography in the English Revolution* (Oxford: Clarendon Press, 1991), 22–48. Milton claims of his history that "quatuor iam libros absolveram" by the time that the republic was established; *The Works of John Milton*, ed. Frank Allen Patterson, 18 vols. (New York: Columbia University Press, 1933), 8:136. All subsequent references to Milton's Latin prose are made to this edition and use its translations; I abbreviate the reference as *CW*.

Britain. Milton wants to fill the "unsightly gap so neer to the begin-ning" of his nation's story (*CPW* 5:41) if not with an epic poem then with a prose history. A fascination with beginnings marks Milton's work throughout his entire career, persisting up to *Paradise Lost* and his wish to know "what cause" led our originary parents to disobey God's command. The *History*'s full scope, relating the national past continuously from Brutus to the Conquest, was precisely the quality that made it attractive to some of its early readers. Edmund Bohum commended its coverage by noting that "few of our English Writers begin (to any purpose) before the Norman Conquest, passing over all those times that went before it with a slight hand."[81]

Yet the *History*'s difference from the proposed national epic emerges with the problem of fiction. Milton's course of historical study in the 1640s appears to have made him uneasy about the status of early British history. After all, when Milton read Geoffrey's *Historia Regum Britanniae* in Jerome Commelin's historical collection, *Rerum Britannicarum* (Heidelberg, 1587), he encountered a narrative even more discredited than it was for Spenser and Drayton. The 1630s saw a reemphasis on Brutus's story, but writers largely restricted this revival to masques and poetry.[82] In their treatments, Geoffrey's narra-tive was conspicuously fictional, fulfilling the process begun, to some degree, by Spenser's own hesitant fictionalization of the story. Milton finds the narrative's status as fiction unacceptable for his national history, famously castigating Geoffrey and those who follow him for their easy credulity: "what he was, and whence his authority . . . will better stand in a Treatise by themselves" (*CPW* 5:9). He laments that the pre-Christian period of English history, the subject of book 1, is "obscur'd and blemisht with fables" (1). Of one historical source, he observes that although it is "oldest seeming, [it] hath by the greater part of judicious antiquaries been long rejected for a modern fable" (3). He finds the story of King Dioclesian's fifty daughters, who mur-dered their husbands and ran off with satyrs, "too absurd and too un-conscionably gross" (6). Indeed, Milton spends a good portion of book 1's narrative complaining about its fictional nature. This complain-ing does not stop after book 1's account of pre-Roman history, how-ever, but continues to some degree throughout the entire narrative.

---

81 Quoted in von Maltzahn, *Milton's "History of Britain,"* 221.
82 See D. R. Woolf, "Erudition and the Idea of History in the Renaissance," *Renaissance Quarterly* 40 (1987): 48.

He condemns the "fables" (133) of the Scottish historian Buchanan, and laments that sixth-century history has been "surcharg'd with all the idle fancies of posterity" (163). Doubting the very existence of King Arthur, Milton comments on Geoffrey's claims about the British king's European conquests with skeptical incredulity (164–71). He worries that Bede's account of Paulinus's conversion of King Edwin stems merely from "Legend" (200). The Saxon chronicler he relies on for tenth-century history "runs on a sudden into such extravagant fansies and metaphors, as bare him quite beside the scope of being understood" (309). Similarly, Malmsbury's account of King Edgar is "fitter for a Novel then a History" (327). Milton bitterly protests that fiction plagues English history from its ancient beginnings to the Norman Conquest.

This sustained vehemence is somewhat puzzling, as a number of critics have noted. Much of the writing Milton produced through the 1630s indicates a willingness to combine history and fiction. For example, the Trinity manuscript suggests that even when Milton considers writing about the genuinely historical figure of King Edgar, he compares such an undertaking to fiction: he toys with focusing "especially at his [Edgar's] issuing out of Edelingsey on the Danes, whose actions are wel like those of Ulysses" (*CW* 18:243). The Ludlow *Mask*, which makes substantial use of early British myths, also implies a belief in the presence of literal truth within fiction: " 'tis not vain or fabulous, / (Though so esteem'd by shallow ignorance) / What the sage Poets taught by th'heav'nly Muse / Storied of Old in high immortal verse" (513–16). Furthermore, his two *Defenses*, written shortly after the first four books of the *History*, express what David Loewenstein has called a "mythopoetic" vision of history.[83] In both texts Milton creatively picks and chooses slices of his nation's history in order to defend English republicanism to a European audience. In his closing remarks in the *Second Defense* he compares his efforts to represent his nation's past deeds to the work of an epic poet (*CW* 8:253). In these examples Milton does not find fiction and history simply opposed to each other. Most puzzling about Milton's attitude in the *History* is that, for all his complaining, he does in fact rehearse Geoffrey's account at considerable length in the *History of Britain*. Milton's text is unique: no other seventeenth-century history devotes

---

[83] David Loewenstein, *Milton and the Drama of History* (Cambridge: Cambridge University Press, 1990), 81.

so much space to events so overtly labeled fabulous. Samuel Johnson's perplexity has been shared by many readers: "Why he should
have given the first part, which he seems not to have believed, and
which is universally rejected, it is difficult to conjecture."[84]

Critics have responded to this perplexity in a number of ways. Von
Maltzahn justly observes that Geoffrey's *Historia* still held some
small *caché* with English historians in the 1640s,[85] and Milton himself acknowledges that the Monmouth narrative has been "defended
by many, deny'd utterly by few" (*CPW* 5:8). Loewenstein suggests
that although Milton may insist on the division between fiction and
history in theory, "[i]n practice, Milton writes mythopoetically, even
as he appears to eschew the fabulous and imaginary."[86] Wyman H.
Herendeen has made a somewhat similar claim, arguing that the
History of Britain bucks against the contemporary trend of "empirical history," instead offering a narrative that "makes history an essential part of [Milton's] poetic."[87] Indeed, Milton's history comprises a collage of secondary sources rather than the results of
antiquarian research; the "truth" of history for him resides in narrative, not in physical evidence. And despite Milton's promise not to
interrupt his story's "plain and lightsome brevity" with historiographic "controversies and quotations" (*CPW* 5:4), Herendeen, von
Maltzahn, and others correctly observe that the *History* is full of editorial interruptions, usually critical comments on the events described. Such elaborations on the bare facts remind us of the didactic
function of fiction, Milton's concession to some readers' inclination
to ignore truth unless they see her "elegantly drest," as he notes
wryly in *Church Government*. Although he condemns the tendency
"to invent [speeches], though *eloquently*, as some Historians have
done," as "an abuse of posterity" (*CPW* 5:80; my emphasis), Milton
elsewhere praises, as we have seen, the exemplary and memorializing "Eloquence" (40 and 127) of historical writers. Such contradic-

---

[84] Samuel Johnson, *Lives of the Poets*, ed. G. B. Hill, 3 vols. (Oxford: Clarendon
Press, 1905), 1:145–46.

[85] Von Maltzahn, *Milton's "History of Britain,"* 90.

[86] Loewenstein, *Milton and the Drama of History*, 83.

[87] Wyman H. Herendeen, "Milton and Machiavelli: The Historical Revolution and
Protestant Poetics," in *Milton in Italy: Contexts, Images, Oppositions*, ed. Mario A
di Cesare (Binghamton, N.Y.: Medieval and Renaissance Texts and Studies, 1991),
430, 431.

tions make it tempting not to take Milton's aspersions on fiction and rhetoric at face value.

Despite this seductive reasoning, we should take these aspersions at face value. In the *History of Britain,* Milton really believes, more firmly than Spenser and Drayton, even more than Bolton or Selden, that fiction disrupts the authenticity of history, robbing history of its truth and value. That Milton *relies* on fable to tell his nation's story should not detract from the seriousness of his condemnation of fable: his use of fiction is a forced contingency, much as his prose history is a second-best choice after his national epic came to seem untenable. Ornamenting history with the vestments of fable makes history more elegant and presentable but also mars its etiological force. The etiological context in fact determines much of the bleak tone and rhetorical conflict of the *History.* In addition to instructing his nation morally, Milton also wants to tell his nation where it came from. If the primary or only goal were an exemplary "Eloquence," then an epic poem would do just as well. No, unlike the *Defenses,* both of which employ British and English history for the sake of building a rhetorical justification of the republic, the *History of Britain* wants to articulate a complete account of the nation's past. Fiction, rather than offering assistance in this effort, moves in Milton's estimation from a necessary evil to an impossible obstacle. Milton ends up taking a position that precisely reverses the position of a writer like Bolton: rather than excepting English history from historiographical rigor (since fiction is the only complete narrative option England has), Milton gives up on English history altogether, finding the fictionality at its narrative root an anathema to the kind of absolutely true etiology he wishes to produce.

We may nonetheless feel inclined to ask with Samuel Johnson why Milton, if he felt so unhappy with his nation's early history, did not simply exclude it, as many of his contemporaries were doing, and begin with the Saxons or the Normans as England's origin. Johnson's question in fact exposes the double bind under which Milton suffered, the conflicting impulses of etiology and historical truth. That Milton refuses to exclude the early history signals how deeply he values a complete nation story. On the other hand, that Milton gives up on his nation's history when he reaches the Norman Conquest signals Milton's realization of how obscure the truth of the English past remains. His position is even more difficult than Spenser's, and he is less inclined to compromise with historical fiction. He refuses to simply fictionalize national history, as Spenser finally does in the Paridell episode of *The Faerie Queene*. Like Spenser in the *View of the State of Ireland*, Milton sees that the desire for pure and ancient national origins stems from narcissistic delusion. Early in the *History* he speculates that the myth of Trojan derivation began with some ignorant British storyteller whose "vanity, not pleas'd with the obscure beginning which truest antiquity affords the nation, labour'd to contrive us a pedigree, as he thought, more noble" (*CPW* 5:7). Yet although Milton acknowledges that obscure origins are the truth of history, he is unwilling to condemn his nation to a belated modernity, as Spenser does in the *View*. He wants the whole story, origin and all.

Of course, Milton could have mitigated this awkward conflict between history and fiction if he had thought of his narrative as an exemplary rather than etiological one. The line between moralizing and memorializing is a fine one in Milton's work, and we must take care not to exaggerate it; nor should we erase it. The two letters to Henry de Brass, both written in 1657, close to when Milton was probably writing the final two books of his history, provide useful examples of the distinction between historical narration and moral persuasion. Again, the fact that Milton sometimes ignores this distinction in his own writing should not lead us to disregard his comments in these letters, which include several ideas quite relevant to the *History of Britain*:

> This then, is my view: that he who would write of worthy deeds worthily must write with mental endowments and experience of affairs not less than were in the doer of the same, so as to be able with equal mind to comprehend and measure even the greatest of them, and, when he has comprehended them, to relate [narrare] them distinctly and gravely in *pure and chaste speech* [sermone puro atque casto]. That he should do so in ornate style, I do not much care about; for I want a Historian, not an Orator. Nor yet would I have frequent maxims, or criticisms on the transactions, prolixly thrown in, lest, by interrupting *the thread of events* [rerum serie], the Historian should invade the office of the Political Writer: for, if the Historian, in explicating counsels and narrating facts, *follows truth most of all*, and not his own fancy or conjecture, he fulfills his proper duty. (*CW* 12:93; my emphasis)

First of all, Milton makes it clear that historiography amounts to more than a rehearsing of facts and dates: the historian must attain a degree of life experience in order to process and interpret the deeds of the past. Yet Milton also makes it clear that such interpretation does not turn the historian into an orator, rhetorician, or political theorist. Two qualities distinguish the work of the historian from that of other writers: his discourse is unornamented ("pure and chaste speech"), and it reports a basically continuous story ("the thread of events"). These two elements appear to compose what Milton calls the "truth" of history. Milton's 1641 injunction against "verbal curiosities" in historical poetry has become more serious in his 1657 definition of the historian proper: the true historian is a plain-speaking etiologist. The point here is not that Milton never imagines contexts in which the roles of historian and orator merge—aside from the *History* he often does—but that he finds it important to define the historian by keeping these roles separate. He repeats the distinction in his second letter, responding to de Brass's concern that Aristotle recommends using maxims to gloss narratives: "the parts of the Orator and Historian are different whether they narrate or prove, just as the Arts themselves are different" (*CW* 12:103).

This distinction sheds light even on some of Milton's most obviously "poetic" treatments of national history. Consider the conclusion of the *Second Defense,* in which Milton compares his historical labors to an epic poet in terms that appear directly to contradict his advice to Henry de Brass:

> I have celebrated, as a testimony to them, I had almost said, a monument, which will not speedily perish, actions which were glorious, lofty, which were almost above all praise; and if I have done nothing else, I have assuredly discharged my trust. But as a poet, who is styled epic, if he adhere strictly to established rules, undertakes to embellish not the whole life of the hero whom he proposes to celebrate in song, but, usually one particular action of his life, as for example, that of Achilles at Troy, or the return of Ulysses, or the arrival of Aeneas in Italy, and leaves alone the rest, so likewise will it suffice for my duty and excuse, that I have at least embellished [exornasse] one of the heroic actions of my countrymen. The rest I past by: for who could do justice to all the great actions of an entire people? (*CW* 8:252–53)

In addition to rhetorically defending the recent actions of the republic, Milton makes clear his desire to preserve these actions for posterity. The role of historian does indeed merge with the role of the orator, and of the poet (Achilles, Ulysses, Aeneas), in this passage. The embellishing or ornamenting (*exornare*) of England's historical deeds associates these deeds with fictional models. Some critics have even read this passage as Milton's claim that his prose treatises constitute an adequate replacement for his abandoned Arthurian epic.[88] Yet we should also note Milton's care to specify the limited scope of his monument: one heroic action rather than the entire story of his people. He wishes to praise the very recent past, selectively using details from earlier English history to ornament this praise. His brief comments about the *History of Britain* earlier in the *Second Defense* emphasize precisely the opposite kind of coverage: "I undertook a history of the nation *from its remotest origin;* intending to bring it down, if I could, *in one unbroken thread* to our own times" (*CW* 8:137; my emphases). In contrast to the *Second Defense*'s "one particular action," Milton's account of his history stresses the nation's "remotest origin [ultima origine]" and makes clear the goal of continuity, the "one unbroken thread [filo perpetuo]" that anticipates the "rerum serie" in the 1557 letter to de Brass. An epic oration, employing fictional ornamentation, properly celebrates a single, recent effort of the English people; an entire national history, entailing etiology and continuity, requires "pure and chaste speech."

Yet Milton's misgivings about the ability of such plain, unornamented speech to represent the English story from beginning to end also manifest themselves in the *Second Defense,* in the two passages about history that we just examined. He concludes his observations about English epic history with the rhetorical question, "who could do justice to all the great actions of an entire people?"—precisely Milton's project in the *History of Britain*—and he qualifies his account of his etiological goal in that history with a conditional: "if I could." These comments, I would argue, reflect Milton's dissatisfaction with the four books of his history he had already completed around 1649 and raise the question of whether his history meets its goals of continuity, plainness, and truth. On the one hand, the *History* succeeds in these respects to a greater degree than any earlier British/English his-

---

[88] See, e.g., Lawrence A. Sasek, "Milton's Patriotic Epic," *Huntington Library Quarterly* 20, 1 (1956): 1–14.

tory. It tells a continuous story, from Brutus to the Conquest. Despite Milton's editorial comments, his account is plain to the point of reticence, as John Oldmixon's early judgment of the style suggests: "Milton . . . has been so careful of Redundancy, that he has not allowed Words enough for his Matter."[89] As for truth, Milton takes assiduous care not to affirm the dubious accuracy (as he sees it) of nearly all of his sources: he urges his readers into a continuous skepticism about what they read. On the other hand, the *History of Britain* represents Milton's greatest failure, the derailment rather than fulfillment of his early plans to write a national epic. The bitter tone of this text, both in the first four books and in the last two, a bitterness that critics have sometimes downplayed,[90] emerges from Milton's keen sense of the English historian's double bind. Truth demands a plain history but also exposes national obscurity and barbarism; fiction makes the past knowable and civilized but also empties the past of its historical content.

Milton expresses this problem, as I have suggested, as a tension between the bare, unornamented truth and the decorative clothing that makes the past visible and attractive. The metaphor of clothing and

---

[89] Quoted in von Maltzahn, *Milton's "History of Britain,"* 177.

[90] E.g., Blake Greenway has noted an optimistic energy in the *History*'s tendency to emphasize the individual actor over the collective, seeing the narrative to some degree as a celebration of "the spirit of inflamed heroism, no matter how unbridled or rash"; Greenway, "Milton's *History of Britain* and the One Just Man," in *Arenas of Conflict: Milton and the Unfettered Mind*, ed. Kristin Pruitt McColgan and Charles W. Durham (Selinsgrove, Pa.: Susquehanna University Press, 1997), 65–75; quotation at 67. Greenway offers an intriguing account of Milton's manipulation of his historical sources but neglects the overall discouraging tone of the narrative, as well as Milton's summary account of his countrymen in the Digression:

> For Britain, to speak a truth not often spoken, as it is Land fruitful enough of Men stout and courageous in War, so is it naturally not over-fertile of Men able to govern justly and prudently in Peace, trusting only in their Mother-Wit; who consider not justly, that Civility, Prudence, love of the Publick Good, more than of Money or vain Honour, are to this Soil in a manner outlandish; grow not here, but in minds well implanted with solid and elaborate Breeding, too impolitick else and rude, if not headstrong and intractable to the industry and vertue either of executing or understanding true Civil Government. Valiant indeed, and prosperous to win a field; but to know the end and reason of winning, unjudicious, and unwise: in good or bad Success alike unteachable. (*CPW* 5:451)

Surely we ought to take this pessimistic condemnation of the "headstrong and intractable" English as a rather severe qualification of unbridled action.

body for the poetic ornamentation of history is an old one. We have already mentioned Puttenham's recommendation of the civilizing ornaments for women and poetry, "such . . . apparel as custom and civility have ordained to cover their naked bodies." In the *View of the State of Ireland,* Irenius laments that the impoverished state of Irish chronicles allows for only "naked conjectures," and Eudoxus likewise complains about the "bare traditions" (43). Drayton describes the unornamented past as "naked yet and bare" (6:285). Yet although these examples emphasize the impropriety of an insufficient and naked history, Milton tends to stress the deceptive quality of garments that cover. In this emphasis Milton corresponds to the observations of another republican historian, Thomas May, in his *History of the Parliament of England* (1647):

> Some historians, who seem to abhor direct falsehood, have, notwithstanding, dressed truth in such improper vestments, as to seem to have brought her forth to act the same part that falsehood would; and to have taught her, by rhetorical disguises, partial concealments and invective expressions, instead of informing, to seduce the reader, and carry the judgment of posterity after that bias which themselves have made.[91]

Likewise, in the *History of Britain,* Milton announces his intention to relate "the naked truth, though as lean as a plain journal" (*CPW* 5:230). He intensifies here his dislike of those rhetorical elements that superfluously make the naked truth "elegantly drest," as he puts it in *Church Government.* He associates naked truth with plain speaking and repeatedly privileges this sense of continuous narrative as the "smooth course of history" (4), "the stream of history" (30), "the plain course of historie" (123), and "the smoothness of history" (239). He almost always conceives of fiction and rhetorical elaboration as interrupting these continuities.

Yet Milton complicates this link between uncovered truth and a straightforward history by associating the barbarity of the ancient Britons and Saxons with their nakedness. Contemptuously comparing the Britons with the "wild Irish," Milton notes that "thir bodies [were] for the most part naked, only painted with woad in sundrie figures" (*CPW* 5:59, 58). These same naked warriors, resisting the so-

---

[91] Thomas May, *History of the Parliament of England* (London, 1647; reprint, Oxford: Oxford University Press, 1854), xv.

phisticated Romans, represent "a barbarous and lunatic rout" (75), and the Saxons that later overrun the Britons are themselves "half-naked Barbarians" (135) and "rude and naked barbarians" (443). The body of truth may be naked, but Milton finds it difficult to speak of such naked savages with the "pure and chaste speech" that he recommended to Henry de Brass. Indeed, the problem with unornamented, chaste discourse is that it represents the truth of English history as shameful.

Part of this shame derives from the sheer inability of the past to take on meaningful patterns for the present, an absence of meaning that Milton comes to suspect constitutes the truth of English history. Aside from Milton's praise of King Alfred as a "miror of Princes" (*CPW* 5:292), he has little good to say about his nation's past actions, a striking contrast with his antiprelatical tracts of the early 1640s and with the two *Defenses* of the early 1650s. Indeed, throughout the *History* Milton vacillates in his willingness to claim the past he relates as his own, alternately referring to both the Britons and Saxons as "us" and "them," as Linda Gregerson has recently observed.[92] Even the continuity of his story, one of the essential goals of the *History*, becomes tedious for Milton. Noting that Geoffrey lists "a long descent of Kings, whose names only for many successions without other memory stand," Milton suggests that the Welsh author is "himself wearie, as it seems, of his own tedious Tale" (*CPW* 5:35). He laments that Bede, whom he relies on for seventh-century Saxon history, offers "a Calendar rather then a History" (229). He notes how tiresome it is "to read of so many bare and reasonless Actions, so many names of Kings one after another, acting little more then mute persons in a Scene" (239). He wonders whether rehearsing the petty battles of Saxon lords is any more useful "then to Chronicle the Wars of Kites, or Crows, flocking and fighting in the Air?" (249). The Danish histories that he consults likewise offer only "the bare names and successions of their uncertain Kings, and their small actions at home" (332).

The meaninglessness of these continuities emerges most distressingly in Milton's observation about the various violent displacements in his nation's history (Romans, Britons, Saxons, Danes, Normans),

---

[92] Linda Gregerson, "Colonials Write the Nation: Spenser, Milton, and England on the Margins," in *Milton and the Imperial Vision*, ed. Balachandra Rajan and Elizabeth Sauer (Pittsburgh, Pa.: Duquesne University Press, 1999), 102.

wherein he sees a palpable but enervating sense of continuity: "But if the Saxons, as is above related, came most of them from Jutland and Anglen, a part of Denmarke, as Danish Writers affirm, and that Danes and Normans are the same; then in this invasion, Danes drove out Danes, thir own posterity. And Normans afterwards, none but antienter Normans" (*CPW* 5:258). Although, in the letter to Manso, Milton imagines national conflict as a form of epic heroism—"as mighty Britons break Saxon battle formations" (*Riverside Milton,* 234)—this repetition of the same perhaps represents Milton's new vision of national union, the bleaker version of Spenser's hopeful "eternall union." Here we have historical homogeneity indeed, but a meaningless one, a narrative sameness that deadens national identity rather than grounding it. The bareness of this history is precisely what motivates early national historians, according to Drayton, to supplement the truth with fictive elaboration: "to those things whose grounds were verie true, / Though naked yet and bare (not having to content / The weyward curious eare) [they] gave fictive ornament" (6:277–86). Milton resists offering such ornament as much as he can, to present "the naked truth, though as lean as a plain journal." His truth is indeed naked, but he does not seem to care much for the thinness of his history.

Milton's wish in the 1630s to produce an epic poem about early British kings subtly marks the *History of Britain,* most significantly in terms of the delicate border between history and poetry. As a national historian Milton wants to free himself of the falseness of poetry but also regrets giving up poetry's inventiveness. At the beginning of book 1, Milton justifies his use of dubious historical sources by pointing out the value that early national history has for poets: "I have therefore determined to bestow the telling over of these reputed tales, be it for nothing else but in favor of our English poets and rhetoricians, who by their art will know how to use them judiciously" (*CPW* 5:3). This justification surely takes on a peculiar resonance when we think about it in the context of Milton's own desire only a decade earlier to use these tales for his "art." The contrast in this sentence between the casualness of his gesture ("be it for nothing else") and the concern that poets will need to be careful of history ("judiciously") suggests how vexed this justification is for Milton. After all, Milton has just observed in the preceding paragraph that "*judicious* Antiquaries" are the ones who rejected Geoffrey's fables in the first place (3; my emphasis). *Can* poets use fables to relate the national past judiciously? If yes, then why didn't Milton himself? Loewenstein has aptly described Milton's difficulty in the *History of Britain* as "the dilemma of the historiographer who simultaneously perceives himself as a poet."[93] Indeed, Milton may feel the dilemma all the more painfully because he sees that the historiographer's zeal for truth must displace the creative powers of the poet. Milton conspicuously does not include himself in the phrase "our English poets" because he fears that a poeticized version of English history will succumb to the contaminating fictionality that obscures his nation's past. The two occasions when he permits himself to use verse in book 1 reflect Milton's refusal of poetic fiction but also his regret at its unavailability. Milton offers his own translation for the Latin prophecy in Commelin's edition of Geoffrey, suggesting a certain poetic pleasure, but carefully labels the passage a "Fable" (15). Likewise, Milton introduces the stanza from *Briton moniments* as something "which our Spencer also thus sings" (20). Yet he then makes a point of noting the stanza's historical unlikeliness: "But Henault, and Brunchild, and Greenesheild, seeme newer names then for a Story pretended thus Antient" (21). Unlike Spenser, Milton tries to keep these poetic moments from ornamenting his historical narrative. To some degree, Milton would like to be Spenser, to recall and embellish the national past with the aid of fiction, even at the risk of emptying its historical content. His commitment to "pure and chaste speech," his demand for the naked truth, prevents him from doing so.

What, then, of the great etiological epic that Milton did eventually write? Interestingly, *Paradise Lost* offers as many fictional details as any national epic could offer. Until Milton told us, who would have suspected that Adam asked God to create Eve, that Eve had dreams about flying, or that the Edenic couple argued about gardening? In light of my discussion, however, the crucial difference between *Paradise Lost* and an Arthurian epic is that the former is guaranteed by the Bible; the basic story is in fact overdetermined as true. This very overdetermination had allowed earlier poets like du Bartas and theologians like Luther to imaginatively and interpretively retell the Genesis story themselves. Milton can indulge his etiological impulse by filling in as many fictional details as he wishes, for the taint of fictionality cannot harm this history. The flip side of this observation, however, is that despite the biblical guarantee of veracity, Milton's

---

[93] Loewenstein, *Milton and the Drama of History,* 84.

etiological project is an audacious one. Piling on so many fictional details strains to the limits the original brief story in Genesis. Milton's claim to divine inspiration by the "heavenly Muse," as well as his frequent negative comparisons of literary fiction to biblical truth, may belie an uneasiness about his obviously fictionalized redaction of this history. In this uneasiness, national history stands as the archetypal instance of fictional contamination for Milton. If the *History of Britain* taught Milton that fiction makes etiology impossible, the project of writing an epic history based on two brief chapters in Genesis taught him the opposite lesson: that fiction is, to some degree, the very condition of any etiology. The ghost of fictionality that Milton hoped to exorcise returns uncannily in his religious epic. Milton therefore strives in *Paradise Lost* to cleanse his fictional details by making early national history the monitory Other of cosmic history. This is why, in his list of legendary armies in book 1 (576–86), he singles out the fictionality of the English, Arthurian army as opposed to any of the others. Ideally, the marginal presence of a degraded Arthurian history—"*fabled* knights / In battles *feigned*" (9:29–31)—negatively and differentially confirms the truth of Milton's epic.

Perhaps this is why Milton associates the fictionality of national history with the demonic. Book 2 of the *History of Britain*, which describes the Roman occupation, is the one place in which Milton speaks confidently about his narrative, because its sources are classical. Relieved to have escaped from the obscure, earlier period of English history, Milton begins book 2 by invoking a metaphor of a traveler: "By this time, like one who had set out on his way by night, and travell'd thro' a region of smooth and idle dreams, our history now arrives on the confines, where daylight and truth meets us with a clear dawn, representing to our view, though at a far distance, true colours and shapes" (*CPW* 5:37). This passage seems to anticipate Milton's journey from Hell to Heaven in book 3 of *Paradise Lost*, when he addresses the "holy light":

> Thee I revisit now with bolder wing,
> Escaped the Stygian pool, though long detained
> In that obscure sojourn, while in my flight
> Though utter and through middle darkness bourne
> With other notes than to the Orphean lyre
> I sung of Chaos and eternal Night,
> Taught by the heavenly Muse to venture down

> The dark descent, and up to reascend,
> Though hard and rare: thee I revisit safe,
> And feel thy sovereign lamp . . .

> (3:13–22)

Much as the movement from fable to true history is a transition from night to daylight, so the journey from the stygian pool to heaven is an escape from dark to light. The parallel between these two passages helps us to track Milton's sense of the relation between the fictional and the true—dark to light, low to high, demonic to angelic. In as far as Milton's demonization of national history is a process that began with the *History of Britain*, we might see it as complete in *Paradise Regained*, when Satan tempts Christ with an elaborate banquet served by women more lovely than those "fabl'd since / Of Fairy Damsels met in Forest wide / By Knights of Logres, or of Lyones, / Lancelot or Pelleas, or Pellenore" (2:359–62). Lancelot, Pelleas, and Pellenore are all entirely Romance figures, not mentioned in Geoffrey and the historians; they are the invention of poets such as Chrétien de Troyes and Mallory. Rather than resisting the fable of national history, Milton now fulfills it in order to make his fictionalization of biblical history as true as possible by contrast.

This reading of *History of Britain* presents a Milton less in control of his national discourse than other recent studies have suggested. Milton does the best he can with a format that is not his first choice (a history rather than an epic poem) and with a history he wishes were more inspiring (English rather than, say, Roman). Although some critics argue that the bitterness of Milton's narrative represents his dissatisfaction with the past as a guide for the present,[94] I suggest that such dissatisfaction characterizes his other prose works much more than the *History*. The *History* really does want the past to guide the present—by linking the present to its origin. Comparing the seventeenth century to the fifth century will give the nation an identity: "if it be a high point of wisdom in every private man, much more is it in a Nation to know it self" (130). This is Milton's etiological side, his

[94] Von Maltzahn suggests that "Milton's dislike for the Saxons translates into a wider unwillingness to research the past for more specific directives for present action" (*Milton's "History of Britain,"* 180). Herendeen argues that *History of Britain* is characterized by "the belief in change—that humanity can be other than it is, that it can step out of the determinist course of history onto a path of reform" ("Milton and Machiavelli," 439).

sense that self-knowledge comes out of the past. In this regard, his bitterness in the *History* stems not only from an unhappiness with the national present but also from his sense that this present must be defined to some degree by the past, a past that the naked truth exposes as either barbarous or obscure. He does of course have another side, one that resists historical continuity and denies tradition as an authority for the present. We explore this anti-etiological quality of his thought in the next chapter. In the *History of Britain*, however, his conflicted attitude toward fiction and national history derives from much the same problematic that encouraged Spenser and Drayton to try to recover the truth of the past with fictional ornament.

5 FROM TRADITION TO INNOVATION
Foxe, Milton, and English Historical Progress

Millennialism and Progress

The three modes of historical writing that we have examined—the antiquarian, the apocalyptic, and the fictional—all derive in part from the disinclination to embrace historical novelty. They all attempt to mitigate or resolve the impression that the national present differs fundamentally from the past, seeking to align the present with tradition. The paradoxical qualities of these modes of writing result, as I have suggested, from the manner in which their efforts to impose temporal continuity infelicitously expose the fact of historical difference. The antiquarian unearthing of early medieval artifacts revealed petty British and Saxon provinces rather than an Arthurian empire. Apocalyptic anticipation pointed to the disparity as much as the commensurability between English history and God's eschatological plan. Fictionalized origins implied deluded national vanity even as they offered etiological grounding. Foxe, Dee, and Spenser never try to assuage these contradictions by simply embracing the novelty that they seem to fear inhabits national community. Indeed, this disinclination constitutes one of the central problems of early English nationhood: an increasing perception of historical difference without a vision of historical progress that could interpret this difference positively. The first book of *The Faerie Queene* tentatively offers a perspective on national history in which human effort may contribute positively to God's apocalyptic plan, a perspective I call historical optimism, but Spenser, like Foxe and Dee, firmly conceives of the Apocalypse as the end of history, a conclusion shortly to arrive. He has no sense of eschatology as a model of *continuing* human progress, in which history emerges as a series of innovations that break with the past. This concluding chapter, in some ways a study of the conclusion of an early phase of national temporality, examines the way that Milton and his contemporaries begin to conceive of millennial history as a form of godly novelty.

One of the most striking differences between the *History of Britain*'s view of the past and Milton's other historical writing is the *History*'s lack of apocalyptic language and perspective. Despite the (uneven) presence of Providential oversight—"Divine vengeance deferr'd not long the punishment of men so impious" (*CPW* 5:196)— Milton's narrative tells England's story outside the scope of eschatology. In the *History*, the nation's five sequential encounters with Romans, Picts, Saxons, Danes, and Normans compose a tedious repetition of the same, leading to nowhere in particular. How contrary to *Of Reformation*'s appeal to the just God, who "after the impetuous rage of five bloody Inundations . . . didst build up this Britannick Empire to a glorious and enviable heighth," a historical development that leads to England's apocalyptic encounter with "the Eternall and shortly-expected King" (*CPW* 1:614, 616). It will not do to say that the difference between *Of Reformation* and the *History* represents a shift from naïve national optimism in 1641 to world-weary national pessimism in 1649. Milton repeatedly qualifies his comments about England's merit in the earlier text, wondering why a nation so favored by God thus far "should now be last, and most unsettl'd in the enjoyment of that Peace, whereof she taught the way to others" (*CPW* 1:525). Yet despite this consciousness of England's shortcomings, in *Of Reformation*, as with *Animadversions*, *Areopagitica*, and the *Defenses*, the expectation of the cosmic end determines—at least in part—the meaning of national history.

In their historical vision, then, these other prose works seem more continuous with Foxe's *Acts and Monuments*, a text that likewise interprets history through an apocalyptic lens, than with *History of Britain*. Yet *Acts and Monuments* and the *History* share an etiological impulse, a sense that present identity must derive from past tradition. Both texts resist the notion of breaking historical continuity and, as a result, have difficulty in interpreting historical difference positively. This is where Milton's apocalypticism, and that of some of his contemporaries, represents a significant departure from earlier evaluations of national time as well as from his etiological emphasis in *History of Britain.* He begins to conceive of national novelty as a positive break from the past, using apocalyptic thought as a model of historical innovation. The strongest version of this chapter's thesis might be stated as follows: seventeenth-century millenarian discourse, with its emphasis on the national future rather than the national past, allows the secular notion of historical progress to begin to emerge in English thought.

What is historical progress? Most answers involve some of the following ideas: inevitable improvement, gradual development, ameliorative innovation, and the human ability to create history rather than simply being created by it. My interest centers on the potential contradiction between the first and last ideas, wherein historical inevitability may render human ability irrelevant, or conversely the human potential for failure may disqualify the claim of inevitability. Many descriptions of the idea of historical progress tend toward one of these poles or the other. Robert Nisbet, for example, emphasizes the notion of inevitability:

> Simply stated, *the idea of progress holds that mankind has advanced in the past—from some aboriginal condition of primitiveness, barbarism, or even nullity—is now advancing, and will continue to advance through the foreseeable future.* . . . The idea must not be thought the companion of mere caprice or accident; it must be thought a part of the very scheme of things in the universe and society.[1]

The view that stresses the natural and inexorable quality of progress often also implies, as is the case here, the wholeness of history, the sense that past, present, and future are profoundly connected to each other. Hence Nisbet's surprising refusal to describe Francis Bacon, who anticipates improvement in the future but sees only cyclical decay in the past, as an authentic voice of historical progress.[2] This "whole time" view thus perceives historical progress as the successor of a Christian worldview in which an individual moment is intelligi-

---

[1] Robert Nisbet, *History of the Idea of Progress* (New York: Basic Books, 1980), 4–5 (emphasis in the original).

[2] Bacon "saw [the past] as an expanse to graze on, to nibble at, to eat from occasionally, to exhibit for rhetorical and illustrative purposes; not as the sacred, indispensable soil that alone makes intelligible the present and any anticipated future" (ibid., 112–15).

ble in relation to a total Providence, an ethos that Lord Clarendon suggested when, in a 1670 essay arguing for a progressivist rather than pessimistic interpretation of history, he insisted that "no Decay attends this fulness of Time."[3] The modern idea of secular progress here borrows its continuity from an older notion of Christian revelation unfolding in history.

Yet the view of progress predicated on the human ability to create history often emphasizes not continuity but rather a break with the past. For example, both Richard Glasser and Ricardo Quinones have argued that in the seventeenth century, people began to experience time in a new fashion: "man became aware that time and life were in his own hands, that they were empty and shapeless in themselves, and that he had to fill and inform them according to his personal sense of liberty and responsibility."[4] Strikingly, the moment history becomes malleable and improvable, it also emerges as alienated or "empty"—hence Glasser's focus on Time as the *edax rerum* in his study of Renaissance French literature. Quinones likewise implies that perceiving time as susceptible to human shaping dislocates it from Clarendon's assured "fulness of Time": "when time comes to be a precious, individual commodity through the effective use of which man can elevate his life and preserve his identity, then energies and possibilities are aroused that force the abandonment of the older, contained universe."[5] The human effort to build progress results here in an incommensurability between present and past, because the past is precisely what you must abandon if you wish to create the future. Significantly, recent theorists of modernity have sometimes described the modern epoch's understanding of itself precisely in terms of such an incommensurability. Hans Blumenberg, arguing against the interpretation of modernity (especially in the seventeenth century) as a secular recapitulation of a Christian worldview, insists, "[f]or modernity, the problem [of self-understanding] is latent in the claim of accomplishing, and of being able to accomplish, a radical break, and in the incongruity of this claim with the reality of history,

---

[3] Edward Clarendon, "Of the Reverence Due to Antiquity" (1670), printed in *A Collection of Several Tracts of the Right Honourable Edward, Earl of Clarendon* (London, 1727), 240.

[4] Richard Glasser, *Time in French Life and Thought*, trans. C. G. Pearson (Manchester, U.K.: Manchester University Press, 1972), 150.

[5] Ricardo Quinones, *The Renaissance Discovery of Time* (Cambridge: Harvard University Press, 1972), 16.

which is never capable of starting anew from the ground up."[6] Modernity, like progress, requires an effort of self-definition (an "accomplishment") that dramatically, if unrealistically, leaves the past behind. Human effort thus seems to produce a break in time, contrary to the notion of historical progress as inevitable, gradual, and continuous.

John Spencer Hill has complained that Glasser and Quinones exaggerate the "secular-humanist" interpretation of history in the Renaissance, neglecting the more normative "Augustinian" dispensation of time as a totality that reflects Providence.[7] I agree with this criticism, especially in terms of how deeply theological structures influenced the Renaissance understanding of time. Yet Hill himself neglects the effect of apocalyptic, and especially millenarian, thinking on seventeenth-century accounts of history, an effect that encompassed both seemingly irreconcilable perspectives on historical progress.[8] That is to say, on the one hand, English millenarian theology anticipates an imminent earthly paradise, usually with national dimensions, as the culmination of God's plan, worked out from beginning of time to Christ's final return, and prophesied in full in the book of Revelation. On the other hand, precisely because this paradise will be *earthly*, English millenarians come to feel that their temporal efforts can influence it, perhaps even hasten it or help shape its dimensions, and so they also come to perceive as positive the apparent disparity between their political beliefs and those of the past. Change and innovation emerge as progression rather than simply mutability, linked to the past through an apocalyptic interpretation of history, yet also breaking with the past through the anticipation of a new national order that will rebuild society "from the ground up," to borrow Blumenburg's phrase. Milton, defending antiprelatical ideology against Joseph Hall's charge of "upstart noveltie," finds it natural in 1641 to invoke the anticipated millennial paradise as a model for human innovation: "the new Jerusalem, which *without your admired linke of succession* descends from Heaven" (*CPW* 1:703; my

---

[6] Hans Blumenberg, *The Legitimacy of the Modern Age*, trans. Robert M. Wallace (Cambridge: MIT Press, 1983), 72.

[7] John Spencer Hill, *Infinity, Faith, and Time: Christian Humanism and Renaissance Literature* (Montreal: McGill-Queen's University Press, 1997), 97–98.

[8] Surprisingly, in Hill's otherwise excellent study of Renaissance time, he includes no discussion of apocalyptic temporality, despite his insistence that Renaissance thinking "tends to privilege the future" (ibid., 98).

emphasis). Millenarian theology, at least in English thought, helps the modern notion of historical progress emerge as a dialectic between inevitable improvement and human effort.

We can fully appreciate this millenarian effect of what we might call "futurist historicism"—conceiving the coming millennium as both the culmination of and break with history—only if we place it in the context of the history of English Reformation apocalypticism that we explored in chapter 3. For both Foxe and Milton, this interpretation responds to a violent break with the past that complicates their sense of England's place in time: for Foxe, the replacement of a centuries-old Catholicism with a new religion; for Milton, the revolution against, and eventual replacement of, the centuries-old prelatical system. In linking these two writers, I hope to draw out their status as the bookends of this work. Foxe represents a habit of historical thinking imposed by the Reformation, a consciousness of the gap between now and then that English writers repressed or revised by recourse to precedent. Milton represents the far side of this consciousness, an emerging willingness to dispense with precedent for the sake of ameliorative innovation. This is not to deny Milton's etiological side as it appears in texts such as the *History of Britain*. Nor does his dismissal of precedent constitute a full-scale "secular" notion of historical progress, as later centuries came to elaborate it, but the dismissal does employ the available apocalyptic interpretation of history as a means to authorize novelty.

Foxe: Historical Novelty and Apocalyptic Continuity

In chapter 1 we considered Foxe's historical problem: his insistence on the continuity of the true church throughout English history necessarily called attention to the national community's opposition to this church before the Reformation. The true church's oppressors, more often than not, were English Catholic monarchs, officials, and clergy. Foxe could have simply abandoned a sense of pious Englishness throughout history and located the recent past as the moment of national rebirth, relegating the nation to modernity. To a limited degree, this is what Sir Henry Spelman does in his denial of a glorious British antiquity, and what Spenser's *View of the State of Ireland* initially does in its denial of pure origins. Yet Foxe in the 1560s and 1570s feels compelled to reconstruct an English genealogy that makes the national past at least somewhat commensurate with the national present—hence his defense of Oldcastle as a patriot as well as a martyr. His insistence on historical continuity, in which the break with Rome represents a restoration rather than interruption of tradition, matches the interpretation to which nearly all his reformist colleagues subscribed.

Yet why did they insist on continuity over innovation? Given the sheer antiquity of the Catholic church, Protestants might have done better—at least regarding their polemical efforts—to trumpet their theology as a positive break from the past, a new-and-improved Christianity. Yet they continued to insist on the language of precedent, despite the rhetorical disadvantage this language imposed on them. This issue circles back to the question of national continuity that we examined in chapter 1, but I now consider the question specifically in terms of the desire for precedent because this will bring into sharper relief the contrast between Foxe and Milton. The question of precedent deserves careful scrutiny in any case in that Protestants express notoriously contradictory notions about this matter. Their reliance on tradition does not negate their painful consciousness of historical difference, as Kevin Sharpe somewhat misleadingly implies when he asserts that "past and present were not conceived as different" by Renaissance writers.[9] Indeed, the vehemence of the Reformers' defenses and polemics suggests they sensed and feared the novelty of their doctrines at some level. Yet their traditionalism does mean that we cannot take the occasional dismissal of precedent by Tudor Protestants at face value. John E. Curran, Jr., in his otherwise excellent book on Galfridian history, slightly misreads the Protestant distrust of medieval Catholic history as the sign of a "fundamental question of whether one should stand on tradition of any kind."[10] Fundamentally, in fact, no such question existed. Superficially, Tudor Protestants, dismayed by the massive historical visibility of the Church of Rome, sometimes observed that God's truth transcended any human tradition. Yet this position was by no means inherently Protestant, because Catholics would certainly grant such a claim outside of polemical debate. Until the mid-seventeenth century, the dis-

---

[9] Kevin Sharpe, *Remapping Early Modern England: The Culture of Seventeenth-Century Politics* (Cambridge: Cambridge University Press, 2000), 87.

[10] John E. Curran, Jr., *Roman Invasions: The British History, Protestant Anti-Romanism, and the Historical Imagination in England, 1530–1660* (Newark, Del.: University of Delaware Press, 2002), 38.

missal of historical tradition remained a rhetorical flourish, a tempo-
rizing measure Protestant writers employed until they mustered evidence (however dubious) to show that their church had at least poked
its head out into the world throughout history. Some Protestants
chose not to use the Arthur narratives as evidence of an originary
pristine British Church, but they eschewed them (as we saw in chap.
4) out of a distaste for fable rather than a distrust of tradition per se.
To deny precedent of any kind was, finally, ludicrous, the butt of
Donne's painful joke about Christ's post-Reformation church:
"Sleeps she a thousand, then peeps up one year?"[11] Indeed, as I have
suggested throughout this book, the ironic dilemma faced by Tudor
and Stuart Protestants is that they recognized the English Church's
isolation from historical tradition yet lacked the conceptual means to
valorize their church apart from tradition.

Again, the language Foxe employs can sometimes make his ultimate reliance on tradition difficult to discern. While discussing the
theological controversy about the doctrine of transubstantiation that
flared up during Edward VI's reign, Foxe invents a dialogue between
the figures of Custom and Verity about the meaning of Christ's words
"This is my body." The opposition between truth and custom itself
appears to suggest Foxe's sense that a proper understanding of the
phrase need not rely on traditional interpretations. Indeed, when
Custom insists that Catholics have accepted transubstantiation
"these fifteen hundred years and more," warning that "I think you
would not withstand a doctrine so long holden and taught, unless you
were enforced by some strong and likely reasons" (1570, GGGg2v),
we naturally expect Verity to give tradition a set down by means of
precisely such reasons. Yet Verity's defense of the new understanding
of Christ's words in fact ends up using precedent to show that there is
nothing new about this understanding at all. Most ancient authors,
claims Verity, essentially agree with Luther's reading, and he tells
Custom that "if they be called to witness, they will give evidence
against you" (GGGg3v). The apparent lack of precedent for the reformed theology stems from a misunderstanding and perversion of
tradition: while the ancient church doctors "deliver their mind with
their right hand, you, Custom, received it with the left" (GGGg4v).
Custom's shortcomings derive not from his reliance on history but

---

[11] Holy Sonnet 18.5, in *John Donne: The Complete English Poems*, ed. A. J. Smith
(New York: Penguin, 1986), 316.

rather from his inability to interpret history properly. Until recently, in fact, the church understood the meaning of Christ's words reasonably well. As Verity repeatedly insists, only in these "late days" has the erroneous Romish interpretation prevailed. Foxe's invented dialogue, although it initially seems to imply the irrelevance of tradition, reveals a determination to use tradition to defend the true church.

Even when Foxe cannot entirely avoid the impression of historical alteration, he does so grudgingly, making clear his distaste of the idea of change for change's sake. For example, early in the 1570 edition of *Acts and Monuments,* Foxe confronts the Catholic criticism that the Reformers have instituted blasphemous innovation in sacramental matters: "our adversaries do moreover charge us with the faith of our fathers and godfathers, wherein we were baptized, accusing and condemning us for that we are now revolted from them and their faith" (a2r). Foxe provides an "answer" in the margin of his text: "No man bound to follow the opinions of his godfathers in all points." Foxe appears quite prepared here to differ from tradition when the truth is at stake. He elaborates this point in the text, explaining that if an earlier generation of Englishmen "held anything which receded from the faith of Christ, therein we now remove ourselves from them, because we would not remove with them from the rule of Christ's doctrine." The performative quality of "we *now* remove ourselves from them" hints at the potential need of the reformed English community to embrace its novelty for the sake of doctrinal purity. Yet Foxe crucially revised this bold statement of historical difference six years later, rewriting the sentence to read, "we now remove ourselves *not because we would differ* from them, but because we would not with them remove from the rule of Christ's doctrine" (1576, A2r; my emphasis). Foxe here tellingly softens his earlier stance, placing the rejection of wanton innovation precisely between the terms of present and past, "us" and "them." Does this new formulation deny entirely the gap between now and then? No. Yet it acknowledges historical difference very reluctantly, insisting that current practice did not come about for the sake of change itself. He does this because he deeply believes that truth and tradition ought to coincide, and he finds it uncomfortable when they do not.

Foxe thus either denies Protestant innovation when he can or minimizes it when he cannot. For those cases in which the evidence is truly dubious, especially regarding the continuity of the church in

English history, Foxe takes a middle path: he theoretically denies the absolute authority of tradition but implies that a proper understanding of the facts places tradition on the Protestant side anyway. We see an example of this strategy when Foxe confronts a central controversy of ecclesiastical antiquity: did England receive the Gospels first from the Church of Rome or from the Greek Church (via Joseph of Arimethaea)?[12] Initially, Foxe declares that readers need not take precedent as the criterion of validity: "For giving this, that England first received the christian faith and religion from Rome . . . yet [the Catholic] purpose followeth not thereby, that we must therefore fetch our religion from thence still, as from the chief well-head and fountain of all godliness" (1570, n1r). For a moment Foxe, hypothetically granting the Catholic claim to antiquity, seems willing to subordinate precedent to well-meaning change. Yet immediately after making this striking statement, he shows it to be irrelevant in that he confidently denies "that our christian faith was first derived from Rome; as I may prove by six or seven good conjectural reasons." And, indeed, after a detailed consideration of the evidence, Foxe concludes: "By all which conjectures it may stand probably to be thought, that the Britons were taught first by the Grecians of the East church, rather than by the Romans" (n1r). In effect, Foxe says: even if the Catholics have antiquity on their side, it doesn't matter, though, in fact, we probably have it on our side. We ought to take Foxe's rhetoric in these passages as a microcosm of the Tudor attitude toward tradition: a theoretical willingness to suspend it that is almost always trumped by a deeper conviction that tradition—what Foxe calls "the well-head and fountain"—ultimately holds the truth.

This reliance on tradition helps to explain why the historical interpretation of the book of Revelation played such an important part in the Reformers' defense of the English Church. We have seen how they used the apocalyptic interpretation of history to characterize the seeming absence of the true church in history as a continuity rather than as an interruption. Foxe, even more than Bale, conceives of the Apocalypse as an unbroken, pre-scripted story, a continuity allowing him "to prosecute, by the merciful grace of Christ, the proceeding and course of times, till we come at length to the fall and ruin of the said Antichrist . . . and how he is now falling apace (the Lord Christ

---

[12] Turning pre-Saxon Britain into England is Foxe's anachronism, not mine, and reveals how strongly he would like his nation's past to be homogeneous.

be thanked for ever!) to his decay and confusion" (1570, T6r). To the degree that Revelation foretold the English Church's break with Rome, this break did not really count as a discontinuity. Yet although Foxe's apocalyptic emphasis allows him to confer a significant degree of continuity on his nation's past, it also creates a formidable difficulty in his conception of the national future. The Elizabethans, as we have seen, were a postmillennialist and antimillenarian bunch; they advanced a historicist rather than futurist interpretation of the Apocalypse. For them, Christ's Second Advent, coming *after* the millennium that had already occurred in history, would bring a sudden and absolute end to earthly existence. Foxe thus writes from a difficult position in that his nation's efforts against Antichrist potentially fuel a sense of England's role in the final eschatological battle, but Tudor antimillenarian theology conceives of the Apocalypse as an erasure of earthly distinctions such as national identity. This sense of postmillennial foreclosure prevents Foxe from articulating a clear sense of what contribution his nation can in fact make to God's cosmic plan. His narrative thus gestures at deferring the Apocalypse in order to create a conceptual space that can imagine an English future.

The problem of postmillennial foreclosure derived from the same situation that prevented the Tudors from abandoning tradition in the defense of their church: the sixteenth-century conception of history lacked a narrative of earthly progress, which regards temporal change as fundamentally meliorist rather than mere mutability. Without such a narrative, there was no ready way for Foxe and his contemporaries to interpret historical difference as positive, nor a means for them to see the eschaton as a threshold to an earthly future. Of course, a few sixteenth-century writers proposed historical patterns that implied progressivism, but they did so to contest the idea of inevitable decay, not to construct a theory of inevitable earthly progress. This was the case, for example, with Jean Bodin's *Methodus* (1566). Apocalypticism, for all its shortcomings, offered one of the few large-scale interpretations of history that mitigated the distressing sense of the English Church's novelty.

At first glance, eschatology's revelation of God's unfolding plan appears to resemble a narrative of progress. The difference remains crucial, however. In the post-Renaissance notion of progress, human institutions improve through time, each event producing a further set of resources or an additional paradigm of knowledge that nonetheless takes on a novel quality, breaking with the past. In apocalyptic history, the eschaton looms closer and closer, but human institutions do not improve in time; if anything, they may degenerate as the end approaches. When Foxe, for example, talks about the ecclesiastical alterations produced by the Reformation, he speaks of the transcendence rather than improvement of human society: "We know that politic men evermore detested all changes: and we must confess, there ensueth some evil upon dissentions, and yet it is our duty evermore in the church to advance God's ordinances *above* human constitutions" (1563, Oo5r; my emphasis). To the degree that it requires change, God's dispensation works beyond rather than within civil institutions. The apocalyptic view of history revealed time proceeding event by event, prophetic sign by prophetic sign, but in the meantime human society did not evolve in preparation for a superior earthly future.

Yet the linear understanding of history, although not progressive, did influence the English Reformers' evaluation of human effort within earthly time, ascribing a magnified significance to this effort. I have called Spenser's revision of Foxe's apocalypticism, wherein the legend of Holiness defers the final end for the sake of national *achievement* as well as merely existence, a form of "historical optimism." I would characterize millenarian writing in the 1640s and 1650s in the same way. Does this mean that Foxe is a historical pessimist? Scholars have often thought of the Tudor conception of history as pessimistic. Ernest Tuveson refers to "Renaissance pessimism"; Richard Bauckham speaks of "apocalyptic pessimism"; Robert Nisbet describes the Renaissance conception of history as "the doldrums"; Marshall Grossman offers a pre-seventeenth-century belief in "a homogenous human history, *winding down* to the appointed moment of messianic apocalypse."[13] It is true that the Tudors tend to view Christ's return as the judgment rather than culmination of history and that they doubt the ability of human action to influence the final effects of God's cosmic plan. Yet this pessimism emerges only in the *relation* between history and the Apocalypse; the Tudors have no more despair about these two things, taken on their own, than did the later millenarians. The Tudors are as optimistic as

---

[13] See Ernest Tuveson, *Millennium and Utopia: A Study in the Background of the Idea of Progress* (Berkeley: University of California Press, 1949), 43; Richard Bauckham, *Tudor Apocalypse* (Oxford: Sutton Courtenay Press, 1978), 133; Nisbet, *History of the Idea of Progress*, 118; and Marshall Grossman, *"Authors to Themselves": Milton and the Revelation of History* (Cambridge: Cambridge University Press, 1987), 14 (my emphasis).

the later millenarians about eschatology, confident in Christ's inevitable victory on the final day. And the millenarians saw as much suffering in history as the Tudors did. The distinction rests in how these two groups interpreted the value of human action.

We are perhaps now in a position to make a more explicit assessment of Foxe's vision of history and how it influenced his sense of human effort. The apocalypticism of *Acts and Monuments* tends to subordinate the cyclical, typological interpretation of history to a linear model. This is not to discount the typological interpretations of Revelation in the Middle Ages, nor to deny Foxe's own use of typology. Like many Reformers, Foxe took keen interest in erecting a figural parallel between the ancient captivity of the Jews and the contemporary church's captivity under Rome: "those Israelites exemplifieth and beareth a prophetical image to us" (1570, KK2v). Yet as early as the emergence of the Joachite interpretation in the late twelfth century, the historical exegesis of the Apocalypse implied a linear movement in history, the fulfillment of prophecy event by event. As such, this model opened a new space in which to contemplate human effort within time. Marjorie Reeves very insightfully describes this consequence of Joachim's historical application of Revelation:

> Joachimism gave historical happenings a unique importance linking past, present, and future moments of time with transcendental purpose. It invited the casting of roles in the final acts of the drama. Above all, it opened up the prospect of new human agencies called to participate in the last decisive works of God in history. The backcloth of apocalyptic drama gave enhanced stature to actors in history.[14]

Apocalyptic historicism thus makes human activity one of the primary signs by which history is to be interpreted. This enlarged scope for human volition allows Foxe to blend to a considerable degree the workings of divine Providence with the efforts of his earthly nation and with the individual struggles of hundreds of godly martyrs. The seemingly innumerable local stories in *Acts and Monuments* articulate and merge with the Providential plan. The apocalyptic, linear

[14] Marjorie Reeves, "The Development of Apocalyptic Thought: Medieval Attitudes," in *The Apocalypse in English Renaissance Thought and Literature*, ed. C. A. Patrides and Joseph Wittreich (Ithaca: Cornell University Press, 1984), 51.

model of history focuses more attention on these local actions than a typological interpretation usually would. Indeed, when Marshall Grossman, in an otherwise fascinating study of action and history in the work of Milton, links the seventeenth-century linear model of history to typology by arguing that "typology emphasizes the historical development of the Christian revelation,"[15] he somewhat exaggerates the linear-historical nature of typological reading. True, typology moves from *figura* to *veritas*, as Auerbach (whom Grossman cites) tells us.[16] Yet Auerbach himself makes clear that in typology, "the horizontal, that is the temporal and causal, connection of occurrences is dissolved; the here and now is no longer a mere link in an earthly chain of events . . . it is something eternal, something omnitemporal, something already consummated in the realm of fragmentary earthly event."[17] Typology, while promising spiritual development, primarily reminds us that sequential time is an illusion, giving us a glimpse of the fact that God sees things all at once, that Eve's transgression and Mary's obedience happen for Him at the same time, or out of time.[18] Such thinking tends to marginalize the meaning of local human action in history. Foxe's linear-apocalyptic narrative produces a quite different effect: it begins to take human actions in history as the raw material by which we can understand God's cosmic plan. Such a history tries to comprehend the God's-eye-view by, among other things, examining the struggles of individual actors. In an important sense, the Elizabethan Reformers received the Apocalypse as a typological edifice and worked hard to bring out its potential as a history of human effort.

In claiming that, in Elizabethan apocalypticism, human activity becomes *one of the signs* by which we interpret history, I choose my words carefully. Foxe's postmillennialism requires an important qualification of his sense of earthly effort: although apocalyptic linearity and continuity imbue local action with cosmic meaning, local action is unable, on its own, to *shape* the cosmic story. The effect travels in

[15] Grossman, *"Authors to Themselves,"* 18.

[16] Erich Auerbach, *Scenes from the Drama of European Literature* (New York: Meridian Books, 1959), 24ff.

[17] Erich Auerbach, *Mimesis: The Representation of Reality in Western Literature,* trans. Willard R. Trask (Princeton: Princeton University Press, 1968), 74.

[18] John Spenser Hill puts it very aptly: "The premise of figural thinking is that earthly life, though real, is still—for all its reality—only the *umbra* of an authentic and ultimate reality" (*Infinity, Faith, and Time,* 129).

only one direction, from heaven to earth, resulting in Foxe's inability to reconcile the expectation of the imminent end of earthly life with a earthly effort to create a national future. Note that this difficulty results only when we try to read human action as *cause* rather than *sign* of cosmic meaning, as Foxe implicitly must do when he attempts to imagine his nation's future colliding with the Apocalypse. When considering his historical moment in terms apart from eschatological pressure, he can quite optimistically speak of "these halcyon days" (1583, ¶2v) that England enjoys under Elizabeth. The Elizabethans were not necessarily pessimist about either history or human action, taken on their own. Although cosmically speaking Antichrist would be defeated only by the preaching of God's word and not by the temporal sword, many Protestants in the 1570s and 1580s, for example, felt a moral necessity to use that sword to intervene in the religious wars on the Continent. That is, Elizabethan Protestants were unequivocal about the *moral* obligation to resist Antichrist, an obligation made all the more urgent by their interpretation of history. But their sense of what their efforts contributed to the *cosmic* conclusion of the apocalyptic story was, in the end, quite modest: Christ would return whether or not the earthly forces of the true church had the upper hand over Antichrist. Apocalyptic theology gave Foxe and the Elizabethan Reformers an excellent means of consolidating a historical dispensation they feared was lost or obscured by recent changes, as well as providing a historicism that valued local human effort. But their postmillennialism ultimately produces a conservative sense of this effort, a human history trumped in one way or another by the imminent end. Foxe has no theological means to imagine a radical future, nor can he extrapolate from his apocalyptic continuity a conception of historical progress. He has no choice but to return conceptually to the image he initially mocks, the "wellhead and fountain" of tradition.

An Earthly Millennium and the Possibility of Failure

When English interpreters of Revelation began to suspect that the millennium referred to in Revelation 20 had not already occurred in history but rather was to occur in the future, after Christ's return, they also began to conceive of this millennium as an earthly paradise. They thus embraced the "carnal" interpretation of Revelation that

Augustine had long ago condemned. This new attitude emerged in a slow and uneven process, hindered no doubt by the earlier conviction that the Apocalypse would result in the absolute destruction of earth and of worldly meaning, followed by *heavenly* bliss for the members of the true church. In chapter 3 I focused on the effect of the 1588 defeat of the Spanish Armada as an event that began to change the Reformers' perception of Christ's return. Yet it would be impossible to locate a single cause of the long-term monumental shift in apocalyptic theology. However, to avoid the impression of an inevitable, "evolutionary" development in English thought, I venture two other local factors.[19] The first is the quasi-apotheosis of Elizabeth in poetic epideixis that proliferated in the 1580s and 1590s. The intensification of her image from godly monarch to goddess, though usually taken at its metaphorical face-value, produced a link in some late-Tudor minds between England and divine favor. It is worth noting that seventeenth-century millenarians such as Joseph Mede took Elizabeth's reign as a potential sign of England's elect status.[20] The second factor is the development of English colonialism in the New World, moving from abysmal failure in the sixteenth century to only moderate failure in the early seventeenth century. The anticipated conversion of the Indians to Christianity appeared to signal an active and global spread of God's Word, suggesting the defeat of Antichrist in the world. Seventeenth-century sermons about both the New England community and the Virginia Plantation suggest that America partakes in a kind of apocalyptic ameliorism.[21] I have offered these three

[19] Bernard Capp argues that the shift to premillennialism "was in fact probably evolutionary. Political successes in the later sixteenth century encouraged Protestants to place more emphasis on the eventual overthrow of Antichrist, which in turn aroused interest in the triumphant period between Rome's fall and Christ's return to Judgment"; Capp, "The Political Dimension of Apocalyptic Thought," in Patrides and Wittreich, *Apocalypse in English Renaissance Thought and Literature*, 101. Yet although events such as the Armada victory surely played a part in the theological shift, "political successes" alone cannot explain why many radicals in the 1640s, feeling marginalized and defeated by the Presbyterian majority, continued to insist on the millenarian expectation of an earthly paradise. They did not revert (like their sixteenth century counterparts, the Marian exiles) to postmillennialism.

[20] On the intensity of Elizabethan apotheosis toward the end of the century, see Beth Quitslund, "Elizabethan Epideixis and the Spenserian Art of State Idolatry," in *European Legacy* 5, 1 (2000): 29–48. On the apocalyptic potential of this apotheosis, see Robin Headlam Wells, *Spenser's "Faerie Queene" and the Cult of Elizabeth* (Totowa, N.J.: Barnes and Noble Books, 1982).

[21] On New England millenarianism, see Stephen J. Stein, "Transatlantic Extentions: Apocalyptic in Early New England," in Patrides and Wittreich, *Apocalypse in*

phenomena as "causes" of English millenarianism, but the various interpretations produced about them could also be taken as "effects" of the new theology. The important thing to keep in mind is that the futurist reading of the Apocalypse interacted with a variety of discourses in the early seventeenth century, especially to the degree that commentators believed that English nationalism was at stake.

Part of the national investment involved the question of human effort: to what degree could the nation participate in the final apocalyptic victory? I have discussed Spenser's nonmillenarian answer to this question, but what about the early millenarians? The often-cited commentary of Thomas Brightman, a Bedfordshire minister, serves as a good example of the uncertain relation between human effort and paradise, because he wrote his work in the final years of Elizabeth's reign (it was published posthumously in Latin in 1609). Though he criticizes the sluggishness of the English Reformation, he identifies his nation's break with Rome as "a most evident proof given us of this eternal Kingdom," a future earthly kingdom that Brightman suggests would provide "great felicity pertaining to *this* life." As is well known, he is one of the first English commentators to predict a period of earthly rule by the saints: "this kingdom of Saints shall be eternal, which shall be begun on earth, neither shall it ever be interrupted, but shall be finally translated into heaven."[22] Brightman's emphasis on continuity in this statement, as well as the idea of "continuance" that he repeatedly underscores in his comments on Revelation 20, results partly from his sense of the limited role human effort will play in summoning the millenarian kingdom. Brightman's scheme tends to subordinate human action (which potentially produces a break with the past, as we saw earlier) to the flow of unbroken tradition. The English people would not bring about the coming paradise through their

---

English Renaissance Thought and Literature, 266–98. On Virginian millenarianism, see Perry Miller, *Errand into the Wilderness* (New York: Harper, 1956), 115–22ff.; see also Beth Quitslund, "The Virginia Company, 1606–1624: Anglicanism's Millennial Adventure," in *The Ends of the Earth: Millennialist Thought from the Reformation to the American Civil War*, ed. Andrew Gow and Richard Conners (Amsterdam: Brill Press, forthcoming).

[22] I quote from the first English translation: Thomas Brightman, *A Revelation of the Apocalypse* (Amsterdam, 1611), 389, 701 (my emphasis), 706. Brightman's treatise serves to remind us that the opposition between "postmillennial" and "premillennial" is sometimes only nominal: Brightman (following Foxe), identifies the thousand-year period of Revelation 20:2 with the historical epoch of 300–1300 C.E. (648) but also predicts a future earthly paradise after Christ's return. He is a postmillennialist millenarian.

own activity; in fact, Brightman insists that Antichrist will become all the stronger just before Christ returns to rule on earth.

However, human effort *does* enter into Brightman's interpretation in a negative sense. Like Foxe, Brightman warns the English to press on with Godly reformation of the church; unlike Foxe, however, Brightman ties this warning to the conclusion of the cosmic story: if the English grow lax, God may "translate his Court and Palace to some other place" (162). Although Brightman offers little hope that worldly activity can stymie Antichrist before Christ's return, he suggests that the English could behave so poorly that God will choose some other nation to favor with paradise. Once English thinkers conceived of the future millennium as *earthly*, and hence localized, they began to fear they would fail to keep it in England. From this perspective, interestingly enough, English colonialism in America threatened millenarian loss as much as it promised success. William Twisse, a scholar deeply interested in the premillennial theology of Joseph Mede and anxious about his nation's poor spiritual state so close to Christ's return, wonders in 1635 if America rather than England might house "the glory of new Jerusalem": "it may serve as a chamber to hide many of God's children, till the indignation pass over, which hastens upon us more and more."[23] Sentiments such as this may shed light on George Herbert's poem of disappointed millennialism, "The Church Militant"—published in 1633—in which America seems to steal the Apocalypse from England: "Religion stands on tip-toe in our land, / Ready to pass to the American strand."[24] Characteristic of the period, Herbert's poem conceives of the Apocalypse occurring (or not occurring) in a precise place.

Yet we should not allow this anxiety about failure to obscure the powerful, implicit, and almost reciprocal connection it assumed between Providence and action. Indeed, the possibility of failure was precisely what allowed human effort to *matter* to the cosmic story. If the millenarians had something to lose, then they also had something to gain. The contrast with *Acts and Monuments* is helpful: for Foxe, resistance to Antichrist may result in the individual Christian's salvation but will not affect the cosmic conclusion of the apocalyptic

---

[23] "Dr. Twisse's Fifth Letter to Mr. Mede, applauding his Conjecture concerning *Gog* and *Magog*, and the first peopling of America" (1635); the letter was printed in Joseph Mede, *Works* (London, 1677), 809.

[24] George Herbert, "The Church Militant," in *George Herbert and Henry Vaughan*, ed. Louis L. Martz (Oxford: Oxford University Press, 1986), 235–36.

narrative. Cosmically speaking, this resistance can neither win nor lose. Whatever role England plays, Christ will make a universal triumph over worldly corruption. The seventeenth-century millenarians were not more "optimistic" than their postmillennialist predecessors about the nation per se, for as often as not they expressed doubt that England would continue to merit the favor God has thus far bestowed on it—a characteristic of their writings that sometimes passes unnoticed by modern readers. Such doubt is not surprising, given that the millenarians frequently saw themselves as an embattled minority, oppressed by a Presbyterian majority in the 1640s and by a turncoat Cromwell in the 1650s. No, rather than simple confidence, their theology allowed them to perceive the future as an *earthly* opportunity, one that they might succeed or fail to grasp. This notion of opportunity implied a conception of history as both predetermined (Christ will come no matter what) and human-made (local effort may or may not manage to center Christ's kingdom in England). Put another way, millenarianism produced an effect similar to the modern dialectic of historical progress, an oscillation between inevitable improvement and human effort.

The vocal and influential "fifth-monarchists" held to the millenarian interpretation of the Apocalypse more consistently than other radical groups did.[25] Yet, as Nigel Smith has noted, "[m]illennialism touched all the radicals, just as it was a fundamental component of all religious outlooks of mid-seventeenth-century English people."[26] The anticipation of an earthly millennium led many English writers of the 1640s and 1650s to conceive of their political activity as possibly shaping God's plan. This sense of shaping power marks the crucial difference between post-Armada apocalyptic discourse and later millenarianism. The millenarians, of course, believed that they needed the blessing of Christ to defeat Antichrist (who now largely took the shape of Charles I, religious formalism, and the like). They conceived of Parliament and its allies as God's elect *instrument*, as Stephen Marshall made clear in 1647 when he told the Commons that God "hath put (as it were) the fates of his Church and Kingdom

---

[25] The best general description of mid-century millenarianism is still that in Bernard Capp, *Fifth Monarchy Men: A Study in Seventeenth-Century English Millenarianism* (London: Faber, 1972). On their sense of active participation in the cosmic story, see especially 131–40.

[26] Nigel Smith, *Perfection Proclaimed: Language and Literature in English Radical Religion, 1640–1660* (Oxford: Clarendon Press, 1989), 9.

in your hands"; "as it were" marks the limiting condition of human agency.[27] Nonetheless, Marshall believed that the cosmic future was at stake in Parliamentary action, implying, contra Spenser, Giffard, and Dent in the 1590s, that the *manner* in which Christ returns to earth would depend to a considerable degree on English effort. These predictions about the future almost always function as a call to action in the present. In 1649, Christopher Syms implied a reciprocal relationship between the divine plan and human action when he asked, "if this British Northern nation be the people chosen of God to accomplish the last wonders of the world, to cleanse the church of heresy, schism, atheism, and hypocrisy, as time will shortly make appear it is, is it not necessary the nation itself be first purged?"[28] Syms has no doubt that England has been "chosen," but he believes that God requires human effort on earth before He will grant an earthly paradise.

Among its many effects, millenarian expectation energized a specifically national activism to an almost unprecedented degree, creating the new possibility that the English community might influence the cosmic end. The national flavor of midcentury radicalism lies precisely in this sense of communal potential. Recent scholarship has emphasized, in contrast, the manner in which millenarian thought extended the scope of individual agency. Thomas Corns, in his excellent survey of radical groups in the period, notes that the revival of the Joachite idea of the post-Advent millennium, when the Holy Ghost would speak directly to each believer, possessed radically divisive implications: "No heresy could be more subversive of the social fabric of the early modern state in that it empowers the conscience of each individual to stand against any received wisdom and against any social or ecclesiastical authority."[29] Certainly true, though Luther's demand that each Christian maintain a personal and unmediated relationship with Christ had created this subversive potential of individual conscience a century earlier. Millenarianism intensified this long-standing emphasis in Reformation theology. Its most distinctive contribution, however, involved the union of apocalyptic and English futures, so that godly resistance to traditional

---

[27] Stephen Marshall, *The Right Understanding of the Times* (London, 1647), E2v.

[28] Christopher Syms, *The Swords Apology* (London 1644), B4v.

[29] Thomas Corns, "Radical Pamphleteering," in *The Cambridge Companion to Writing of the English Revolution*, ed. N. H. Keeble (New York: Cambridge University Press, 2001), 77.

forms took on a communal, national significance. The millenarians, unlike their Tudor predecessors, saw their efforts contributing to the national future as much as to the welfare of their individual souls. As we saw in chapter 3, although George Giffard in 1596 very much believes England can contribute to Antichirst's overthrow, English soldiers ultimately can be responsible only for their individual salvation. Compare this sentiment to Marshall's 1643 tract addressing the House of Commons:

> More than the salvation of your own souls depends upon you; the glory of Christ; the establishment of this Church and Kingdom; yea the welfare of all Christendom, in great measure, are all embarked in that vessel, the steering whereof is in great part committed unto you. You are in part *one of the Angels* who are to pour out the vial of the wrath of God.[30]

Marshall's apocalyptic futurism leads him to extend the purview of human effort from personal salvation to cosmic polity. The fate of Christ's church on earth lies in English hands.

The millenarian interpretation of Christ's return thus shifted emphasis from the apocalyptic judgment of individual souls to the apocalyptic culmination of national effort. The outcome of this effort, as commentators make clear, remained uncertain, and hence the notion of an "elect nation" fails to capture the provisional quality of most millenarian thought. These writers seek a future English paradise while acknowledging that their efforts may fail; in this respect they sometimes see themselves in competition with other nations. The title page of Gerrard Winstanley's *Law of Freedom* (1652) includes verses that invoke this interplay of hope, caution, and competition:

> In thee, O England, is the Law arising up to shine,
> If thou receive and practice it, the crown it will be thine.
> If thou reject, and still remain a froward Son to be,
> Another Land will it receive, and take the crown from thee.[31]

---

[30] Stephen Marshall, *Song of Moses* (London, 1643), F3r (emphasis in original).

[31] Gerrard Winstanley, *Law of Freedom* (London, 1652), title page. See David Loewenstein's discussion of this tract in *Representing Revolution in Milton and His Contemporaries: Religion, Politics, and Polemics in Radical Puritanism* (Cambridge: Cambridge University Press, 2001), 80–89.

Voicing a theme that runs through much millenarian writing, Winstanley insists that the English must exercise sufficient spiritual discipline. He had made the same claim, in a more pointed reference to the Apocalypse, two years earlier while defending the efforts of the Diggers, one of the most politically radical groups of the period, to create a communist society:

> England is the first of nations that is upon the point of reforming: and if England must be the tenth part of the city, Babylon, that falls off from the beast first, and would have that honour, he must cheerfully (and dally no longer) cast out kingly covetous propriety, and set the crown upon Christ's head, who is the universal love or free community, and so be the leader of the happy restoration to all nations of the world. And if England refuse, some other nation may be chosen before him. . . . Therefore, you rulers of England, be not ashamed nor afraid of Levellers, hate them not. Christ comes to you riding upon these clouds. . . . You have set Christ upon his throne in England by your promises, engagements, oaths, and two acts of Parliament, the one to cast out kingly power, the other to make England a free commonwealth. Put all these into sincere action, and you shall see the work is done, and you with others shall sing Hallelujah to him that sits upon the throne, and to the Lamb for evermore.[32]

I quote Winstanley at length to point out that he sees the distinct possibility, not certainty, of an English millennium: "*if* England . . . *would* have that honour." Yet the lack of certainty does not cause him to anticipate anything but an earthly paradise, one in which Christ comes to the earth "riding upon these clouds," rather than the earth being "caught up into the clouds," as Bishop Jewel put it seven decades earlier. The imminence of an earthly millennium serves as a call to radical political action now, in the world. Once again in this millenarian tract we can observe the dialectic between inevitability ("Christ comes to you") and human effort ("you have set Christ upon his throne in England").

This implied proximity between human and divine provenance made some writers uneasy. Shortly after the execution of Charles I,

---

[32] Gerrard Winstanley, *A New-Year's Gift* (London, 1650); reprinted in *The Works of Gerrard Winstanley*, ed. George H. Sabine (Ithaca: Cornell University Press, 1941), 385–86.

Thomas Gataker, editing a posthumously published interpretation of Revelation by Robert Parker, seems primarily motivated to curb the political implications of Parker's exegesis: "But whatsoever the Interpretation of these abstract and mystical points in the Revelation, it is not safe for any men to ground any action upon presumption or confidence that now the time is come when things shall be fulfilled, and that it doth belong to them to execute the Wrath of God against Papists or any others."[33] Yet many of them already believed that the time had come, or was about to, convinced that their political efforts in the present prepared for a worldly paradise in the future. Of course, they also believed they were acting out the role God had given them, but it was a role that put the fate of the world in their hands.

Miltonic Apocalypticism

The link in Milton's work between eschatology and Englishness has been well established.[34] In addition to his two most extensive millennial references—the apocalyptic prayers in *Of Reformation* and *Animadversions* (*CPW* 1:613–17, 705–7)—critics commonly note that Milton often insists on God's particular esteem for England, arguing that the Creator "hath yet ever had this Iland under the speciall indulgent eye of his providence . . . pittying us the first of all other Nations" (704) and calling his countrymen "the elect people of God" (861). Recent commentary on Milton also sometimes argues for an apocalyptic "reluctance" in his work, pointing out how often he voices doubt about his nation's worthiness in God's eyes.[35] Indeed, although Milton often links national privilege with the coming end, observing, for example, that God permitted England to "blow the

---

[33] Robert Parker, *An Exposition of the Pouring out of the Fourth Vial*, ed. Thomas Gataker (London, 1650), 15.

[34] For introduction on this topic, see Michael Fixler, *Milton and the Kingdoms of God* (Evanston, Ill.: Northwestern University Press, 1964); and C. A. Patrides, "'Something like Prophetic strain': Apocalyptic Configurations in Milton," in Patrides and Wittreich, *Apocalypse in English Renaissance Thought and Literature*, 207–37.

[35] E.g., Patrides links Milton's hesitation about Revelation's "emphasis on judgment" to his ambivalence about England's merit: "Equally, the nationalistic strain would eventually be qualified . . . into a cosmic vision distinctly more appropriate to a poet with stated prophetic aspirations" ("Apocalyptic Configurations in Milton," 225).

first Evangelick Trumpet" of Revelation 8:7, he just as often takes the same occasion, as we have seen, to wonder why his nation "should now be the last, and most unsettl'd in the enjoyment of that Peace, whereof she taught the way to others" (*CPW* 1:525). Yet by placing statements like this one in the context of other millenarian writing, we can see that Milton's fear of national failure is not simply a sign of apocalyptic reluctance but rather the element that brings human effort into play in the first place. He warns his fellow citizens in *Animadversions* that if they hesitate to push on with reformation, "let us feare lest the Sunne for ever hide himselfe, and turne his orient steps from our ingratefull Horizon justly condemn'd to be eternally benighted" (*CPW* 1:705). By the phrase "eternally benighted," Milton does not deny that God may save individual deserving Englishmen, but rather he fears that England will fail to merit God's attention *as a nation* ("our ingratefull Horizon"). As an *earthly* community, England has something to lose (and therefore possibly to gain) in the future. David Loewenstein, discussing the millennialism of Milton's early prose, poses a primary question about Milton's work: "how large a part can human agents . . . assume in the cosmic drama of history?"[36] This is aptly put, since it makes clear the distinction between the moral drama of earthly life (a ubiquitous element of Christian theology) and the cosmic drama of eschatology (brought to a human level by the anticipation of an earthly paradise). The answer to Loewenstein's question is "a quite large part," provided we understand that only the possibility of failure makes this large part intelligible.

I have been assuming that Milton expects an earthly future to reward his nation's earthly effort, but his oeuvre makes this issue far from self-evident. One way to approach Milton's "futurism" is to ask: was Milton in fact a millenarian, in the way that many of his Puritan contemporaries had become? Christopher Hill and others have argued that he is; Janel Mueller and others argue the opposite.[37] To begin, we should examine the explicit millenarianism in *De Doctrina Christiana*, which insists that

---

[36] David Loewenstein, *Milton and the Drama of History: Historical Vision, Iconoclasm, and the Literary Imagination* (Cambridge: Cambridge University Press, 1992), 26.

[37] For Christopher Hill's interpretation, see Hill, *Milton and the English Revolution* (New York: Viking, 1977), 279–84.

there are any number of texts which show that Christ's reign will take place on earth. . . . This *judgment* [of Luke 22:29], it seems, will not last for one day only but for a considerable length of time, and will really be a reign, rather than a judicial session. . . . After a thousand years Satan will come again, raging, and will besiege the church with huge forces, with all the enemies of the church collected together. But he will be thrown down by fire from heaven and condemned to everlasting punishment. (*CPW* 6:624–25)

I am inclined to take this passage as rather definitive, but given the recent controversy about the authorship of *De Doctrina Christiana*,[38] we should perhaps refer the question to the less explicit millennialism of Milton's other prose. Mueller justly observes that *Of Reformation* imagines the apocalyptic glorification of the saints in heaven, not earth, and she quotes from the concluding apocalyptic invocation of the treatise: "the . . . beatific Vision progressing the dateless and irrevoluble Circle of Eternity" (*CPW* 1:616).[39] Not much millenarian earthliness here, to be sure. But just one sentence earlier in this final invocation, Milton hopes that his fellow Englishmen

may press on hard . . . to be found the soberest, wisest, and most Christian People at that day when thou the Eternal and shortly-expected King shalt open the Clouds to judge the several kingdoms of the World, and *distributing National Honours and Rewards for Religious and just Commonwealths*, shalt put an end to all Earthly Tyrannies, proclaiming thy universal and mild Monarchy through Heaven and Earth. (1:614; my emphasis)

The millenarian question is not quite so obvious in this passage. If Christ's Second Coming will yield only "a heaven beyond time," as

---

[38] See William B. Hunter, *Visitation Unimplored: Milton and the Authorship of "De Doctrina Christiana"* (Pittsburgh, Pa.: Duquesne University Press, 1998); also see Barbara K. Lewalski's response in "Milton and *De Doctrina Christiana*: Evidences of Authorship," *Milton Studies* 36 (1998): 203–28.

[39] Mueller introduces this passage by arguing that "[t]rue . . . to the premium Milton lays on transmundane glory as the end of human activism, there is no room for millenarianism in *Of Reformation*." See Janel Mueller, "Embodying Glory: The Apocalyptic Strain in Milton's *Of Reformation*," in *Politics, Poetics, and Hermeneutics in Milton's Prose*, ed. David Loewenstein and James Grantham Turner (Cambridge: Cambridge University Press, 1990), 19.

Mueller suggests,[40] what sense are we to make of "National Honours"? At the least, Milton has moved far past the Elizabethan scheme by suggesting that some worldly distinctions—such as national identity—will be meaningful after Christ's arrival. C. A. Patrides aptly describes the ambiguity of Milton's apocalyptic vision: "the millennial reign would seem to be the final event within time-bound history and yet coterminous with or protracted into eternity."[41] And as we have seen in Milton's contemporaries, the issue of *national* merit appears to be the factor that encourages this protraction.

Indeed, despite Milton's common privileging of the spiritual over the physical, we see ambiguous interpenetrations between time and eternity fairly often in his writing, especially in those places where he voices a sense of eschatological pressure. For example, although Milton certainly conceives of the New Jerusalem as a spiritual place, he interprets the golden reed of Revelation 21:15 to mean that the millennial paradise possesses a high degree of what sounds like worldly organization: "The state also of the blessed in Paradise, though never so perfect, is not therefore left without discipline, whose golden survaying reed marks out and measure every quarter and circuit of new Jerusalem" (*CPW* 1:752). Similarly, in *Reason of Church Government* Milton, likening the presence of the prelaty to life-killing winter, speaks of the time "when the gentle west winds shall open the fruitful bosome of the earth thus over-girded by your imprisonment, then the flowers put forth and spring, and then the Sunne shall scatter the mists, and the manuring hand of the Tiller shall root up all the burdens of the soile without thank to your bondage" (1:785). If we take the "Tiller" as a kind of apocalyptic Christ, as Thomas Corns suggests,[42] then what does Milton believe this Christ will do at the end of time? We could read "rooting up" as the destruction of earthly existence, but "manuring hand" suggests cultivation as well as deracination. Further, the Tiller comes in the midst of an earthly spring in which "the gentle west winds shall open the fruitful bosome of the earth." Millenarian writers often use the summer image as a metaphor for end time, as Winstanley does in a reference to Song of Solomon 2:11: "but now the Winter is past, the

---

[40] Ibid.
[41] Patrides, "Apocalyptic Configurations in Milton," 226.
[42] Thomas Corns, *John Milton: The Prose Works* (London: Twayne, 1998), 33.

Summer is come, the flowers appear in the earth: that is, the glorious workings of the Anointing, in the spirit of the Saints."[43] Milton's eschatological setting hovers suggestively between heaven and earth.

Milton expresses this sense of the earthly nature of paradise in some of his earliest writings. Toward the end of *Prolusion VII* Milton confronts the discouraging argument of "Ignorance" that, because "we live under the shadow of the world's old age and decrepitude, and of the impending dissolution of all things," there is no point in pursuing learning. Rather than denying this apocalyptic imminence, Milton embraces it, reinflecting the nature and significance of this end:

> But we may hope for an eternal life, which will never allow the memory of good deeds we performed on earth to perish; in which, if we have done well here, we shall ourselves be present to hear our praise; and in which, according to a wise philosophy held by many, those who have lived temperately and devoted all their time to noble arts, and have thus been of service to mankind, will be rewarded by the bestowal of a wisdom matchless and supreme over all others. (*CPW* 1:302)

The pressure of end time leads Milton not to quiescence or apocalyptic reluctance but rather urges him to imagine a commensurability between earthly and heavenly life. This commensurability remains ambiguous, for Milton does not make clear where this "eternal life" will unfold. He insists, however, on a continued colloquy between the spiritual and earthly, an eternity in which we will "hear" the commentary of temporality. The "wisdom matchless" that Milton hopes to achieve does not sound like a spiritual relinquishing of earthly knowledge (the inference that Ignorance wishes us to make) but rather an extension of such knowledge.

Again, the protraction of earthly meaning into the divine future implicitly links human action with eschatology. In his analysis of *Prolusion VII* Robert Appelbaum shrewdly argues that Milton "tries to open up a space for human conduct within the constraints of temporality," a project he pursues in this early text by imagining eternity "not only as the judgment of history, but also its culmination, the fulfillment of its this-worldly objectives."[44] For Milton, like many of

---

[43] Gerrard Winstanley, *The Breaking of the Day of God* (London, 1649), F1r.
[44] Robert Appelbaum, "Tip-toeing to the Apocalypse: Herbert, Milton, and the Modern Sense of Time," *George Herbert Journal* 19, 1–2 (1995–96): 39, 45.

his contemporaries, earthliness creates a possibility for human impact on the cosmic scheme. Indeed, although Mueller resists the idea
of millenarianism in Milton's work, she argues that Milton
"projects . . . an unprecedented role for human agency in and beyond
history," concluding that "he recast[s] native apocalypticism as a uni-
tary framework where a divine design finds realization in and
through the struggles of the English people toward ever more perfect
forms of individual and institutional life."[45] My interpretation of
Milton's millennialism attempts to combine this sense of human activity with Appelbaum's description of Milton's earthly eternity. Milton interprets the coming Apocalypse as a *product* of historical
progress by imagining an affiliation between the apocalyptic future
and the earthly, English future.

Does Milton value the nation as much as he does Christ's kingdom? Certainly not. Like Foxe, he always chooses the true church
over the faithful nation, if he must choose. As Linda Gregerson has
observed in an analysis of *History of Britain* and *Paradise Regained,*
"Nation was always for Milton an interim measure, a means of struc-
turing hope and performing fidelity during the interval between two
Comings. The conceptual and practical problem, both before and
after the Restoration, was how to inhabit the meantime. It is not nation the poet rejects in *Paradise Regained;* it is nation for its own
sake."[46] An England not directed toward God becomes a meaningless
community. Yet in much of his writing in the 1640s, Milton expresses hope that the nation, whatever its interim reality, will continue to reform, purifying itself until it becomes nearly continuous
with the paradise that Christ may bring to earth. Although there is no
denying Milton's bias toward the church over the nation, this does
not represent a reluctance about England's potential, because all English millenarians held the same bias. Compare Stephan Marshall's
observations on this matter:

> I go not about to determine what the event of these troubles will be to
> England, as England is a Civil, or Political State, or Commonwealth;
> Christ breaks and moulds Commonwealths at his pleasure. He hath

---

[45] Mueller, "Embodying Glory," 10, 35.
[46] Linda Gregerson, "Colonials Write the Nation: Spenser, Milton, and England on
the Margins," in *Edmund Spenser: Essays on Culture and Allegory,* ed. Matthew
Greenfield (Burlington, Vt.: Ashgate, 2000), 102.

not spoke much in his word, how long they shall last, or what he intends to do with them. . . . But it is the cause of the Church, the blessed event of these things to the Church of Christ, which I speak of, the welfare and good success of Religion, in which Cause you are properly engaged and interested, and which I hope is dearer to you than ten thousand Englands.[47]

When it comes to a choice, England always gives way to Christ. But for Marshall, and Milton, it does not always have to come to a choice, and this quoted passage does not negate Marshall's earlier demand that his readers "behold the wonders of these two or three last years in England and Scotland, ponder them seriously, they are the Lord's doings, and ought to be wonderful in your eyes: think yet further how wonderful he will be when he comes to be admired in his Saints at the last day" (E3r). Like Marshall, Milton provides no full-fledged description of a future earthly paradise, yet he repeatedly suggests England's paradisal potential (as well as his fear of England's failure). His eschatology is fraught with worldly content.

Innovation and Secular Time

The desire for historical continuity was alive and well in the 1640s and 1650s. Like their Elizabethan predecessors, seventeenth-century antiroyalists and antiformalists combated the painful impression of novelty (writing against the grain of centuries-old monarchical and prelatical organization) by appealing to long-standing native traditions (real or imagined). Keith Thomas has discussed how the antiroyalists used political prophecy (often medieval manuscripts that had ostensibly "predicted" the execution of the king) as a means to make their actions appear continuous with past tradition.[48] English Parliamentarians also often articulated their position in terms of "ancient" English (or Saxon or British) constitutional principles.[49] Fur-

---

[47] Marshall, *Song of Moses*, G4r.

[48] Keith Thomas, *Religion and the Decline of Magic* (New York: Charles Scribner's, 1971), 409–13, 422–32.

[49] David Norbrook notes that "both sides in the Civil War were to present themselves as defending the ancient constitution, from the encroachments of a usurping Parliament or a tyrannical ruler." See Norbrook, "The English Revolution and English Historiography," in Keeble, *Cambridge Companion to Writing of the English Revolution*, 234.

thermore, even the emerging idea that humans could impact the millennial scheme did not automatically disqualify the hope for historical continuity. Ralph Cudworth describes historical events with a theatrical metaphor: "we men [are] Histrionical Actors upon the Stage, who notwithstanding insert something of our Own into the poem too; but God Almighty is that Skillful Dramatist who always connecteth that of ours which went before with what of his follows after, into good Coherent Sense; and will at last make it appear that a Thread of exact Justice did run through all."[50] Although Cudworth suggests human actors can alter the prewritten script, he emphasizes God's ultimate shaping power to create coherency out of what might otherwise appear as mere contingency, the "Thread" that connects past, present, and future.

Nonetheless, alongside this commitment to tradition there emerged among many English writers the impression that novelty was good in itself. Their comments about historical change begin to resemble what Habermas describes as the dispensation of secular, modern time: "Whereas in the Christian West the 'new world' had meant the still-to-come age of the world of the future, which was to dawn only on the last day . . . the secular concept of modernity expresses the conviction that the future has already begun: It is the epoch that lives for the future, that opens itself up to *the novelty of the future.*"[51] Yet although Habermas opposes this new sense of time to Christian cosmology, apocalyptic thinking in fact helps English writers to conceive of novelty as a positive phenomenon in history. The notion of a future earthly paradise, one radically different from the present, provided a model of godly innovation. Postmillennialism's promise of universal destruction, making individual or national effort irrelevant on a cosmic level, did not provide Foxe and his contemporaries with a concept of history as dynamic, progressive change. In the seventeenth century, however, millenarians begin to describe their future expectations in terms we would call historical progress. They employ apocalyptic rhetoric not to confer continuity on the past but rather to urge a break with tradition in order to refine society in the present and near future. Stephen Marshall anticipates a

---

[50] Ralph Cudworth, *True Intellectual System of the Universe* (London, 1678), 879–80.

[51] Jürgen Habermas, *The Philosophical Discourse of Modernity*, trans. Frederick G. Lawrence (Cambridge: MIT Press, 1987), 5 (my emphasis).

future golden world whose glory will lie in its difference rather than continuity with the past: "God hath cast your lot so, that if you be rightly instructed in this one Lesson, you may make our times differ as much from former times, as Nebuchadnezzar's Golden head did from the feet of iron and clay; Golden times indeed might be brought about, if God vouchsafe but to teach you this one Lesson."[52] Gerrard Winstanley prefaces the millenarian passage I quoted earlier by denying that tradition authorizes action in the present, thus linking the idea of historical change to Christ's imminent earthly paradise. When told that his communist ideal "is not practiced in any nation in the world," Winstanley does not reach back to Plato or other predecessors to defend himself. Rather, he answers:

> It was true. Property came in, you see, by the sword, therefore the curse; for the murderer brought it in, and upholds him by his power, and it makes a division in the creation, casting many under bondage; therefore it is not the blessing, or the promised seed. And what other lands do, England is not to take [as a] pattern; for England (as well as other lands) has lain under the power of that beast, kingly property.[53]

Immediately after this criticism of custom or "pattern," Winstanley moves into his millenarian hope for England. For him, the future, not the past, authorizes his innovative politics. Indeed, his cosmology allows him to theorize a radical culture in a way that Foxe and the Elizabethans could not. He responds to an apocalyptic directive to break with a corrupt lineage and rebuild society from the ground up.

The same is largely true for Milton, except that Milton expresses an even more intense willingness to break with the past. This is not to deny his etiological and historicist impulses. His early, undergraduate claim that the study of history will make the historian "coeval with time itself" (*CPW* 1:297), his wish in the early 1640s to write a national epic so that his countrymen "should not willingly let [our history] die" (810), his extensive though abortive *History of Britain*, and his motivating desire in *Paradise Lost* to determine "what cause" (*Riverside Milton* 1:28) precipitated that Fall—all these instances and more illustrate how deeply Milton cares about the past. Nonetheless, as we discussed in chapter 4, he rarely cares about it as a moral au-

---

[52] Marshall, *Right Understanding of the Times*, E3v.
[53] *Works of Winstanley*, 385.

thority for behavior in the present. As Achsah Guibbory has observed, the "belief that people (with God's help) can replace the cyclical pattern of the past with a future pattern of progress underlies Milton's sense of his own role in the pamphlets."[54] In her book on Milton's progressivism, Guibbory says little about eschatology, and Milton's sense of the Apocalypse's relation to the past is a difficult matter. On the one hand, as Milton tells the traditionalist Joseph Hall, Christ's return absolutely breaks with and owes nothing to all previous patterns: the New Jerusalem "descends from Heaven," "without your admired link of succession" (CPW 1:703). On the other hand, the Apocalypse will be a result of historical activity (not historical tradition), shaped by history rather than simply trumping it. Unlike Foxe, who seeks to represent the Reformation break with traditional religion as an apocalyptic continuity, Milton writes of the Puritan break with church tradition as apocalyptic precisely because it *is* discontinuous, because it stems from the human effort to change history.

This combination of eschatology, innovation, and civic activity makes Milton's relation to the early modern nation somewhat difficult to pin down. Does he represent an emerging voice of the modern, secular nation or a concluding murmur from a traditional religious community? On the one hand, the nationalist Milton we see in the apocalyptic tracts approximates the one elegantly described by Paul Stevens's recent work, a Milton committed to "the dissolution of the old links" and "the forging of new ones," imagining an English community that will allow its members "to fashion their own lives, to invent aspirations and realize vocations free from the deadening weight of custom." This description presents us with a surprisingly modern figure, and Stevens himself acknowledges that "[t]his vision may well be utterly bourgeois in its genesis."[55] Other studies depict a more premodern Milton by emphasizing his thoroughly religious rather than civic commitments. Still other critics such as David Loewenstein imply that we should not even try to distinguish between the political and religious Milton.[56] Yet I do not so much wish to deny all va-

---

[54] Achsah Guibbory, *The Map of Time: Seventeenth-Century English Literature and Ideas of Pattern in History* (Urbana: University of Illinois Press, 1986), 172.

[55] Paul Stevens, "Milton's Janus-Faced Nationalism: Soliloquy, Subject, and the Modern Nation State," *Journal of English and German Philology* 100, 2 (2001): 247–68, at 257 and 267.

[56] Loewenstein, *Representing Revolution*, esp. 3–6.

lidity to the religious-traditional/secular-modern division as to observe that this division fails to capture what is new in mid-seventeenth-century thought. Milton's "modern" understanding of national temporality emerges not only in spite of his religious millenarianism but also as a result of it. It sets him apart from Foxe, Dee, and Spenser but also distinguishes him from later nationalists who more thoroughly translate religious energy into civic expression. In the remainder of this chapter, I describe Milton's peculiar position between the early modern and modern nation.

For all their similarities—their dual commitment to church and nation, their wish to locate England within a larger pattern of history—Foxe and Milton hold radically different historical sensibilities. We can aptly distinguish between Foxe's and Milton's conception of tradition, for example, by contrasting their metaphorical understanding of history as a river. In *Acts and Monuments*, as we have seen, Foxe refers to the past from which he cannot escape as "the chief well-head and fountain" (1570, n1r). Although he expresses a theoretical willingness to depart from tradition, all his defenses of Protestant practices return to the past: the "well-head" ultimately authorizes the river of history. For Milton, the movement of the river itself, the flow of its streams, produces its own authority and reveals the truth. As he tells us in *Animadversions*, error arises chiefly in still water: the traditionalists "feel themselves strook in the transparent streams of divine Truth, they would plunge, and tumble, and thinke to ly hid in the foul weeds, and muddy waters, where no plummet can read the bottome" (*CPW* 1:569). Milton reiterates this idea famously in *Areopagitica*, when he notes that "Truth is compar'd in Scripture to a streaming fountain; if her waters flow not in a perpetuall progression, they sick'n into a muddy pool of conformity and tradition" (2:543). For Milton, truth emerges within the process of temporal change; history progresses, or is at least susceptible to progression, when a godly people work to improve it.

For Foxe, then, the servants of the true church must do their work within a Providential narrative stretched between the Alpha and Omega, between the "chief well-head" of the ancient past and the apocalyptic judgment looming in the future. In such a view of temporality, human action is subordinate to and derives its meaning from history. By contrast, in Milton's vision of progressive time, human action *creates* history, and God's servants work to construct their future rather than wait for this future to happen to them. Gordon

Teskey has astutely described this sense of human capacity in terms of Milton's distinction between narrative and moral choice. That is, whereas earlier romance narratives carry characters into and out of moral scenarios, "in the Miltonic narrative [errors] cannot be wandered into like the adventures encountered by errant knights of romance: they must be entered by deliberate choice."[57] This imperative to actively choose a future becomes especially pressing as humankind moves into the last age, as Milton suggests: "God is decreeing to begin some new and great period in his Church, ev'n to the reforming of the Reformation itself: what does he then but reveal Himself to his servants, and as his manner is, first to his English men" (2:553). The final apocalyptic period is poised to move to culmination, but this movement seems to be a historical one, deriving from the "perpetual progression" of Truth's waters and infused with a national flavor. The Apocalypse is not only the fulfillment of human effort but also a spur to think of history as progressive and responsive to this effort.

But if humans, anticipating a worldly paradise, can innovatively create history, then what part exactly does God play in temporal progression? Milton's famous Arminianism only makes this a more difficult question to answer. Men certainly have free will, but Milton concedes that many of their bad choices may result from God's plan. For example, in *Of Reformation* Milton acknowledges that his countrymen may not be entirely responsible for their sluggish attempts at reformation: "yet will I not insist on that which may seeme to be the cause on Gods part" (*CPW* 1:527). By way of determining God's role in temporal action, we might consider how fragile history potentially becomes when placed in the hands of human agents. Let us start, in *Animadversions*, with Milton's metaphor of antiquity as a giant,

> this unactive, and livelesse Colossus, that like a carved Gyant terribly menacing to children, and weaklings lifts up his club, but strikes not, and is subject to the muting of every Sparrow. If you let him rest upon his Basis, hee may perhaps delight the eyes of some with his huge and mountainous Bulk, and the quaint workmanship of his massie limbs; but if yee goe about to take him in pieces, yee marre him; and if you thinke like Pigmees to turne and wind him whole as hee is, besides

---

[57] Gordon Teskey, "From Allegory to Dialectic: Imagining Error in Spenser and Milton," *Publications of the Modern Language Association* 101, 1 (1986): 9–23, at 9.

your vaine toile and sweat, he may chance to fall upon your owne
heads. (*CPW* 1:699–700)

Interestingly, Milton presents an idol of antiquity that is both impo-
tent and implacable. It can frighten only children and weaklings, it
dare not use its club, birds shit on it, and close scrutiny ("take him in
pieces") destroys it. This Colossus looks fierce on the outside but in
fact has no power. Yet, if you try to move this massive giant whole, as
did the foolish Pygmies, it will likely destroy you. Milton stresses antiquity's simultaneous weight and fragility to suggest that idolizing
history makes it inaccessible to human manipulation and understanding. You can neither study it in detail nor grasp it as a whole.
Humankind has no relation to a history thus reified, transformed as
it were from flowing streams to still, muddy waters.

Milton returns to this image in *Areopagitica*, metaphorizing in this
case not antiquity but rather Truth itself. A startling contrast with
the massive Colossus, this famous image of Truth presents a broken,
ruined body, dismembered and scattered, awaiting the Apocalypse:

> Truth indeed came once into the world with her divine Master, and was
> a perfect shape most glorious to look on: but when he ascended, and his
> Apostles after him were laid asleep, then strait arose a wicked race of
> deceivers, who as that story goes of the *Aegyptian Typhon* with his
> conspirators, how they dealt with the good *Osiris*, took the Virgin
> Truth, hewd her lovely form into a thousand pieces, and scattered them
> to the four winds. From that time ever since, the sad friends of Truth,
> such as durst appear, imitating the careful search that *Isis* made for the
> mangl'd body of *Osiris*, went up and down gathering up limb by limb
> still as they could find them. We have not yet found them all, Lords and
> Commons, nor ever shall do, till her Master's second coming; he shall
> bring together every joint and member, and shall mold them into an
> immortal feature of loveliness and perfection. (*CPW* 2:549)

To deal first with the positive aspect of this violent passage: Truth's
dismemberment radically involves humankind in the temporal re-
creation of Truth in which the godly persist "up and down gathering
up limb by limb still as they could find them." The human effort to
rebuild truth leads up to the final act of restoration, at the Apocalypse. Unlike the idolatrous stasis imposed by the Colossus of antiquity, the scattered body of Truth produces a dynamic effect, a con-

tiguous rather than continuous history in which human action takes on meaning event by event rather than only in terms of a Providential plan. As Milton insists later in his treatise, the house of God "cannot be united into a continuity, it can but be contiguous in this world" (*CPW* 2:555). This dismembered body functions like "the transparent streams of divine Truth"—both of them resist a reification that would exclude humans from the historical process.

Yet this refusal of hypostasis also implies that the human activation of history relies on a profound loss. A history susceptible to human manipulation is also a history from which God has withdrawn, to some degree. Milton's sense of this loss goes beyond the fact that Truth's original "perfect shape" was ruined. The curious choice to liken Truth's dismemberment to Osiris's fate hinges on the famous sexual nuance of the Egyptian story, namely, that at his final restoration Osiris still lacked his penis.[58] As Milton would have read in Plutarch's "Isis and Osiris,"

> Typhon, when he was hunting by night in the moonlight, came upon [the coffin of Osiris]. He recognized the body, and having cut it into fourteen parts, he scattered them. When she heard of this, Isis searched for them in a papyrus boat, sailing through the marshes. . . . The only part of Osiris which Isis did not find was his male member [to aidoion]; for no sooner was it thrown into the river than the lepidotus, phagrus and oxyrhynchus ate of it, fish which [the Egyptians] most of all abhor. In its place Isis fashioned a likeness of it and consecrated the phallus, in honor of which the Egyptians even today hold festival.[59]

Plutarch's account emphasizes the symbolic equation between penis and phallus ("in its place"), allowing the loss of the physical member to make possible a cultural posterity. Osiris's "castration" thus represents a founding moment in Egyptian civilization, an originary loss that initiates a compensatory, productive history. Milton's redaction of the pagan tale, rather than merely revising it along the lines of the *virgo intacta*, "recastrates" Osiris by replacing him with the female

---

[58] Certainly Osiris's "resurrection" and provenance as god of the dead make him a reasonable candidate, but there are any number of classical deities who would fit as well, and Milton says especially unpleasant things about Isis and Osiris in the "Nativity Ode" (210–20).

[59] *Plutarch's "De Iside et Osiride,"* ed. and trans. J. Gwyn Griffiths (Cambridge: University of Wales Press, 1970), 144–45.

"Virgin Truth," who lacks a penis in the first place. There is no phallus—no symbol of metaphysical presence—to recover because there
was no penis to begin with. Milton's scheme deprives history of
Plutarch's symbolic compensation, emphasizing instead the implacable absence that confronts human effort. There are no festivals of remembrance, no traditions of recovery, that can guide action in the
present. After Truth's dismemberment, then, the ongoing process of
human activity depends on a "recastrated" history, one not merely
fallen from previous wholeness but always already marked with absence.[60]

Yet although this conception of history and truth may further rein-
force the priority of contiguity over continuity, it also suggests the
cosmic futility of the human effort to unite truth, creating a distance
between historical progress and the Apocalypse: "We have not found
them all, Lords and Commons, nor ever shall doe, till her Masters
second Comming." For a moment in this almost melancholy comment, Milton seems to divide the Apocalypse from the historical
search for Truth, because Christ's reunification will occur regardless
of how much or how little progress humans have made in their endeavor. Stanley Fish has recently argued just the opposite of this passage, insisting that the impossibility of final action "sounds discouraging and even despairing, but in fact it is full of hope—hope that the
task will never be accomplished and that therefore the efforts to accomplish it will never cease."[61] Fish is partly right—for Milton, historical despair represents a version of future hope. Yet Fish does not
take seriously enough Milton's eschatology. Milton does not believe
that human effort "will never cease"; on the contrary, it will cease, or
at least radically alter, at Christ's return. From a cosmic perspective,

---

[60] Lana Cable, without reference to the sexual detail in Plutarch's account, similarly argues against a determinant interpretation of Truth's original wholeness that
humans could theoretically restore: "To seekers of Milton's determinant program,
the Egyptian myth encourages the supposition that truth is a sundered whole that requires only putting together again for all to come out right–for fallen humanity at
last to restore order. . . . Yet the Osiris portrait . . . remains in the end an iconoclastic
image. If the 'image of God in the eye' is beyond visualization, the image of Truth we
get with the Osiris portrait can be visualized only as a dismembered god, a shattered
icon whose parts remain incapable of reuniting by human agency." See Cable, *Carnal
Rhetoric: Milton's Iconoclasm and the Poetics of Desire* (Durham, N.C.: Duke University Press, 1995), 127–28.

[61] Stanley Fish, *How Milton Works* (Cambridge: Harvard University Press, 2001),
564.

then, a certain illogic emerges in the continued effort to restore Truth, an illogic that threatens to turn Truth herself into a kind of idol as the passage continues. Milton urges Parliament not to set limitations on the servants of Truth who "continue seeking, that continue to do our obsequies to the torn body of our martyr'd Saint" (*CPW* 2:549–50). "Saint" is not an automatically negative word in Milton, as the first line of his sonnet "Methought I saw my late espoused Saint" makes clear. Yet in the context of Milton's iconoclastic historicism, the sentence has a rather peculiar resonance, as if truth's followers had taken on a passive servitude ("do our obsequies" rather than "gathering up") to a Catholic-sounding mistress.

Indeed, Milton cannot entirely escape the illogic of human action in eschatological history because he has no notion of a "post-Christian" idea of progress in which inevitable improvement is only metaphorically divine. Although unlike Foxe he believes that human effort can create historical progress, he does not believe, as do later theorists of progress, that historical events are *immanently* meaningful without deriving their significance from a divine Providence. He is not Macaulay, nor even Spinoza. Some scholars maintain that post-Enlightenment secular progress is simply a mystified derivation of Christian revelation. Yet one would have to decide how seriously Macaulay takes his metaphors of divinity when, in a discussion about the revolutions of the seventeenth century, he describes historical progress:

> time advances, facts accumulate, doubts arise. Faint glimpses of truth begin to appear, and shine more and more unto the perfect day. The highest intellects, like the tops of mountains, are the first to catch and to reflect the dawn. They are bright, while the level below is still in darkness. But soon the light, which at first illuminated only the loftiest eminences, descends on the plain, and penetrates to the deepest valley. First come hints, then fragments of systems, then defective systems, then complete and harmonious systems. The sound opinion, held for a time by one bold speculator, becomes the opinion of a small minority, of a strong minority, of a majority of mankind. Thus, the great progress goes on.[62]

---

[62] Thomas Babington Macaulay, "History of the Revolution in England in 1688," *Edinburgh Review* 124 (July 1835); reprinted in *The Edinburgh Review*, 250 vols., American ed. (New York: Leonard Scott, 1813–1929), 61:150.

No doubt Macaulay derives this vision of cultural development from an earlier Christian model of spiritual development. Indeed, part of my argument in this chapter is that the millenarian nationalism of Milton and his contemporaries made it possible to interpret historical change positively rather than as only a loss. Macaulay's dialectic between human effort ("bold speculator") and inevitability ("Time advances," "the great progress goes on") emerges in part from the seventeenth-century dialectic between godly action on earth and divine Providence.

Yet despite its glittering metaphysical traces, Macaulay's passage is able to treat progress as earthbound and nondivine in a way that seventeenth-century writers could not. The theistic element of progress must be literally present for Milton in a way it need not be for Macaulay, and this makes a difference. Milton's apocalyptic historicism in fact deviates from Catherine Gimelli Martin's fascinating thesis that Milton optimistically represents the cosmos "both as organic and as immanently numinous remnants of a divine hierarchy," a cosmos characterized by "enriched possibilities of meaningfulness."[63] That is to say, although Milton makes history accessible to human effort as Martin's thesis would predict, he does not imagine that divine hierarchy has entirely melted into immanence. He believes that the apocalyptic inevitability of progress is *literally* divine, not just metaphorically so, that it really derives from Christ above on one side of the dialectic, while human effort activates it or at least shapes it on the other side. The two sides do not meet on an immanent or organic middle ground; their division remains as traumatic as the violent dismembering of a beautiful body. As much as he wants to make worldly activity commensurate with the millennial paradise that may come to England, he can bring humankind into the cosmic scheme only by postulating a doubly castrated history, one fallen from (and also free from) divine overdetermination. This is the limitation and capability of his historical moment.

Milton and his contemporaries thus begin to "solve" the national problem of historical loss by interpreting discontinuity as innovation, but at the cost of a history conceived as whole. While Foxe, Dee, and Spenser struggle to realign the nation with tradition, Milton tries to embrace it as a product of modernity, a community that has really

---

[63] Catherine Gimelli Martin, *The Ruins of Allegory: "Paradise Lost" and the Metamorphosis of Epic Convention* (Durham, N.C.: Duke University Press, 1998), 4.

only emerged "just now." If I suggest that Milton's conception of national history is "modern" in a way that the other three writers' conceptions are not, I simply mean that historical progress is one of the primary constructs by which nations in the eighteenth, nineteenth, and twentieth centuries came to terms with the contradiction of a past that inevitably shaped the present, on the one hand, and a present that refused to remain aligned with the past, on the other. Modernity is not the only way to conceive of a nation, which can never simply escape from tradition, nor do its members usually want to do so. Yet modernity is the quality that has most consistently distinguished nations from other forms of community—religious, regional, racial, even imperial. Milton and other seventeenth-century writers, by developing a futurist apocalypticism that accommodated local human effort on a cosmic scale, laid the groundwork for a future conception of historical progress whose godlessness would have appalled them.

Even though Milton can represent human effort only in a contiguous history marked with an absence, he nonetheless demonstrates how closely this effort can come to resemble Christ. Shortly after his description of the body of Truth, Milton lashes out against those who want to limit free intellectual inquiry:

> They are the troublers, they are the dividers of unity, who neglect and permit not others to unite those dissever'd peeces which are yet wanting to the body of Truth. To be still searching what we know not, by what we know, still closing up truth to truth as we find it (for all her body is homogeneal, and proportionall) this is the golden rule in Theology as well as in Arithmetick, and makes up the best harmony in a Church. (*CPW* 2:550–51)

Although Truth's servants do not replace Christ, they begin to imitate him: much as He "shall bring together every joint and member" of Truth, humans now "unite" the scattered pieces, and in so doing achieve a kind of "harmony." This passage recuperates their role as active and productive creators of truth. The earlier mention of the Master's second coming, rather than indicating the cosmic limitation of human effort, ultimately links this effort to the Apocalypse. Even in this passage, the earthly content of apocalyptic form crucially allows Milton to interpret historical change as progressive, just as it allowed his contemporaries to imagine radical versions of the future.

These gains do come at a cost. Unlike Foxe, Milton imagines an English future linked to the divine; but also unlike Foxe, Milton replaces a history of divine Providence with a history of human effort, an imperfect, tentative history capable of progressing to magnificent success or devolving to abysmal failure, a history partly emptied of its divine content that we now call, with appropriate redundancy, secular history.

CONCLUSION

It has been argued that eighteenth- and nineteenth-century national consciousness encouraged the adoption of a developmental model of historical change—the so-called Whig interpretation of history—that nations then tautologically used to describe their own pasts. The nation creates a history that creates the nation. Does this study of national temporality, in concluding with the emergence of "secular" history, subscribe to the Whig interpretation of history? Perhaps, in the sense that it assumes that the concept of community is historical, that its many manifestations emerge and fade through time, and that we can usefully interpret the various local phenomena comprised by antiquarian, apocalyptic, and poetical history as contributing to a "development" of English national consciousness. By calling the sixteenth-century phase of this development "early," I posit a structure of similitude between the historical discourses of the Renaissance and those of later centuries. Indeed, only by positing such a similitude do questions about differences become meaningful: What difference does it make that the Renaissance did not avail itself of a conception of historical progress, whereas the eighteenth and nineteenth centuries did? What happens to narratives of nationhood when the narrative ethos shifts from historical precedent (the early Reformers) to historical novelty (the Civil War radicals)? These may be embarrassingly large questions, but the study of nationalism as a long-term and continuing phenomenon obliges us to ask them, and this book has tried to provide answers.

Yet this work also diverges from the Whig interpretation of history in that it by no means takes the development of either English nationhood or modern historical sensibility to have been inevitable, organic, ameliorative, or steady. Although the English people may have made their own history, they did not make it under circumstances chosen by themselves. As far as nationhood goes, the Renaissance was an era of bad timing, equipped (burdened?) with a sense of historical difference but lacking (free of the mystification of?) a narrative of historical progress. Foucault's "scarcity principle" was very much in operation: English writers tried to address the problem of historical novelty with the resources they had at hand, however imperfectly suited, using antiquarian, apocalyptic, and poetical history to reestablish a continuity they felt was in peril.[1] English national temporality emerged awkwardly, in fits and starts, subject to the contingencies of early Reformation polemic, monastic library spoliation, colonialism in Ireland, failures in the New World, Union debates, and heated Civil War rhetoric.

After the Renaissance, the terms of the problem of historical loss changed, and English society developed new resources for dealing with it. In claiming this, I do not wish to suggest that the problem of historical loss vanished from the national scene after Milton and the Civil War writers. As Eric Hobsbawm has noted, modern nations continue to yearn for tradition as a means of maintaining a sense of connection with the past, even if these traditions must be fabricated:

> the peculiarity of "invented" traditions is that the continuity with [a historic past] is largely factitious. In short, they are responses to novel situations which take the form of reference to old situations, or which establish their own past by quasi-obligatory repetition. It is the contrast between the constant change and innovation of the modern world and the attempt to structure at least some parts of social life within it as unchanging and invariant, that makes the "invention of tradition" so interesting for historians of the past two centuries.[2]

[1] See Michel Foucault, *The Archaeology of Knowledge*, trans. A. M. Sheridan Smith (New York: Pantheon Books, 1972).

[2] Eric Hobsbawm, "Introduction: Inventing Traditions," in *The Invention of Tradition*, ed. Eric Hobsbawm and Terence Ranger (Cambridge: Cambridge University Press, 1983), 2.

In this view, nations of the nineteenth and twentieth centuries have sought to create continuity precisely as a result of the feeling that modern changes have left the past too far behind. The phenomenon this book has described thus clearly endures past the Civil War. Yet I think that the sense of a lost past reaches its most urgent expression in the Renaissance, given the Tudor and Stuart inclination to interpret historical change as decay rather than evolution. However melancholic Victorian historical writing might have become, nineteenth-century English people had at their disposal a progressivist model of change that allowed them to interpret the loss of the past as a gain for the future. Although they did not always choose to apply this model, it represents an available tool mostly denied to the Renaissance.

It is worth stressing how crucially progressivism affected post-Renaissance historical writing, especially national history. We looked, in chapter 5, at Macaulay's sense of how "the great progress goes on," a view that offers, I suggested, a secular version of Milton's account of millenarian revelation. Indeed, this secularism produces a thoroughly *modern* Milton in Macaulay's invented dialogue between the Puritan poet and the royalist Abraham Cowley, set in 1665, in which Milton's religious principles are translated into entirely political ones. Macaulay has Milton respond to Cowley's disparaging comparison between the recent political upheavals and a destructive flood with an image that he probably drew from Milton's own writings:

> I hold it not to be such a deluge as that of which you speak; but rather a blessed flood, like those of the Nile, which in its overflow doth indeed wash away ancient landmarks, and confound boundaries, and sweep away dwellings, yea, doth give birth to many foul and dangerous reptiles. Yet hence is the fullness of the granary, the beauty of the garden, the nurture of all living things.[3]

Although for the Milton of *Animadversions* and *Areopagitica* this overflowing river ultimately leads to Christ's fulfillment of a divine plan, for Macaulay's imaginary nineteenth-century Milton the flood leads to the continual improvement of human society and the replen-

---

[3] Thomas Babington Macaulay, "A Conversation between Mr. Abraham Cowley and Mr. John Milton Touching the Great Civil War," *Knight's Quarterly Magazine* (August 1824); reprinted in *Critical, Historical, and Miscellaneous Essays and Poems by Thomas Babington Macaulay*, vol. 1 (New York: Lovell, Coryell, n.d.), 88.

ishment of its resources. Macaulay's secularization of Milton, however much we might now associate it with naïve, Whiggish history, allows the essayist to link progress to what he takes to be the glimmerings of modern democracy. Macaulay's essay "History" (1828) similarly uses the idea of progress to compare the English moderns favorably with the Greek and Roman ancients:

> It is not, indeed, strange that the Greeks and Romans should not have carried the science of government, or any other experimental science, so far as it has been carried in our time, for the experimental sciences are generally in a state of progression. They were better understood in the seventeenth century than in the sixteenth, and in the eighteenth than in the seventeenth.[4]

The moral sciences have likewise made progress denied to the ancients: "All the metaphysical discoveries of all the philosophers, from the time of Socrates to the northern invasion, are not to be compared in importance with those which have been made in England every fifty years since the time of Elizabeth" (294). That Macaulay links Englishness in particular with progress points to his general association of the nation with modernity, especially with modern English political freedom: "Our liberty is neither Greek nor Roman, but essentially English" (286).

In pointing out this faith in progress, I do not wish to overstate Macaulay's modernity or his break from earlier, less optimistic dispensations. He does not simply ignore the limitations of historiography, but often freely acknowledges that no history could capture every detail of the past, that all stories are selective (277). His own *History of England* (1848) embraced this selectivity by supplementing the main narrative with what seemed like stray anecdotes and everyday details. Likewise, in his essay "History," a proper history of England, which for him should resemble the development of the plot of a novel, would openly accept the assistance of fiction: "The early part of our imaginary history would be rich with coloring from romance, ballad, and chronicle. We should find ourselves in the company of knights such as those of Froissart, and of pilgrims such as those who rode with Chaucer from the Tabard" (307). Such an atti-

---

[4] Thomas Babington Macaulay, "History," *Edinburgh Review* (May 1828); reprinted in *Critical, Historical, and Miscellaneous Essays and Poems*, 294.

tude should surely make us think twice about the "historical revolution" that supposedly began in the Renaissance, reputedly demanding greater and greater empirical precision up through modern times. Even a late-Renaissance progressivist like Milton will not tolerate such fabling in early English history as Macaulay proposes. Clearly, we cannot simply invoke empirical method to distinguish a modern Macaulay from an early modern Milton. Yet Macaulay's tolerance of fiction does suggest an aspect of his historiographic modernity: he accepts quasi-fabled origins partly because for him we need no longer expect historical writers to account for the most ancient origins or the final ends. Instead, the modern historian (for Macaulay at least) traces the progress of society as it evolves toward modernity. This sense of historiography may help account for Macaulay's treatment of the Civil War, the moment of political awakening for the English people, in his view; he concludes his hypothetical history with this conflict and begins his *History of England* with it as well. History leads to or follows from the threshold of modernity—creating new problems of historical process, new complexities in the negotiation between past and future—but also potentially assuaging the earlier Renaissance anxiety about obscure beginnings and the end of time.

I thus use Macaulay as a brief example of how post-Renaissance English historians could use the discourse of progress to respond to the problem of historical loss. Yet, as I have already noted, modern writers did not always avail themselves of the progressivist model, and some of them express a keen sense of England's lost past. Perhaps the best example of this melancholic tone is Thomas Carlyle, who, like Macaulay, recognized historiography's inability to capture the past whole. Yet Carlyle did not turn to progress as a compensation for historical loss but rather saw the historian's limitations as a cause for lamentation. His essay "On Biography" (1832), for example, commenting on the character of Clarendon's *History of the Rebellion in England* (1704–7), fastens on a detail from the account of Charles II's flight from the Battle of Worcester: a pair of old shoes loaned to the king by a helpful peasant. Carlyle celebrates this detail as an authentic piece of the history of the ordinary English citizen—"a genuine flesh-and-blood Rustic of the year 1651"—and, like Macaulay, seems to perceive the Civil War as a threshold of modernity for English society. Yet rather than treating this moment as an anticipation of future English development, Carlyle goes on to discuss it as an exception to the general rule of vanishing history:

How comes it, that he alone of all the British rustics who tilled and lived along with him, on whom the blessed sun on that same "fifth of September" was shining, should have chanced to rise on us . . . ? We see him but for a moment; for one moment, the blanket of the Night is rent asunder, so that we behold and see, and then closes over him—forever.[5]

Here we have a dramatic sense of historical loss, the past that disappears even as you seek for it. Though written over two centuries later, Carlyle's lament resonates with Camden's caution in the preface to his *Britannia*: "who is so skillful that, struggling with time in the foggy dark sea of antiquity, may not run upon the rocks?"[6] Like the Elizabethan antiquaries Leland, Dee, and Weever, Carlyle both praises the value of history and associates it with death. As he comments in his essay "On History" (1830), "[w]ell may we say that of our History the more important part is lost without recovery, and . . . look with reverence into the dark untenanted places of the Past, where, in formless oblivion, our chief benefactors, with all their sedulous endeavors, but not with the fruit of these, lie entombed."[7] To look for the past exposes its demise. We might see Carlyle's attitude as the structural opposite of Hobsbawm's "invention of tradition," a sense of historical difference that provokes not the creation of continuity but rather the expression (I am tempted almost to say a Renaissance expression) of overwhelming anxiety. If Macaulay is a latter-day Milton, Carlyle postfigures the Spenser of *Briton moniments*.

The Romantic period's anxiety about history is the subject of a recent, extraordinary book by Ann Rigney, who argues that a new, egalitarian impulse to capture history whole—"a democratizing attempt to ensure the representation of all aspects of the experience of all member of society"—proliferated contrasting views of the past, highlighting the necessary imperfection of any given account.[8] She is not concerned with national history per se, but her emphasis on democratic historiography resonates with the sense of demotic comradeship—however imaginary—associated with modern nationalism. Rigney's chapter on Carlyle focuses on the issue of historical unrep-

[5] Thomas Carlyle, "On Biography," in *Critical and Miscellaneous Essays*, 7 vols. (London: Chapman and Hall, 1872), 4:60, 61.

[6] William Camden, *Britain*, trans. Philemon Holland (London, 1610), *5v.

[7] Thomas Carlyle, "On History," in *Critical and Miscellaneous Essays*, 2:63.

[8] Ann Rigney, *Imperfect Histories: The Elusive Past and the Legacy of Romantic Historicism* (Ithaca: Cornell University Press, 2001), 1–2.

resentability and the sublime, the manner in which the essayist not only complained about the elusiveness of the past but also cultivated this quality in his narratives for aesthetic effect. As Rigney puts it,

> the aesthetic effect particular to historical representation derives precisely from the realization that there is so much of the past beyond the historical text that is still unknown, and that understanding the past as a whole is an almost unimaginably complex enterprise. It follows from this that the more historians meet the resistance of their material by going as far as they can into its complexity, and the more they can express this resistance, the greater the aesthetic appeal of their work. . . . Carlyle's conception of historical ignorance, with its emphasis on the boundlessness, obscurity, and the almost unimaginable complexity of the past was clearly influenced by the eighteenth-century discourse of the sublime. (114, 115)

Historiographical limitation may thus represent, for the Romantics and afterward, Edmund Burke's "delightful horror." The yawning gap between past and present can aesthetically satisfy readers at the same time it frustrates or worries them. Rigney's account of the pleasures of historical loss corresponds at least faintly with the response of Spenser's Prince Arthur, who initially feels "offence" at the imperfection of the history he reads but then experiences "secret pleasure" (*FQ* II.x.68.8).

Yet Rigney's study of nineteenth-century imperfect histories also reveals the limits of such correspondences. Much as Macaulay's progressivism follows from yet transmutes Civil War millenarianism, Carlyle's early-nineteenth-century expression of loss is marked by its distance from as well as proximity to the Renaissance anxiety about historical otherness. That Carlyle can invoke historical absence as an aesthetic *principle,* that he can assume history's imperfection will yield delight as well as despair, stems from a view of the past that readily grants the contingency of historical origins. Whatever the metaphysical longings of post-Renaissance English imperalism, whatever the mystifications of English historical progress, Carlyle lives in a culture that no longer imagines history as literally synonymous with Virgil's *imperium sine fine.* Imperfection comes with the historical territory in a way that the Tudors and Stuarts would be loath to acknowledge. Furthermore, as we saw with Macaulay, post-Renaissance thinkers could treat the breaks in the past as signs of ameliorative innovation. He may be a skeptic, but Carlyle knows that where he sees lacunae, many of his fellow citizens see progress. This is not to deny that Carlyle genuinely worries about the elusive past nor that Foxe, Dee, Spenser, and Milton thematize the issue of elusiveness as well as lament it. Yet the distinctiveness of Renaissance historical loss, the quality that places it awkwardly between premodern and modern, lies in the Tudor and Stuart recognition of historical difference, on the one hand, and their unwillingness to relinquish the metaphysical pattern of historical continuity, on the other. As for national history, at least, the Renaissance lacked the category of the sublime as a compensation for a chaotic past. Historical loss was the price those writers paid for the nation's novelty rather than an effect they could freely cultivate as a means of artistic consolation.

Again, the Renaissance "lacked," the nineteenth century "acknowledged"; the Tudors "experienced," the Romantics "cultivated." Shades of the Whig interpretation of history? I hope my account here of the basic incommensurability between the two periods, with their local contingencies and modalities, resists the most naïve version of this interpretation. If the narrative of development continues to reemerge in my description of English national temporality, it does so partly as an effect of the lasting consequences Renaissance historical loss had for England's national identity, and indeed on the modern conception of nations generally. It partly explains why a writer such as Macaulay can invoke a sense of liberty that is "essentially English"—a category he apparently finds so self-evident that he offers no concrete examples—while acknowledging that the roots of this Englishness must remain partly unknown, even fictional. Modern nations emerge in history; they are not coterminous with it, however large a historical role they imagine for themselves. Renaissance national novelty forces Foxe, Dee, Spenser, and Milton to confront this impression, but they do the best they can to combat it with tools at their disposal: the physical artifact, the Apocalypse, and the poetic imagination.

Index of Names

INDEX OF SUBJECTS